Field Guide to Child Welfare

Volume III

Judith S. Rycus & Ronald C. Hughes

CWLA Press
Washington, DC

Institute for Human Services
Columbus, OH

CWLA Press is an imprint of the Child Welfare League of America. The Child Welfare League of America (CWLA) is a privately supported, nonprofit, membership-based organization committed to preserving, protecting, and promoting the well-being of all children and their families. Believing that children are our most valuable resource, CWLA, through its membership, advocates for high standards, sound public policies, and quality services for children in need and their families.

CHILD WELFARE LEAGUE OF AMERICA, INC.
440 First Street, NW, Third Floor, Washington, DC 20001-2085
Email: books@cwla.org

CURRENT PRINTING (last digit)
10 9 8 7 6 5 4 3

Cover and text design by James Graham
Photographs by Jeffrey A. Rycus

Printed in the United States of America

ISBN # 0–87868-619-3

Rycus, Judith S.
    Field guide to child welfare / Judith S. Rycus & Ronald C. Hughes.
        p.   cm.
    Includes bibliographical references and index.
        ISBN 0-87868-617-7 (v. 1). -- ISBN 0-87868-618-5 (v. 2). - - ISBN
    0-87868-619-3 (v. 3). -- ISBN 0-87868-620-7 (v. 4)
        1. Child welfare--United States.   2. Social case work with
children--United States.   3. Family social work--United States.
I. Hughes, Ronald C.   II. Title
HV741.R94   1998   98-4701
362.7'0973--dc21   CIP

CONTENTS

Volume III

CHILD DEVELOPMENT AND CHILD WELFARE

VI. The Effects of Abuse and Neglect on Child Development...**439**

    A. Child Development in Child Welfare.................................441

    B. The Effects of Maltreatment on Infants and Toddlers 455

    C. The Effects of Maltreatment on Preschool Children 483

    D. The Effects of Maltreatment on School-Age Children 505

    E. The Effects of Maltreatment on Adolescents.................................523

VII. Child Welfare Services for Children with Developmental Disabilities **547**

    A. Understanding Developmental Disabilities 549

    B. Myths and Misconceptions About Developmental Disabilities 563

    C. The Primary Developmental Disabilities: Identification and Early Intervention.............................577

    D. Services for Children with Developmental Disabilities and Their Families..................................629

    E. Child Welfare Services for the Catastrophically Ill Neonate 655

VI. THE EFFECTS OF ABUSE AND NEGLECT ON CHILD DEVELOPMENT

A. Child Development in Child Welfare

B. The Effects of Maltreatment on Infants and Toddlers

C. The Effects of Maltreatment on Preschool Children

D. The Effects of Maltreatment on School-Age Children

E. The Effects of Maltreatment on Adolescents

A. CHILD DEVELOPMENT IN CHILD WELFARE

1. Conceptual Framework

2. Application

Conceptual Framework

Abuse, neglect, and traumatic separation often have pervasive detrimental effects on children's development. The more obvious consequences include permanent physical injury, disability, illness, and even death. However, abuse, neglect, and traumatic separation can also insidiously alter the normal processes of development, often with serious, albeit less obvious, consequences.

Many maltreated and traumatized children continue to exhibit developmental delays and problems, even after abuse and neglect have essentially ceased, and their placements are stable. To effectively help maltreated children develop to their maximum potential, workers must recognize detrimental outcomes of maltreatment, and integrate developmental and remedial services into individual case plans.

CONCEPTS OF DEVELOPMENT

Understanding the effects of maltreatment on development means first understanding the fundamental principles of developmental processes. There are many theories of development, and various disciplines approach the study of development from different perspectives. Yet, despite differing conceptions, there are many principles that are agreed upon by the majority of developmentalists.

Development Is an Ongoing Process

Individual development begins with conception and does not end until death. In a broader sense, development is really not bounded by the existential limits of conception and death. Much of what we are was determined by our parents, and generations of parents before them; and, much of what we are will be perpetuated in and by our children. This view of development is called phylogenetic, and it recognizes the continuing evolution of life and human characteristics across generations. It can also help explain our concern for children's welfare, and our attempts to foster a caring future of which we will not always be a part.

However, in this chapter, our primary concern is the development of the individual, referred to as ontogenetic development. Ontogenetic development begins with fertilization, and ends with the death of the individual.

Early in its history, developmental psychology suggested that all important developmental milestones were achieved before adulthood. This is not so. Human development is an ongoing process, with important and necessary developmental stages and milestones occurring throughout the life span [Baltes & Reese 1984].

Development Is a Dynamic Process

Human development is dynamic rather than static; it involves continuous change. This change is sometimes referred to as growth. While the rate and degree of change may vary at different times in the life cycle and among individuals, it is always a continuous process.

Development Is Directional

Most developmental processes evolve in predictable and identifiable ways, and development is always directed toward some end. Individual human development can be defined as growth and change toward more adaptive capability. At different stages of life, different capabilities are needed to successfully negotiate life's challenges and opportunities. Development is this ongoing and purposeful metamorphosis.

Development typically proceeds from the simple to the complex. We see the same basic pattern repeated in all developmental processes and domains. For example, we all begin as a single cell, and develop into a complex organism with many millions of cells that are highly differentiated in both structure and function. These cells are organized into more and more complex and integrated structures as development proceeds.

Another example of the directionality of development can be seen in the evolution of motor development. The rudimentary and uncoordinated motor movements of a newborn infant become increasingly complicated, integrated, and efficient as the child grows. Early uncoordinated and undirected movements evolve into complicated patterns of gross and fine motor skills and eye–hand coordination, allowing the individual to maneuver through the environment. Continued development finally culminates in a polyphony of integrated physical capacities, expressed in such activities as playing a piano or playing basketball.

Development May Involve Stages

At certain predictable times in the developmental process, new and different capabilities emerge. These developmental plateaus are often referred to as stages. Stages often represent a qualitative change in development, which results in the emergence of an ability or trait that has no obvious precursors from earlier developmental periods. An example is the emergence of stranger anxiety in an infant who was previously happy being held by anyone.

After the emergence of a new skill or behavior, there is usually a period of leveling off, when the new abilities are practiced, mastered, and integrated. For example, after a toddler has taken his or her first steps, the child will spend several months perfecting walking to achieve balance, coordination, and stability. When perfected, the skill becomes habituated, or performed without conscious thought, and the child can attend to another developmental challenge, such as climbing.

Stages represent the emergence of more complex behavior patterns that often refine or replace earlier, less effective ones. A four year old, who has well-developed language and social skills, is less likely to respond in frustrating situations by having a tantrum than would a two year old in the same situation. The preschooler's ability to communicate the problem to a trusted adult is more effective in removing the source of frustration and negotiating a solution.

Stage development is an essential concept for many theories of child development, including those of Jean Piaget, Erik Erikson, Lawrence Kohlberg, and Sigmund Freud.

Development Is Cumulative

Early developmental tasks provide critical skills or traits that form the foundation for the development of later, more complicated tasks. For example, the ability to engage in reciprocal and intimate relationships is based upon the development of trust, a critical milestone of the first year of life. A child who fails to master early tasks will have more difficulty mastering the demands of later stages, and without remedial intervention, the child's development becomes more delayed, or shows increasingly abnormal patterns over time. This is a critical concept in understanding the importance of early recognition and intervention when children are developmentally delayed.

The negative effects of early developmental deficits increase as the child grows and as environmental demands become more complex. A circumscribed deficit, such as the inability to recognize letters of the alphabet, does not critically affect the life of a six year old. However, an adult who cannot read faces serious difficulties in social and economic functioning.

FACTORS THAT DETERMINE DEVELOPMENTAL OUTCOMES

The factors that affect development are generally divided into two major categories: hereditary contributors and environmental contributors.

While there has historically been considerable debate regarding the relative importance of these two factors, most developmentalists agree that development is shaped by the extremely complex interaction of the individual's genetic predisposition with the environments in which the individual lives and grows.

The Influence of Heredity

All human beings have a common genetic structure that determines the course of much of development. This common heredity accounts for the basic similarities in the structure and functions of our bodies, as well as the differences between humans and other species. Many traits are inherited, including eye color, hair color, body type, height, and skin color. The expression of these traits is genetically determined.

When development occurs as a direct result of the expression of genetic potential, it is called maturation. Maturational developmental milestones generally occur in predictable patterns, even in varying environments or cultures. Early motor abilities are one example of maturational development. Grasping, sitting, crawling, standing, and walking occur in a predictable sequence and time frame, and increase in complexity in direct proportion to the degree of physical maturation. A child cannot walk until the bones, muscles, and other physical structures have developed sufficiently to support upright body posture and to bear weight.

Infants in all cultures are biologically ready to walk somewhere between nine and 15 months. However, environment may influence when a child actually begins to walk. A child who is carried on his mother's back for the first three years of life will not walk at a year. Were that same child to be allowed to roam freely on the ground, he would likely walk within the typical time frame for all infants.

Abilities that result from maturation do not have to be taught in the same way we teach a child to hold a paintbrush or ride a bicycle. The child will have to practice a maturational skill to be proficient; however, the emergence of the skill is not dependent upon environmental factors.

Physical maturation is the easiest type of maturational development to observe. There are many other traits, however, in which maturation is thought to play a primary role. One is the emergence of cognitive skills.

Piaget identified four predictable stages in cognitive development, each of which is exemplified by the emergence of distinctly different abilities. They are: 1) sensorimotor cognition in infants; 2) symbolic thought in the toddler; 3) concrete operations in the early school years; and, 4) formal operations in adolescence. Piaget believed these stages were maturational in origin. As an example, infants are not capable of symbolic thought and, therefore, lack the ability to learn complex language until well into the second year of life. As a result of maturation, the structure and organization of a two-year-old's brain are qualitatively different from that of the infant, making it possible for the two year old to conceptualize symbols. The ability to learn a language is, therefore, genetically determined, even though the particular language a child learns depends on his culture and environment. When an entirely new ability emerges without obvious learned precursors, it is believed to represent a strong maturational influence.

Erik Erikson's stages of psychosocial development (trust, autonomy, initiative, industry, identity, etc.) are also believed to be maturational. Again, environment will affect the ways these traits are expressed; however, the emergence of the trait is not dependent upon the child's contact with the environment.

Despite genetic similarities of all humans, the information carried by our genes varies between individuals. This can account for differences between people in the rates of maturational development. However, maturational traits are generally confined within a well-defined range.

The Influence of Environment

Environment can be defined as the total complex of external (nongenetic) influences that affect the survival and development of the child.

While children are born with different potentials, the capacity for each child to achieve the highest levels of potential is dependent upon a nurturing and supportive environment. Even the most basic genetic expressions of development are essentially interwoven with environmental factors. It is easy to understand why this should be so. The evolution of genetic traits is a factor of environmental pressures. We have evolved certain traits because they work to help us function and survive in our environment. Genetic evolution and expression are the effects of environmental intercession. It is because we understand the fundamental importance of environmental factors in genetic expression that social work intervention becomes so important in our work with abused and neglected children and their families. By working to change a harmful or even benign environment into a supportive and empowering one, we facilitate the expression of the highest developmental potential of children in our care.

In reality, there are multiple environments that influence the course of development. The prenatal environment includes the chemical balance of the mother's body, and the presence of conditions or substances that can alter developmental processes, either positively or negatively. Examples are a nutritious diet and vitamins, or conversely, the mother's use of drugs or alcohol during pregnancy.

Other environmental influences are the physical environment in which the child grows, including the quality of the air the child breathes, the nutritional value of food the child eats, or exposure to conditions that can lead to disease, accident, or injury, including child abuse and neglect. The child's social and cultural environment consists of the norms, values, belief systems, morals, and, in general, standards of behavior that regulate life in the cultural group in which the child is raised. The learning environment consists of the degree and type of stimulation available in the child's immediate environment. There is considerable data to suggest that sensory input stimulates and shapes cognitive development. Cognitive stimulation, in adequate quantity and intensity, promotes establishment of, and "shapes," neural pathways in the brain. Finally, the emotional environment includes the nature of the child's interpersonal relationships, and the degree of psychological nurturance available to the child. The emotional environment shapes personality, and affects the development of self–esteem, identity, trust, social responsibility, the ability to enter into intimate relationships, and personal resilience.

Maturation is an underlying variable in all development. It creates a biological readiness for the child's encounters with the environment. The continuous interactions of the maturing child with the environment determine the final outcomes of development. These interactions between human potential and environment determine the person. It is the child welfare field's responsibility to attempt to make the environmental side of this equation as safe, supportive, nurturing, and enabling as possible.

What is "Normal"?

We must know what constitutes "normal" development to establish an accurate baseline from which to evaluate and understand delayed or "abnormal" development.

Normal is a statistical concept. "Normal" represents what is typical, or expected, for the majority of members of a group. We determine what is "normal" child development by observing a representative group of children, by identifying the traits and processes displayed by most children, and by determining the time frames for the emergence of each trait or process.

For example, if we wanted to determine the normal age range for walking, we would observe and record the ages at which a group of children first walked. Our study group should be representative; that is, randomly chosen and proportionately the same in composition as the entire population we are studying. If our study group is truly representative, we can properly assume that what we learn about the children in our sample is most likely true for all children in the population our sample represents.

Once we have collected our data, we can record the information on a graph, such as the one illustrated below.

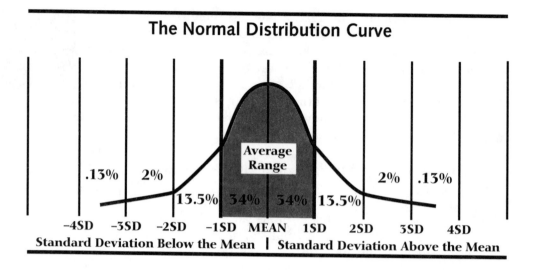

The Normal Distribution Curve

Average Range

.13% 2% 13.5% 34% 34% 13.5% 2% .13%

−4SD −3SD −2SD −1SD MEAN 1SD 2SD 3SD 4SD

Standard Deviation Below the Mean | Standard Deviation Above the Mean

This graph, known as the "normal distribution curve," is used to depict the distribution of many typical traits in a population. The horizontal axis records children's ages from birth to two years. The vertical axis records numbers of children.

The top of the curve represents the greatest number of children. The highest point in a normal distribution is usually the mean, which represents what is average for the population. For example, the mean, or average age at which children walk is 12 months. In a normal distribution, the middle of the curve is also the median; this means that approximately 50% of children walk before, and 50% walk after 12 months of age.

A statistical measure called a standard deviation designates a fixed distance from the mean. One standard deviation from the mean includes approximately 34% of the population. When applied to the age at which children walk, one standard deviation is approximately two months. Therefore, 68% of children walk between the ages of 10 and 14 months. This is generally referred to as the average or normal range. Statistically, as shown above, approximately 96% of the population is included within two standard deviations either side of the mean. Two standard deviations is still broadly within normal limits, but it represents the extreme ends of normal. Walking before 10 months or after 14 months is statistically uncommon.

Few would disagree that children who walk between 10 and 14 months are within normal limits. It is difficult, however, to say with certainty just when "abnormality" begins. A child who is not walking at 18 months is definitely delayed. What about a child who walks at 16 months? 15 months? 14 months, eight days? Where does abnormality begin?

It is not possible to draw strict delineations of normal and abnormal, because, as the normal curve demonstrates, development occurs in a population on a continuum. We must consider development a process, not an event occurring at a fixed point in time. To label a child delayed or abnormal simply on the basis of a statistical delay in performance is of little use. However, statistically determined delays should be considered an indicator of potential developmental problems, and should serve as an inducement to further explore the problems and their origins.

The rate of a child's development may also vary between traits. A child may develop physical skills earlier and language skills later than average, but still be within normal limits. Earlier development may, at times, be genetically determined; or, it may be promoted in traits or skill areas that are favored and reinforced by the child's culture and environment. Therefore, the term "normal" most appropriately refers to a trait, not to the child; and, the rate and progress of a child's development must be evaluated separately for each developmental trait or domain.

Understanding Developmental Domains

To facilitate the study of development, developmental tasks are typically divided into four primary categories, referred to as domains. The four primary developmental domains are *physical, cognitive, social,* and *emotional.*

Physical development consists of the development of the body structures, including muscles, bones, and organ systems. Physical development generally comprises sensory development, dealing with the organ systems underlying the senses and perception; motor development, dealing with the actions of the muscles; and the nervous system's coordination of both sensation and movement.

Motor activity depends upon both muscle strength and coordination. Gross motor activities, such as standing, sitting, walking, and running, involve the large muscles of the body. Fine motor activities, which involve the small muscles of the body, include speech, vision, and the use of hands and fingers. Both large and small muscle activities are controlled and coordinated by the central nervous system.

Sensory development includes the development of vision, hearing, taste, touch, and smell, and the coordination and integration of perceptual input from these systems by the central nervous system. Vision has both motor and sensory components. Muscles regulate the physical structures of the eye to permit focusing; neurological pathways then transmit visual input to the brain.

For the first year of life, children's development is most pronounced in the sensory and motor domains. For this reason, Piaget has named this early stage of development "sensorimotor."

Cognitive development is sometimes referred to as "intellectual" or "mental" development. Cognitive is the more appropriate term. Cognitive activities include thinking, memory, reasoning, language, concept development, problem–solving ability, and abstract thinking. Language, with its requirements of symbolization and memory, is one of the most important and complicated cognitive activities.

Language and speech are not synonymous. Understanding and formulating language is a complex cognitive activity, while speaking is a motor activity. Language and speech are controlled by different portions of the brain.

Social development includes the child's interactions with other people as well as involvement in social groups. The earliest social task is the development of attachment to consistent primary caregivers. Other social tasks include the development of relationships with adults and peers, the assumption of social roles, the development of an integrated system of morals and values, the adoption of group norms and standards, and eventually assuming a productive role in society.

Emotional development includes the development of personal traits and characteristics including a personal identity, self-esteem, the ability to enter into reciprocal emotional relationships, and mood and affect (feelings and emotions) that are appropriate for a person's age and for the situation.

While each of these four developmental domains can be examined individually, it is misleading to suggest that development occurs separately in each of the four domains. Development in any domain affects, and is affected by, development in all of the other domains. This can be illustrated by considering the effects of a developmental disability in one domain on development in other domains:

- How does a blind child learn the concepts of "near," "far," "round," and "hazy"? All these concepts (cognitive development) are normally learned through primarily visual (sensory) input. The absence of visual stimuli may thereby affect cognitive development.

- How will a child with a cognitive deficit, such as mental retardation, learn and understand the complicated social cues, rules, and roles that guide interpersonal relationships? The cognitive deficit can affect the child's acquisition of social skills.

- A child with emotional problems, such as poor self-esteem and lack of confidence, is likely to be fearful and anxious when confronted with difficult physical tasks, and may avoid these activities. The child's physical coordination, mastery of his or her own body, and motor skills will be affected as a result.

As a rule, children should show some degree of consistency in their developmental rates in the four domains. However, most normally developing children will be more advanced in some areas than they are in others, and yet they will be within normal limits in all domains. More rapid development in a developmental domain may be a precursor of a strength in that area. For example, many children who learn to talk very early continue to display exceptional verbal ability as they grow; and, a child who shows early physical skill and mastery will often continue to be well coordinated and agile.

The greater the disparity in the rates of development between the four domains, the more difficult the developmental process becomes for the child. Significant delays in all domains may indicate the presence of a disability, such as mental retardation. A significant delay in one developmental domain might indicate a circumscribed developmental problem, such as a speech problem, learning disability, or emotional problems.

Application

Many of the job responsibilities of child welfare caseworkers require a thorough knowledge of both normal child development and the potential detrimental effects of maltreatment on the developmental process. Knowledge of normal, or statistically typical development permits early recognition of developmental delay and disability, and can help the worker design intervention plans for children and their families that stimulate and reinforce growth and mastery of new skills.

Child welfare workers will utilize information about typical and atypical child development in several ways.

The caseworker must be able to recognize the negative effects of abuse and neglect on a child's development.

Children who have been abused or neglected are often delayed in their development, and they may display abnormal patterns of development. The caseworker should be able to recognize developmental delay in all domains, identify the nature of the child's developmental problems, refer the child for further assessment and diagnosis, and include developmental and remedial services in the family case plan. Early recognition of delays or unusual developmental patterns, and proper intervention by the caseworker, can greatly minimize the potential negative effects of maltreatment on the child's development. (See related discussion in Chapter VII, Child Welfare Services for Children with Developmental Disabilities.)

The caseworker should know age-appropriate behavioral expectations, and should be able to educate and counsel parents and other caregivers regarding proper child care practices and discipline strategies.

A common contributing factor for both child abuse and neglect is parents' unrealistic expectations for their children's behavior. For this reason, identifying and correcting parents' misconceptions about their children's development can help to prevent future maltreatment.

A poor understanding of age–related developmental capabilities also contributes to the development of unreasonable expectations for behavior. A parent who believes her five year old to be capable of babysitting for the six month old while she goes to the store does not understand the realistic capabilities of a five year old. Other examples would be a parent who expects a two year old to fully and correctly dress himself, an eight year old to find her own way home on a bus from downtown, and a nine month old to keep quiet while the parent is watching television.

Parents of abused and neglected children may also use discipline strategies that are not appropriate for their children's level of development. Behavior management strategies that are not age appropriate might include: 1) the use of "reasoning" with a one–year–old, who can understand neither complex language nor logic; 2) the excessive use of force with a two–year–old, who is developing autonomous behavior, which may promote overreaction by parents and battles for control; and, 3) the use of physical discipline with an infant, who lacks the cognitive ability to put the discipline into context, and therefore, experiences the discipline as a painful and disorienting intrusion, with no effect on modifying behavior.

A lack of knowledge about development can also contribute to a parent's mis-interpretation of children's actions. For example, a two–year–old child, who exer-cises normal autonomy by using the potty only when he wants to, may be per-ceived by his parent as "plotting ways to get back at me." It is not uncommon for two- and three–year–old children to be stubborn; the child's attempt to control his own body functions is an expression of developing autonomy. The child at this age is not capable of "plotting" in the manner the parent attributes to him.

Similarly, a crying infant who cannot be comforted may be perceived as "ungrateful and unappreciative" of the parent's care, and a three–year–old, who is totally absorbed in "Sesame Street" and does not respond to a parental request, might be accused of "deliberately ignoring me." Infants cannot exhibit "appreci-ation" in the planful and reciprocating manner that is typical of adults. Many three–year–olds may not be able to fully attend to more than one stimulus at a time. This may also be a cognitive style of some children and adults, not repre-sentative of selfish or antagonistic behavior.

Discipline strategies that are not appropriate for a child's developmental level are typically ineffective in changing behavior. They can also create high levels of frustration for the parent, which increases emotional conflict between the parent and the child, and may promote additional disruptive behavior in the future.

In many families, parent education is an important component of casework intervention. However, parent education, by itself, is not usually enough to pre-vent maltreatment. The other personal and environmental factors that contribute to abuse or neglect must concurrently be addressed. (See Section II–B, "Dynamics of Child Maltreatment," for further discussion.) However, we can help parents set realistic expectations for their children and accurately interpret the meaning of their children's behaviors. We can help them learn not to interpret their chil-dren's actions as evidence of their own lack of competence and worth, and we can help them manage their children in more pragmatic and effective ways.

> *Caseworkers should be able to assist parents and foster caregivers to access ser-vices and activities to meet children's special needs, and to enhance development.*

Caseworkers should help caregivers identify and access social, recreational, psychological, and educational services and resources that can promote healthy development for a child, and help overcome developmental problems. These activities might include the provision of:

- Health and medical services to address physical problems resulting from abuse or neglect;

- Special school programs to address academic delays;

- Recreation programs to teach social skills and interpersonal relationships;

- Physical education activities to develop motor coordination and skill;

- Participation in activities that are designed to help a child develop positive self-esteem; and

- Speech therapy, infant stimulation, psychological counseling, play therapy, and other types of treatment for developmental and emotional problems.

A thorough assessment of a child's development will enable the worker to recognize developmental needs, and link the child to the most appropriate resources to meet those needs.

Caseworkers should be able to identify early warning signs and symptoms of developmental disability, and begin early intervention services.

There is a high correlation between abuse or neglect of children, and subsequent developmental disabilities. Child welfare workers should be able to recognize the early warning signs of the primary developmental disabilities, including mental retardation, epilepsy, and cerebral palsy. A knowledgeable child welfare worker will not only recognize when children on their caseloads exhibit early warning signs of serious developmental problems, but can initiate the proper early intervention services. Early intervention is critical to reduce the long-range detrimental effects of a disabling condition on a child's development. Children with serious developmental problems or disabilities may also be at a higher risk of maltreatment. By recognizing such delays and disabilities, workers can often provide supportive and counseling services to parents, thereby reducing stress in the family and potentially preventing maltreatment. (More detailed information on the relationship between maltreatment and developmental disabilities, and services to these children and their families, can be found in Chapter VII, Child Welfare Services for Children with Developmental Disabilities.)

Knowledge of child development is necessary to prevent crisis for the child during placement into substitute care.

Accurate knowledge of a child's cognitive and emotional capabilities can help caseworkers understand the child's experience during separation and placement into substitute care. The worker can plan and implement placement activities that minimize the child's stress, and that help the child cope with the placement experience. This can help prevent emotional crisis and subsequent negative effects on the child's development. (Refer to discussion in Section VIII-C, "Placement Strategies to Prevent Trauma.")

In summary, to perform many essential child welfare activities, the worker should have the following knowledge and skill related to child development:

- Knowledge of the stages and processes of normal development in all domains for children ages birth through adolescence;

- The ability to observe and assess a child's development in the primary developmental domains;

- Knowledge of the early warning signs of developmental delay or disability, and the ability to recognize indicators of developmental problems in children;

- Knowledge of appropriate agency and community resources for developmental assessment and for remedial services, and how to properly access these resources;

- Knowledge of developmental opportunities for children available through community resources, including special service providers; and the ability to incorporate developmental services into case plans;

- Knowledge of the most appropriate and effective parenting and discipline strategies for children at different stages of development; and

- The ability to counsel and educate parents and caregivers regarding normal developmental expectations for their children.

Workers who adopt a developmental approach to child welfare services can have a pronounced impact on the long-term well-being of the abused and neglected children in their care.

B. THE EFFECTS OF MALTREATMENT ON INFANTS AND TODDLERS

1. Conceptual Framework

2. Application

3. Case Example

Conceptual Framework

Infants and toddlers are particularly vulnerable to maltreatment by their care-givers, and they are very likely to suffer permanent and serious developmental problems as a result of maltreatment. The signs of developmental problems are often observable within the first weeks and months after birth; however, these are typically not recognized until much later, sometimes not until the child first attends school. This is very unfortunate, since early intervention is the single most important variable in minimizing the long–term negative consequences of early developmental insults.

A child welfare caseworker with training and skill in child development will routinely assess the developmental status of all children, but will be particular-ly concerned about recognizing signs of developmental problems in infants and toddlers. By doing so, the worker can make a profound impact on the long–term prognosis for these children, and can potentially prevent later maltreatment.

The detailed information in this chapter is presented to enable caseworkers to do brief developmental assessments of children on their caseloads, and to refer children suspected of having developmental problems for formal assessment and, where appropriate, intensive developmental services.

DEVELOPMENTAL MILESTONES, BIRTH TO THREE YEARS

The Newborn

The newborn appears thin, with scrawny arms and legs, and a large, rounded belly. The skinny extremities result from limited muscle development, and is apparent even in a heavier newborn. Feet and legs may be bowed and turned inward, knees are often bent up toward the chest, and arms are kept close to the body.

The infant's head represents about one fourth of its total body length. In adults, the head is approximately one seventh of the body. The large head size of the newborn results from rapid prenatal development of the brain relative to the rest of the body. This illustrates an important developmental concept: devel-opment progresses from the head down (cephalocaudal, which literally means from "head to tail"), and from the inside out (proxidistmal). The brain and cen-tral nervous system are the first systems to begin development after conception. The upper body develops before the legs and feet; and, the internal organs develop before the extremities.

Newborn infants can see, but their eyes cannot focus well at all distances. They focus best at objects that are eight to ten inches from them.

The newborn infant displays numerous reflexes, many of which disappear within a few months. One of these, the asymmetric tonic neck reflex (ATNR), is sometimes called the "fencing posture." When the infant's head turns to one side, the arm on that side of the body extends, and the arm on the opposite side bends up toward the ear. This is normal for a newborn. Persistence of this reflex beyond a few months may indicate developmental problems, such as cerebral palsy.

Other reflexes are the grasping reflex (the child will reflexively close his hand around an object placed in his palm); the sucking reflex (the child will turn his head toward an object brushing his cheek and will make sucking movements with his mouth); the startle reflex (in which the child jerks in response to loud noises or sudden movement); and the Babinski reflex (reflexive extension of the foot when the bottom is stroked).

A newborn's general health is rated in the delivery room using the Apgar scale, named after Virginia Apgar, the physician who developed it. The Apgar score is determined twice; once within a minute of birth, and again at three to five minutes. Up to two points are given for each of five criteria; heart rate, respiration, muscle tone, color, and reflexes. An Apgar rating of seven to ten points generally indicates a healthy infant; an Apgar under five often indicates that the child is in distress. A low Apgar at the five-minute reading may indicate the infant is ill, injured, or otherwise at risk. Infants with developmental disabilities often have low Apgar ratings at birth.

Healthy newborns exhibit a lot of gross motor activity, with particularly active movement of arms and legs. Most of these movements are rough, random, and unrefined. Large muscle activity is often jerky and very uncoordinated. There is very little fine motor coordination.

The newborn's head control is also limited, due to immature muscle development. The back and neck muscles are not strong enough to support the head, and it will wobble if not supported. However, all newborns should be able to lift and turn their faces to the side when placed face down. This prevents suffocation. Hypotonic infants (with very poor muscle tone) are often not able to do this.

The newborn's legs will not support any weight. Instead, when the foot touches the ground you can see the "stepping reflex," a reflexive withdrawal of one leg and an extension of the other leg. The baby looks like she is "walking in air."

Some early developmental theorists thought that infants were born as "blank slates." Recent research has demonstrated that infants are born with many abilities.

They can see. They like to look at things with high stimulus value, such as contrasting colors, and interesting patterns. They delight in looking at human faces. They see best at a distance of eight to ten inches, which is the approximate distance between a nursing infant and the mother's face.

Infants hear well, even *in utero*. They orient to sounds by turning in the direction of the sound. They recognize the voices of their significant caretakers within a few days of birth.

Their senses of touch, smell, and taste are also developed. When they are fed sour or salty foods, they will grimace and make faces. They like to be touched. Newborns are often more comfortable when their skin is covered, and will often settle better when wrapped tightly in a blanket.

Several states of alertness and awareness have been observed in infants. In the *active alert* state the infant looks around, listens, and responds vigorously to stimuli. In the *quiet alert* state, the infant is quieter and less physically active, but seems to be "taking things in" by looking and listening. A *drowsy* state occurs just before the infant is ready to fall asleep. The child is physically very quiet, and will not normally respond to stimuli.

Parents and caseworkers should be able to recognize the various states for several reasons.

An assessment of the infant's development should be conducted during the active alert state. An assessment during the drowsy state may lead to misjudgments about the child's development.

Parents should try to interact with their infants during the active alert state, when the child is naturally involved with the environment. An infant is not likely to respond to a parent's attention when quiet or drowsy. The worker may have to teach the parent that this doesn't mean the infant is not interested in the parent.

Infants in the quiet alert state who become cranky can often be soothed by simply turning them to a different view, changing rooms, or providing new stimuli.

Even a very young infant will show considerable awareness and interest in people and the environment, will explore visually, and will initiate visual contact. It is easy to observe such evidence of early cognitive development in all healthy newborns.

By about five or six weeks, the infant displays improved gross motor ability. The first muscles to develop strength and control are those of the head, neck and shoulders, following the cephalocaudal, or head-to-toe pattern. By five weeks, when lying face down, the infant should be able to raise his head and shoulders.

Fine motor control develops later. The infant's hands will generally be fisted when at rest during the first three to four months of life.

By five weeks the infant's eyes are well focused, and she can keep an object in view as it moves from the periphery (edges) of her visual field to the "midline," which is an imaginary line that transects the center of the body from head to toe. Following an object with the eyes is called tracking. At five weeks, healthy infants can track to the midline, but cannot track through the midline to the other side of the visual field.

Attachment between a parent and the infant is visible in the way the parent holds, cuddles, and responds to the infant's needs. The attachment process is satisfying to both the parent and the infant. The infant's needs for security and comfort are met; parents' feelings of love and competence are increased when the infant conforms comfortably into their arms and quiets. The infant's first smile strengthens the attachment.

Attachment responses are instinctive between most parents and their infants. They should not, however, be taken for granted. Some parents who, as children, never developed strong attachments may not recognize these cues, but they can often be trained to do so.

One of the signs of healthy attachment is when the parent engages the infant in the "en face" position. In this position, the infant can easily gaze at the parent's face and maintain direct eye contact. Brothers and sisters also form strong attachments to the infant.

Three to Five Months

By three months we see advances in muscle strength and control. The infant has adequate head and neck control to hold her head at a 90° angle from the floor. To determine the angle, you draw an imaginary line from the top of the infant's head through her ear to the floor. The newborn could barely raise her head. A two–month–old infant should be able to raise her head to a 45 degree angle. The three–month–old infant can also use her arms and shoulders to support her upper body. Recall the principle of cephalocaudal (head to toe) development. The muscles of the arms, chest, and shoulders are next to develop after those of the head and neck.

The infant's head control is not as well developed, however, when pulled up by the arms from a position lying on the back. The head will drop backwards in what is referred to as a head lag. This head lag is normal for an infant of three months. It will disappear at about five months, when the muscles in the neck and back are stronger.

Three-month–old infants experiment with their bodies. They are beginning to use the large muscle groups in their abdomens and legs, and they strengthen them by trying out new physical activities. A three month old can bear some weight on the legs, but is very unsteady.

Alertness, intense interest, and curiosity about people and the environment continue to be early signs of cognitive development. These signs are often absent in abused or neglected infants.

At three months the infant can visually track an object all the way through the midline. The infant focuses on an object at the midline, and will follow it visually as it moves toward the edge of the visual field. The infant often will turn his head far to the side in order to keep the object in view.

One visual problem that can often be identified in infancy is called strabismus. The eyes appear crossed or otherwise out of line. Strabismus is the result of a muscle weakness in the eyes. It usually corrects itself as the child develops. Untreated strabismus can, however, lead to serious vision defects. Infants with abnormal eye positioning should be evaluated by an ophthalmologist as soon as the problem is noted. Surgery can correct the condition if performed before the child is age two. Surgery after this time may not fully restore normal vision.

A three-month–old infant is not strong enough to sit unassisted. When the infant's body is propped, head and neck control are good. However, the infant cannot maintain balance, and will slump forward or fall over, if not held.

By four months the infant is very interested in handling objects. While she won't yet reach for objects, she will close her hand around an object that is placed in her palm. Fine motor control is still pretty primitive, and the grasp is awkward. At four months it's hard to know if an infant's grasp is reflexive or purposeful. The early grasping reflex is replaced by purposeful, goal–directed activity by four to five months. It is also common for infants this age to put objects into their mouths. This is a way for the infant to explore objects, as well as to suck.

Attending to and responding to objects is also an indication of early cognitive development. The infant will focus intently on objects and often responds by excitedly flailing arms and hands, or by squealing or laughing. By this age, infants are beginning to anticipate events, and may become visibly excited when they see a familiar object.

By the end of five months, the infant will have made significant gains in motor development. The head is now routinely held at a full 90 degree (right) angle, and the infant will prop on her hands and push her shoulders and chest up off the floor. Upper body control is much improved, and the infant will turn her head and body around to see what is going on.

The five-month-old baby is developing improved coordination in the lower body, and much of his physical activity now involves the legs and feet. The baby will play by stretching his legs and touching his feet, and by pulling the knees up to the chest deliberately; this is no longer reflexive.

Babies learn new skills while playing and experimenting. For example, quite by accident the baby may swing her legs far to the side, and her shoulders will automatically follow. She has discovered how to roll over onto her stomach from her back. Once a new motor skill is learned, the baby will repeat it many times until she becomes proficient. Then she integrates it into her regular activities and uses it, as in learning to roll to the opposite corner of the room and back again.

By five months the baby can also support weight on her legs, and appears strong and steady, with excellent head control. The head lag referred to earlier should have also disappeared by five months, since the head and neck are now supported by much stronger muscles.

A five-month-old baby's hands are rarely fisted, unless they are purposefully closed for grasping objects. Hands that remain tightly fisted in older infants may be an early warning sign of cerebral palsy.

The five-month-old baby will reach for objects, practicing and perfecting both fine motor control and eye-hand coordination. The baby will reach directly for and grasp an object such as a rattle, and will manipulate it in front of her face, while continuing to keep it in view. This is no longer reflexive behavior; it is purposeful and goal directed.

By five months, babies can transfer objects from one hand to the other across the midline. Babies use both hands interchangeably with no clear hand preference for the first year to 18 months. They will usually reach for an object with the hand that is closest to it, and will rarely reach across their bodies. A clear hand preference before 12 to 18 months, or failure to transfer objects from hand to hand across the midline, may be symptoms of cerebral palsy. The smaller muscles of the hand and fingers are also developing, resulting in improved fine motor coordination. This illustrates the developmental principle of proxidistmal development, as the muscles of the hands and fingers develop later than do muscles closer to the center of the body.

The five month old is very responsive to social stimuli. When something interesting happens, she responds with vigorous physical activity, direct eye contact, big smiles, and loud vocalizations. Other people can easily recognize the baby's emotional states, including pleasure, anger, fear, pain, and protest. The baby is more animated and interactive, and most parents feel they can communicate better with their baby. The baby's responsiveness can be very pleasurable and reinforcing for the parent.

Seven to Eight Months

By seven months many babies will have progressed to sitting without assistance. Some still cannot "get to sitting" by themselves, and must be placed in the sitting position. At first, the baby can maintain balance only as long as he sits in a "tripod" position, with knees bent and feet placed together in front of him. If the baby moves, he will lose his balance and topple over. Sitting without propping does free the baby's hands, enabling him to manipulate objects.

By seven months, the baby has developed considerable upper body strength, and can prop on hands and arms and push the chest and abdomen up off the floor. Add leg movements, which were learned and perfected during earlier periods of lower body play, and the baby is now in a position to begin the next major gross motor task of crawling. At seven to eight months the baby can support weight on his legs with ease, but may not be able to balance in a standing position without being held.

The baby's fine motor coordination has also improved, but finger–thumb opposition has not yet developed. A typical hand position for babies between six to eight months is sometimes called "raking." The baby drags the whole hand across an object, like one would use a rake, and then closes all five fingers around the object and grasps it in the palm.

Babies this age are attracted to objects because of their shapes, colors, and textures. The baby has a primitive understanding of objects. He will have discovered how to remove sticks from holes, but he doesn't yet understand that they can be put back in. The baby will amuse himself for several minutes by repeating the same activity many times in succession, apparently receiving pleasure from repetition and mastery. We begin to see the development of an extended attention span.

Nine to Ten Months

The nine month old should be able to sit comfortably without having to prop himself with his hands. The baby can also get to and from a sitting position by himself, or lean over to reach for an object and return to sitting without losing balance or falling.

By nine months the baby should also be crawling. Not all children crawl in the typical manner–that is, on hands and knees–but they do develop some way of getting from place to place before they learn to walk. Some scoot like a snake, or roll across the floor, or pull with their arms (the G.I. Joe Crawl). Some "early walkers" progress quickly to standing and walking without a long period of coordinated crawling.

A nine-month-old baby can usually crawl to furniture and pull up to a standing position, and can stand for long periods, as long as he holds onto something. The baby has increased strength, but as yet lacks balance. The baby may be able to stand alone, but often for only a few seconds. Arms may be held in an outstretched position to retain balance, and when first standing, the child's legs may be bowed; they are not quite ready to fully support his weight.

The nine month old has well-developed eye–hand coordination. The child still uses both hands equally; it is still too early to have developed a clear hand preference.

Fine motor development will have improved. By this age, the child will have developed finger–thumb opposition, sometimes called the "pincer grasp," and he can hold objects with the fingertips of one hand. With the development of finger–thumb opposition, the baby graduates from "raking" to "finger feeding," and easily self-feeds foods like breakfast cereal, one at a time, closing thumb and forefinger around each one.

The nine month old demonstrates rudimentary problem solving and goal–directed behaviors. The baby does things with an end in mind. He also has a beginning understanding of how activities may be sequenced to reach a desired end. This is evidence of increased cognitive development.

At this age, the baby is very social and interactive. He is playful, affectionate, and responsive to people to whom he is closely attached. He will not play with or easily relate to people he does not know well. The baby's ability to discriminate between people, and to relate differently to them, is both an advance in cognitive development, and a sign of healthy and strong attachment.

The ability to differentiate between people often results in "stranger anxiety." Between nine and ten months old, many children display an initial suspiciousness and fear of people they do not know. They withdraw and observe from a distance. If a stranger moves closer, they will react by withdrawing further or crying. When permitted to go at their own pace, most children will eventually warm to the stranger and go about their activities. Stranger anxiety may develop in children who previously were happy interacting with almost anyone. Stranger anxiety results from the baby's cognitive ability to discriminate between people, plus the development of stronger attachments to important people.

Separation anxiety may also develop around this same time. Children may cry any time they are separated from their parent or primary caregiver, even if the caregiver is only in the next room. They are usually most comfortable if their parent is clearly in view.

Cultural variables may affect children's responses to separation and to strangers. A child who is rarely left in the care of others may show greater anxiety or distress when separated from the parent. A child who is cared for by multiple caregivers, and is often with large groups of people may show little or no distress when separated from the parent, or when in the presence of strangers. Some children will warm quickly to new people after an initial period of shyness or hesitancy. Constitutional factors and temperament also influence the degree of a child's distress in strange situations.

One Year

Most children begin to walk, on average, at about a year. It takes many months to perfect the skill of walking. Walking involves balance, coordination, and excellent motor control. When children are first learning to walk, we can see their intense concentration. They will often walk with arms outstretched to help balance them. Children often revert to earlier methods of getting around, such as crawling or standing holding on, especially when they are tired.

Walking ushers in a new sense of freedom and independence for the child, and the child enters the developmental stage of autonomy. Children will voluntarily separate from the parent for short periods of time to explore the environment, but will return to the parent periodically for reassurance or comfort, or when distressed.

Insecure or poorly attached children cannot find comfort from their parent when under stress, nor can they resume exploration after a reunion with the parent. This inhibits their willingness to explore their environments.

Physical independence has its parallel in emotional development. This developmental period is often referred to as "the terrible twos," even though it may begin as early as 12 to 18 months. The age of onset of this stage, and the degree to which the child will express autonomy, varies. In general, however, the placid, friendly, responsive and cooperative child of last year suddenly becomes willful, uncooperative, and stubborn. Nonverbal children often express their autonomy through tantrums. Verbal children may also exhibit autonomy through language. (The two year old's favorite words are NO!, ME DO IT!, and MINE!)

Early in the second year, children begin to develop symbolic thinking. This is a major step in cognitive development. Children begin to look at books or magazines, and will look for familiar objects. They will point to objects and figures of interest, often in response to a verbal cue. Attaching names to familiar objects is the beginning of language development.

There is a wide age range within which children develop language. Some children can produce meaningful words at a year; and some don't begin to talk until they are age two or older. Most children develop receptive language many months before expressive language; that is, they can understand language earlier than they can speak it.

A primary cognitive milestone of the first year is the development of object permanence. Object permanence is the concept that objects do not vanish or cease to exist when they are removed from view. Infants under a year of age quickly forget objects that are not in view, and they don't search for them, even if they have watched the object being hidden. However, once children have developed object permanence, they will search for the object because they know it still exists. They will look for it in the place they had last seen it. They are aware that the object has a permanent existence, independent of their immediate perception of it.

One and a Half Years

By this time, most children will have been walking for several months and will demonstrate good balance and stability. They need no longer think about each step; the skill has been mastered and integrated. They are developing more complex motor skills such as climbing, which they use to get up and down the stairs, or up into a chair. They can also "stoop and recover," bending or squatting to reach an object and returning to standing without having to use arms and hands for balance.

Fine motor skills, including finger–thumb opposition, are more refined and coordinated. Children will routinely finger-feed themselves, and can drink from a cup unassisted. They will hold most objects using their fingertips, rather than grasping with their whole hand.

Cognitive development is reflected in their more complex use of objects. For example, play with plastic beads includes removing them from, and returning them to, a container. Children this age also understand that certain objects are to be used for particular purposes. They know, for example, that a toy lawn mower should be pushed, that a ball is to be thrown, a comb is used to comb hair, and keys unlock doors.

The imitation of complex behaviors begins at this time. This can affect the rate with which children acquire new skills, as children may learn more quickly when they have opportunities to observe and model the actions of other children and of adults.

The 15- to 18-month old is very social. He learns and repeats simple games, such as "patty cake," "peek-a-boo," or "gimme five," and will play them upon verbal request. The child's responsiveness to verbal cues also illustrates his comprehension of spoken language.

Two Years

The primary cognitive milestone for the two year old is the development of language.

Infants produce their first purposeful sounds at around three months, when they appear to discover they have a voice that is under their control. They babble and imitate sounds at around six months. This must be considered vocalization rather than language, because the sounds are random, and have no symbolic meaning.

Most children begin to consistently produce spoken language between 18 months and two years. The development of language is dependent upon a cognitive leap that occurs during the second year, the emergence of symbolic thought.

Sounds that were originally unattached vocalizations and spontaneous expressions become associated with specific objects, people, or activities. At some point, the child realizes that a particular pattern of sounds can represent the object or an action. The sounds take on meaning for the child. This ability characterizes basic symbolic thought. Once the child achieves this understanding, language develops rapidly. The typical pattern of language development makes sense, when it is viewed within the context of the child's world view.

The child's development during the first year is centered around two primary areas; mastery of his own body, and an understanding of objects. At the end of the first year, the child has mastered many gross and fine motor tasks. The child has also learned that objects exist, and then that they have permanent identities and characteristics.

It is, therefore, not surprising that the first words the child understands, and speaks, are the names of things he knows and understands. This includes the objects and people that are important to him (mama, dada, bottle, juice, baby, Teddy, apple, ball, kitty, chair); and, his activities (sit, eat, play, sleep, go bye-bye).

The next milestone occurs when the child combines two words into a duo, a phrase that usually combines the object and the action, or the object and a place. The duo is shorthand language. The meaning of the duo greatly exceeds that which is reflected by the two words. For example, "ball chair" might mean the ball is in the chair, the ball is under the chair, or the ball was thrown at the chair. The child at this age typically understands more than he can verbally communicate; again, receptive language is more highly developed than expressive language.

Imitation continues to be a primary means of play and learning for the two year old. The determination to imitate another child is often an incentive for the child to try new activities. We must consider the importance of growing up in an environment that stimulates and supports this type of learning.

Two year olds like to be helpful. They will attempt to imitate even difficult activities. Mastery and autonomy are important, and despite the evident difficulty of the task, they will often insist, "Me do it."

The complexity of a child's toys and the way she uses them provide additional clues to the child's level of cognitive development. In play, the child demonstrates both imitative learning, and trial and error problem solving. The child may choose to play with more complex toys that require pieces to be placed in a particular order, or uniquely shaped objects be placed into their appropriate holes. Fine motor skills and eye–hand coordination have also improved. Two year old children can easily build a tower of four blocks without toppling it.

The child's ability to symbolize thought is expressed through play. The child recreates with toys many things he has seen in the world, such as constructing a fence or pushing a toy truck. Toddlers begin imaginative play as well, as in putting a stick between their legs and riding it like a horse, or racing through the house with arms extended, pretending to be an airplane.

The primary task in emotional development of the two year old is autonomy. Autonomy is a state of mind, and it is reflected in all the child's activities. If secure, the two year old will trot off–out the door, down the street, through the supermarket, or into the woods, confidently striking out ahead. Healthy toddlers are alert to their surroundings, and eager to find out what's around the next corner. We talk about this child being "into everything," and naturally curious. Explorations provide the impetus for learning, and the mastery of important skills.

There are differences in how children express their autonomy. Some children are more outgoing and self-directed, others more quiet and receptive. Cultural factors can affect the way in which the child expresses autonomy. However, the emergence of autonomy, and the mastery of situations, characterize activities of all normally developing children at this age.

At age two, children are still very self–centered, and their interactive play skills are poorly developed. They do not cooperate, and they don't usually share. They lack the cognitive ability to understand another child's perspective. This is an aspect of egocentric thinking which will be more fully discussed later. Two year olds will often be totally engrossed in playing with a toy, and oblivious to other children. Playing in the presence of other children is called parallel play. Children will watch each other play, or may even play side by side with the same toys, but they cooperate in only the most rudimentary fashion.

Two and a Half Years

At two and a half, most children talk in phrases or in complete sentences. They understand the concepts that support words like "in," "out," "under," and "over." They also use connecting words such as "and" to string phrases together into often complicated communications, albeit not always grammatically correct. Assessing a child's language at this age means determining whether the content of the child's communication can be understood, not whether the child is skilled at pronunciation or grammar.

The child's gross motor skills have developed to permit skillful running, tumbling, and climbing. Most children this age can master a tricycle or other wheeled toys. Their fine motor coordination has also greatly improved. If children are given the opportunity to use pencils or crayons, they can draw. A two and a half year old can identify shapes, including a circle and an X, both of which he can draw on paper.

Autonomy means wanting to do things independently. If allowed, the child will try to dress, wash, and feed himself, even though he may have difficulty in completing the task. While not very efficient, letting children practice these skills allows them to perfect them, and gives them a feeling of pride and accomplishment.

Between age two and three, children's play patterns begin to change, and we begin to see interactive play. The emergence of interactive play is stimulated by children's ability to communicate with each other. However, early social interactions don't always go smoothly, and things are not always peaceful and pleasant. The two to three year old wants his own way, and often responds to frustration with aggression, including hitting, biting, and temper tantrums. The autonomous child is emotionally impulsive and has not yet developed internal controls. Adults have to step in to resolve the battles and prevent children from hurting each other. By the age of three, children will often prefer, and will be more adept at, interactive play.

Children in different cultures may display different amounts of aggression, depending upon whether aggressive behavior is permitted. Aggression may be valued as being "tough," and "standing up for yourself;" or, it may be viewed as a negative attribute that should be suppressed in the interests of group cohesion and cooperativeness. Some cultures are more tolerant of aggression in boys than in girls. Therefore, children may show different amounts of aggression depending upon each child's temperament and culture.

Three Years

By age three, children have truly mastered basic gross motor skills such as walking, running, and climbing, and can perform them easily without much concentration. These skills are developed by children in a wide variety of physical play activities, such as maintaining balance on a jungle gym, throwing and catching a ball, climbing a ladder, hopping on one foot, or sliding down the slide.

Three year olds love playground equipment and active physical play. They will repeat new motor skills continuously, even though they may have mastered the task; they appear to enjoy performing for its own sake, as when they slide down the slide for the 30th time in as many minutes.

The increasing complexity of the three year old's toys is evidence of advancing cognitive skills. Three–year–old children are adept at putting together puzzles, which require that the child recognize shapes and colors, and see the relationships between the puzzle pieces. They must also understand that the parts together comprise a whole. While younger children work puzzles by trial and error, or imitation, the three year old can discriminate each piece, and knows where it fits in the picture.

Three year olds are also adept at imaginative play with toys; they are often creative, and play with objects in a symbolic manner. For example, a child may stack up boxes or blocks and announce he has, "built a wall so my horses can't get out," demonstrating his understanding of the concepts of open and closed, the nature of horses and their tendency to escape, and the purpose of fences in keeping them from doing so.

The three year old recognizes colors, and can sort objects into groups by color, as well as by size and similarity of type. This is early evidence of a cognitive ability that becomes important during the school years–the ability to classify objects with similar characteristics into groups.

Improved eye–hand coordination permits the child to build complex structures that require the balanced placement of objects, such as a tower of many blocks. Eye-hand coordination also permits the development of self-help skills. At three years children can put on their shoes, even though tying them is a complicated fine motor skill that will not normally be mastered until age four or five. Children will put toothpaste on a toothbrush and brush their own teeth, will wash their hands, and will try to meet most of their own toileting needs.

Application

TOILET TRAINING

Toilet training is one of the most challenging parenting tasks during the second and third years. It warrants more extensive discussion, because toileting accidents, and other problems in toilet training, are a common precipitant in the abuse of toddlers.

Toilet training problems may occur for several reasons:

- The parent begins toilet training before the child is ready, and the child, therefore, does not comply.

- The toilet training process becomes a battle for control between the parent and the child.

- The parent may have unrealistic developmental expectations for the child, and may misinterpret the child's lack of bladder or bowel control as deliberate defiance.

- Some children have problems with constipation. Painful bowel movements may result in children holding off the movement as long as possible. This results in more pain, which leads to further withholding. This can be misinterpreted by parents and other persons as uncooperativeness.

By waiting until the child demonstrates readiness to be trained, the toilet training process will be of shorter duration and will be less of a struggle for the parent. In general, girls are ready to be trained somewhat earlier than boys. However, each child must be evaluated individually. Very few children are ready to begin before the age of two. Most children are ready to begin by age two and a half, unless the child is developmentally delayed, or there are complicating physical problems. Some children will have occasional accidents as late as age five or six. It is usually because they are busy doing something they like, and don't want to stop to go to the toilet, until it's too late.

Several factors contribute to a child's readiness to be trained:

- The child has developed sufficient language to understand words that describe toileting activities, such as "potty," "poop," "BM," "pee pee," "toilet," and "diaper."

- The child has communication skills to let the parent know when she is about to wet or soil, or has already done so. These may be gestures or single words.

- The child knows the difference between a wet diaper and a dry diaper, and shows discomfort when wet or soiled, either verbally or by pulling at her clothes, crying, etc.

- The child has developed adequate urinary control, and remains dry for periods of at least two hours at a time during the day. Bowel movements should be regular.

- The child demonstrates interest and willingness to try out the toilet or potty chair.

- There are no complicating physical or medical problems.

The caseworker can help a parent develop realistic expectations for toilet training, and help the parent approach it with a patient and positive attitude.

The worker should communicate that early in toilet training, frequent accidents are normal. The parent must not feel pressured that toilet training has to occur within a designated period of time.

The parent should be reassured that accidents are not deliberate and do not automatically represent defiance, even from a very autonomous child. The parent must be able to accept accidents matter-of-factly, without scolding or punishing the child.

The more consistent the parent is in making toileting part of a daily routine, the easier it will be. Knowing at what times of day the child normally wets or soils helps.

The parent will probably want the child to be out of diapers before the child is ready. This will probably be frustrating for the parent. However, if the child isn't interested, it's easier to change diapers for a while longer than to battle daily with the child.

The parent must be willing to provide the child with tangible rewards for successes. Some parents may resist giving rewards, believing them to be a type of bribery, and expect that the child should want to comply on her own. The worker should explain that the parent's expectation for social cooperation is unrealistic for a two year old, whose primary developmental concern is autonomy. Rewards serve as an incentive for the two year old to choose to use the toilet. Providing rewards for success will not be necessary when the child is a little older and better motivated, and when toileting becomes a less important focus of emotional energy for the child.

There are several parenting techniques that promote toilet training in a child who demonstrates readiness. Parents can do the following:

- Point out to the child when she is wetting or soiling, or has done so. "David went peepee in the diaper." "Susie pooped. Let's put on a clean diaper."

- Introduce the potty chair, and let the child become accustomed to it before she is expected to use it.

- Take the child to the potty each time she demonstrates she needs to use it, without expectation that she will. If she does, reward her. If she doesn't, don't make a fuss. Don't leave her there for more than a few minutes, and don't give her toys and let her play.

- Always reward for success. The reward should be something that the child likes.

- Ignore accidents, and clean up in a matter-of-fact manner. Never punish the child for wetting or soiling.

- Allow the child to watch and model children who are a few years older. Being "a big girl like Molly" is a good incentive for younger children to imitate siblings, and help to train themselves.

- If a battle begins, and the parent finds herself feeling angry and frustrated, stop for a while, and try again later, when the child may be more ready or willing. Don't push.

The norms for toilet training in some cultures may be different from those of most Americans. For instance, parents in some cultures do not formally "train" their children, but the children are allowed to model and learn to use the toilet by watching others, including their parents. They become "trained" at their own rate. The caseworker should understand the sanctioned parenting practices of these cultures, particularly if a family has recently emigrated from another country.

THE EFFECTS OF ABUSE AND NEGLECT ON INFANTS AND TODDLERS

Infants and toddlers are at especially high risk of abuse and neglect from parents who are predisposed to maltreat them. Several characteristics typical of very young children place them at higher risk of maltreatment:

- Infants are demanding. They require constant attention and a great commitment of time, and rarely do they respect the parent's needs or schedule. Sleep is frequently interrupted, and new parents are chronically tired. This is inherently stressful to even the most competent parent.

- Infants cry at times for no apparent reason, and at times they cannot be comforted. A crying or screaming infant can be extremely distressing and frustrating to a parent, particularly if the parent is unable to quiet the infant, despite considerable effort.

- Newborns may be perceived as unattractive and strange looking. They tend to be red, spotty, wrinkled, and bent into awkward positions, and they may appear deformed to an uneducated parent. Their appearance may frighten a parent, or may stimulate a parent's feelings of poor self-esteem.

- Newborns are not very social for the first three or four months. They demand a lot and give little in return. The parent must derive any pleasure from providing care, rather than expecting expressions of gratitude or recognition from the infant.

- Infants who are premature, sickly, irritable, colicky, have medical conditions, or otherwise require special care, are most susceptible to abuse. Sickly or premature infants are more demanding in their care needs than healthy infants. Separations as a result of hospitalization or illness of the infant may also interfere with the early attachment process.

- The toddler's principal developmental task is autonomy, and typical behaviors of this stage often include stubbornness, rebelliousness, tantrums, angry outbursts, aggressiveness, obstinacy, and oppositional behavior. Struggles for power and control may develop between toddlers and parents. Oppositional behaviors can try the patience of even the most knowledgeable and understanding parent.

- Toilet training can be one of the most stressful developmental tasks for both children and parents. Trying to toilet train a child before he is ready can lead to extreme frustration and feelings of failure on the parent's part. The child experiences criticism and punishment for reasons he does not understand. Toilet training can become a battleground between a parent who wants social compliance, and a child whose major developmental task is to remain in control of his own body, and his environment.

Infants and toddlers are also especially susceptible to serious negative developmental outcomes from maltreatment:

- Infants and toddlers cannot protect themselves. They can't run, scream, or go for help. They are dependent and vulnerable. They will die if they are not properly cared for.

- Very rapid brain and body growth during the first two years makes the infant extremely susceptible to the effects of malnutrition. Mental retardation and growth deficiencies can result.

- The infant's soft skull and unprotected body are very susceptible to injury. Head injuries easily lead to severe brain damage. The soft bones of the skull are more likely to fracture from a blow.

- Muscles are not developed adequately to protect the trunk and abdomen, and blows to this part of the body will cause serious internal injuries.

- Head and neck muscles are not strong enough to withstand even a mild shaking without potential brain and spinal cord injury.

- Infants are more susceptible to infection; they have not yet developed immunity to many environmental agents.

- Infants and toddlers use their bodies to explore their environments, to manipulate objects, to solve problems, and to master many tasks. Physical injury, therefore, can have serious implications for cognitive, as well as physical, development.

- Infants and toddlers are particularly vulnerable to the emotional effects of abuse and neglect. They are likely to experience abuse and neglect as raw, diffuse, pervasive, and incomprehensible pain. Abuse and neglect create barriers to attachment and the subsequent development of trust. This can permanently impair the child's relationship ability, and lead to the development of serious personality problems.

Consequences of Abuse and Neglect on Physical Development

There are several potential negative consequences of abuse or neglect on the physical development of infants or toddlers. These include:

- Chronic malnutrition of infants and toddlers results in growth retardation, brain damage, and potentially, mental retardation. This is prevalent in situations of serious neglect and failure to thrive.

- Head injury can result in severe brain damage or death. Direct blows to the head can create swelling of brain tissue and subdural hematomas (pools of blood in the brain), that destroy brain tissue and can result in brain stem compression and herniation, blindness, deafness, mental retardation, epilepsy, cerebral palsy, skull fracture, paralysis, and coma.

- Less severe but repeated blows to the head can also result in equally serious brain damage. When injured, the infant's soft brain tissue swells. Pressure inside the skull leads to a decrease in oxygen supply to the brain, and involved nerve cells die. This type of injury may be impossible to detect, or may be detectable only by sophisticated imaging technologies such as MRI (Magnetic Resonance Imaging) or CT Scans (Computerized Tomography). In the absence of obvious signs of external trauma, these injuries may go unidentified.

- Injury to the hypothalamus and pituitary glands in the brain can result in growth impairment and inadequate sexual development.

- Blows or slaps to the side of the head over the ear can injure the inner ear mechanism and cause partial or complete hearing loss.

- Shaking can result in brain injury equal to that caused by a direct blow to the head. Additionally, bones in the neck and spine can be injured, resulting in a break or collapse of the vertebrae. Spinal cord injury can result in paralysis, or various degrees of other sensory, motor, or autonomic dysfunction.

- Internal injuries from blows to the abdomen and soft body parts can lead to permanent physical disability or death.

- Medical neglect, such as withholding treatment for treatable conditions, can lead to permanent physical disability, such as hearing loss from untreated ear infections, vision problems from untreated strabismus (crossing of the eyes), respiratory damage from pneumonia chronic bronchitis, or other medical conditions that can lead to significant injury or death if left untreated.

- Neglected infants and toddlers have poor muscle tone and poor motor control, exhibit delays in gross and fine motor development and coordination, and often fail to develop basic motor skills. Since most of an infant's cognitive development is facilitated by motor and sensory interaction with the environment, physical delays contribute to cognitive delays as well.

Consequences of Abuse and Neglect on Cognitive Development

Abuse or neglect can have serious negative consequences on the cognitive development of infants or toddlers.

- An absence of stimulation interferes with the growth and development of the brain, and generalized cognitive delay can result. In situations of serious neglect, a significant lack of stimulation for a long period of time can lead to mental retardation. Brain damage from injury or malnutrition can also lead to mental retardation.

- Abused and neglected toddlers typically exhibit language and speech delays. They fail to use language to communicate with others, and some do not talk at all, even though they may have the motor ability to speak. This represents a cognitive delay that can also affect social development, including the development of peer relationships.

- Maltreated infants are often apathetic, listless, placid, or immobile. They often do not manipulate objects, or do so in repetitive, primitive ways. They are often inactive, lack curiosity, and do not explore their environments. This lack of interactive experience often restricts opportunities for learning. Maltreated infants may not master even basic concepts such as object permanence, and may not develop basic problem–solving skills.

Consequences of Abuse and Neglect on Social Development

The negative consequences of abuse or neglect on the social development of infants or toddlers include the following:

- Abuse teaches a child that interpersonal encounters are typically painful and unpredictable. Neglected infants are deprived of opportunities for meaningful or pleasurable interpersonal encounters. Both experiences interfere with the basic attachment process and the development of trust. Maltreated infants often fail to form attachments to primary caregivers, or may demonstrate insecure attachment, characterized by anxiety, forlorn clinging, and an inability to be comforted when distressed.

- Maltreated infants often do not react to separation from the parent, and may not develop separation or stranger anxiety. Maltreated infants and toddlers may willingly "go to anyone." This failure to discriminate significant people, and the resulting disruption in the attachment process is one of the most striking characteristics of abused and neglected children.

- Maltreated infants are often passive, apathetic, and unresponsive to others. They may not maintain eye contact, may not become excited when talked to or approached, and often cannot be engaged into vocalizing (cooing or babbling) with an adult. These infants may not develop non-verbal communications that attract and hold an adult's attention.

- Abused or neglected toddlers may not develop play skills, and often cannot be engaged into reciprocal, interactive play. Their play skills may be very immature and primitive. This can affect their relationships with other children.

Consequences of Abuse and Neglect on Emotional Development

The effects of maltreatment on the emotional development of infants and toddlers can have consequences that interfere with personal and interpersonal development throughout life. The most devastating effect of maltreatment is the failure to develop basic trust during the first year of life. This has the potential to impair the development of healthy personality, including the ability to engage in trusting, intimate relationships. The absence of trust also deprives the child of the building blocks necessary for the achievement of subsequent developmental tasks, including autonomy, initiative, industry, and eventually, identity.

Maltreated infants show many signs of emotional distress and disturbance. They are often withdrawn, listless, apathetic, depressed, and unresponsive to the environment. They may also display rocking, head–banging, or other self–stimulatory behaviors. They may cry excessively, or not at all. Abused and neglected toddlers may be fearful and anxious, or depressed and withdrawn. They may also become aggressive and hurt others.

Abused infants often exhibit a state of "frozen watchfulness," that is, remaining passive and immobile, but intently observant of the environment. This appears to be a protective strategy in response to a fear of attack. It is as if the child were "on guard."

Abused toddlers may believe themselves to be "bad children." Excessive punishment for self–directed and autonomous tasks, combined with verbal criticism, can have a pervasive negative effect on the child's development of self–esteem. Punishment (abuse) in response to normal exploratory or autonomous behavior can interfere with the development of a healthy personality. Erikson defines shame and doubt as the negative outcomes of failure to develop autonomy. Such children may become chronically dependent and depressed, subversive, or openly rebellious and aggressive.

SPECIAL DEVELOPMENTAL PROBLEMS OF INFANTS

Several developmental conditions may result from abuse or neglect. We will describe two of them here. Additional information on other conditions that affect infants and young children, including mental retardation, cerebral palsy, autism, epilepsy, spina bifida, learning disabilities, fetal alcohol syndrome, and prenatal exposure to cocaine and other drugs can be found in Chapter VII, Child Welfare Services for Children with Developmental Disabilities.

Malnutrition and Growth Retardation ("Failure to Thrive")

The term "failure to thrive" has been used to describe a wide variety of conditions in which infants fail to achieve age appropriate weight and height levels. Kempe & Goldbloom [1987] suggest that the term "failure to thrive" does not adequately describe the serious deficits in nutrition and growth, and the other developmental characteristics, that are associated with this syndrome.

The common variable in all situations of failure to thrive is insufficient nutritional intake. In some infants, feeding problems and abnormally low weight are the result of an underlying physical or medical condition, not the result of neglect. However, treatment approaches for failure to thrive must include both medical and environmental management, regardless of the underlying cause.

Children with malnutrition associated with deprivation have the following physical characteristics:

- Most appear emaciated, pale, and weak; they have little subcutaneous fat and decreased muscle mass.

- The infants are often below their birth weight, indicating weight loss; or their weight is well below the normal range for their age.

- Most are listless, apathetic, and motionless, and at times, irritable.

- Some infants are unresponsive or resistant to social involvement. Others become actively distressed when approached. Many show a preference for inanimate objects.

- Infants may sleep for longer periods of time than is appropriate for their age.

- Infants may display physical posturing that is more appropriate for new-born or very young infants, including lying with hands held near or behind the head; legs flexed in a "frog" position; thumbs closed inside fists.

- Some children display self–stimulatory rocking, head banging, or rumination (vomiting and swallowing).

- Developmental assessment will likely reveal noticeable delays in gross motor and social domains.

Kempe and Goldbloom [1987] cite several studies that delineate common characteristics of parents whose infants are diagnosed with failure to thrive. Research has specifically described mothers of underfed children as depressed, socially isolated, withdrawn, and anxious, and, not surprisingly, abused, neglected, or deprived of positive attachments in their own early childhoods. They subsequently failed to interact in a nurturing and empathetic manner with their infants. Parents of failure–to–thrive infants also demonstrated little ability to empathize with their infants, and often misunderstood or ignored their infant's cues.

While many parents expressed sincere concern about their infants, they appeared to not know how to involve their babies in meaningful activity. There was little interpersonal activity between the parents and their infants. Many parents were overwhelmed by chronic stress, which was exacerbated by the demands of caring for their infant. They often behaved in ways that met their own needs rather than the needs of their infants. Some parents played with their infants in a competitive, rather than nurturant, manner [Kempe & Goldbloom 1987].

Difficulties in caregiving became most evident when the infants were fed. Some parents created an unpleasant or painful feeding situation for the infant; as a result, the infant did not cooperate and rejected food. The parents were often impatient, force–fed the infant, or removed food abruptly. When the infant resisted, or failed to eat, the parent often assumed the infant was not hungry, and discontinued the feeding.

There are several reasons that parents may not acknowledge the feeding problems. The parent often does not realize the infant is failing to grow, nor recognize the low weight and emaciation. In some cases, the infant's feeding problems may have been noticed, but were thought to be the result of vomiting, diarrhea, or other physical illness, rather than problems in the feeding situation itself. The parent may believe the infant is being adequately fed.

The parent may not be able to accurately report feeding times, schedules, or the quantity of formula the infant has taken. The parent may not be assuring adequate caloric intake. The parent may also allow long periods of time to elapse between feedings because "the baby doesn't appear to be hungry." Apathy and listlessness that result from low caloric intake are mistaken for the absence of hunger.

Breast-fed infants can be undernourished if the mother does not produce adequate milk or does not know how to nurse her infant. Breast-fed infants over the age of five months may not be able to get adequate nutrition from breast milk alone.

Treatment strategies for malnourished infants and their families must involve the entire family. Initially, immediate hospitalization of the infant is necessary, with a treatment program that provides caloric intake far in excess of that needed for maintenance under normal conditions. This typically leads to rapid weight gain, called "catch-up growth," in infants who are undernourished from underfeeding. Some infants achieve age-appropriate weight within a couple of weeks. Rapid "catch-up growth" during hospitalization is diagnostically significant for this syndrome, particularly when the infant is fed in the hospital with the same formula used at home. Some secondary physical conditions affecting the infant, as well as apathy and depression, appear to be resolved as a result of intensive feeding programs.

Parents should be directly involved in all aspects of the treatment program. Supportive counseling and education by a caring, nurturing professional can help parents feel less guilty, anxious, and depressed, can teach and reinforce proper feeding methods, and can improve parent-infant interactions. This treatment program should begin in the hospital. If the parents are not involved in treatment, the infant's condition can be expected to quickly deteriorate when returned home. Kempe & Goldbloom [1987] stress that the parents' problems are not simply the result of a lack of knowledge of proper parenting methods, and they warn that most parents of failure-to-thrive infants cannot be "treated" with a few educational sessions on proper feeding techniques. They state:

> The immaturity, neediness, and feelings of helplessness of the neglectful mother are not transformed into empathic nurturing by one or two lectures. She herself must experience from someone the empathy and nurturing she is expected to give her baby, and she must be able to depend on this support while she learns how to be a more sensitive parent for the infant's benefit. [Kempe & Goldbloom 1987]

If the parents appear unable to improve their care of the infant under controlled hospital conditions, foster placement should be considered. Koel [Kempe & Goldbloom 1987] reported that a number of infants who had been hospitalized for malnutrition and returned home were later found to be seriously, even fatally, abused.

Failure to thrive is common in infants with fragile-X syndrome, a genetically caused syndrome of mental retardation and autistic-like behavior that occurs in approximately 1-1000 live births [Goldson & Hagerman 1993; Wiebe & Wiebe 1994]. The syndrome is caused by an abnormal X chromosome in the chromosome pair that determines gender. The effects of fragile-X syndrome are considerably more serious in males than in females. These infants often have feeding problems that include vomiting, diarrhea, gastroesophageal reflux, tactile defensiveness around the mouth, food refusal, and frequent gagging. These feeding problems are thought to result from the laxity in connective tissue and poor muscle tone that are typical symptoms of fragile-X syndrome [Goldson & Hagerman 1993]. The resulting malnutrition results in failure to gain weight. Genetic screening is recommended if fragile-X syndrome is suspected. (See Section VIII-C, "The Primary Developmental Disabilities: Identification and Early Intervention," for a more extensive discussion on fragile-X syndrome.)

Special Care for Severely Abused Infants

Infants who have been abused severely at an early age demonstrate predictable developmental patterns and delays. The clinical picture of these infants has been described by Dr. H. Otto Kaak [1977], who refers to them as "clams" who have "closed up in their shells," and refuse to interact with the outside world. Dr. Kaak suggests that this is the children's reaction to extremely painful early experiences. This pattern is consistent with the condition of "frozen watchfulness," as described and discussed by others. Dr. Kaak's description of these babies includes these characteristics:

- They are withdrawn, unresponsive, and apathetic, and look weak and sickly.

- They permit others to manipulate their bodies without display of protest. They exhibit a generalized passive compliance.

- They do not often cry. They may occasionally whimper, or wail. They do not vocalize in response to other people.

- They do not appear to enjoy being touched or held, and are not responsive to affectionate handling. They do not conform to the adult's body when held. They do not cling to parents or other adults in threatening situations.

- They appear to enjoy nothing. They do not laugh or smile, they show no interest in objects or people. They do not take pleasure in feeding, bathing, play, or other normal activities.

- They do not risk contact with people. They appear to feel best when they are left alone.

- Their movements are slow and cautious; they display limited mobility. They may stay in one place for long periods of time.

Specialized treatment methods are necessary if we are to help these babies. Simply eliminating the abuse is not enough. Parents and foster caregivers must be trained to nurture such a child in a predictable, measured fashion. "Too much too soon" can overwhelm the child and have the effect of further closing him off. As a result, treatment may take many months. Dr. Kaak suggests the following general treatment strategies:

- Move SLOWLY! Take care to approach the child slowly at all times, and do not institute too many changes at once.

- Create a calm, comfortable environment. The environment should not, however, be sterile and devoid of stimulation. Stimulation must be given in measured doses. A foster home with five noisy and active children may not be the best environment for this child.

- Read the child's cues regarding her needs. When the child withdraws from an approach, back off, and approach again more slowly or tentatively. The child will have to become acclimated. There is a fine line between providing nurturance and overwhelming the child.

- Kaak suggests "selective attention and inattention." Choose times in which to interact with the infant, and keep these times short at first.

- Talk to the child using a soft, affectionate tone of voice. Quiet and comforting is the rule.

- Introduce pleasure into caregiving. Any interaction with the child, including feeding, bathing, and changing clothes should be performed gently, allowing the child to experience normal pleasures. Adequate time should be taken; these activities should not be rushed.

- The child should not be harshly or firmly disciplined. If the child approaches a dangerous situation, she should be gently redirected or removed.

- The parent or caregiver must allow latitude in permitting the child to behave in ways that are developmentally more appropriate for a young infant. For example, messing with food, spitting, splashing in the bath, and otherwise "making a mess" are preferable to withdrawal and immobility. After several months, gentle limits may be set.

- Do not force physical affection. Begin with gentle touching, patting, and stroking. When holding the child, hold lightly. Cuddling is fine when the child appears to respond positively by conforming to the adult's body, or "settling in." Follow the child's cues about physical affection.

- After a period of time the child may exhibit such behaviors as thumb sucking, clinging, other dependent behaviors, frequent crying, stranger anxiety, separation anxiety, and other signs of social need. These must be viewed as progress rather than as problem behaviors.

Kaak suggests that beyond the age of three and a half to four, there is a point of closure after which the child appears unable to "recapture infantile pleasures," and the child's long-term emotional development is threatened.

Case Example

GENERAL DEVELOPMENTAL DELAY FROM SERIOUS NEGLECT

⚲ Betsy

Betsy was eight months old when the child welfare worker first saw her. The Walker family had been referred to the agency by the school nurse, who was concerned about the family's six-year-old daughter, Sherry. Sherry appeared to be undernourished, dirty, and listless. She also missed school regularly.

During the initial home visit, the worker confirmed that the mother's care of Sherry was, indeed, marginal at best. The eight month old, however, concerned her greatly. Betsy was lying in her crib on dirty sheets when the worker first saw her. She lay quietly on her back, elbows bent and hands beside her head on the mattress, legs thin and bowed. She appeared to be staring into space and did not respond when the worker entered the room and began to talk to her. The worker picked Betsy up and noticed that she felt heavy, like a sack of potatoes. The worker attributed this to Betsy's limp and listless physical posture and absence of muscle tone. Betsy was small for eight months, and thin, but she did not have the emaciated look of a failure-to-thrive infant. Betsy allowed herself to be picked up, put on the worker's shoulder, and eventually in her lap, without protest and without acknowledgement of the worker's presence. The worker noticed that the back of Betsy's head was flattened and the hair was thin, suggesting that Betsy had spent a lot of time lying on her back.

Betsy had good head control, but when placed on the floor on her stomach, she raised her head only to a 45° angle. She did not use her arms and hands to prop, and she stayed where she was placed on the floor. She was unable to support weight on her legs, and she would collapse when held standing in the worker's lap. She would close her hand around an object placed in her palm but would soon drop it. She would not reach for objects. She did not vocalize; occasionally she would wail pathetically, but would soon stop. She made eye contact only when the worker placed herself in Betsy's direct line of view. The worker could not get Betsy to babble, coo, or smile at her. She was listless, apathetic, and withdrawn. During the visit, six-year-old Sherry appeared with a bottle of milk, and informed the worker that it was time to give the baby her dinner. Mrs. Walker was willing to let Sherry care for Betsy, and told the worker Sherry was considerable help to her.

After a lengthy interview, the worker learned that the children's father had deserted Mrs. Walker when she was six months pregnant with Betsy. She had serious financial problems, and considerable health problems after a difficult cesearean delivery. Mrs. Walker described herself as always tired and moody, that she slept a lot, and didn't feel like doing much. She also cried a lot. Her doctor attributed it to postpartum depression, and told her it would eventually go away. She said she hadn't always been that way, and that taking care of Sherry had been easy compared to caring for Betsy. The worker concluded that the mother was probably depressed, most likely precipitated by the loss of her husband, and her care of both children was extremely neglectful as a result.

The worker's gross assessment of Betsy's developmental age was no more than two or three months, and she determined that Betsy was in need of immediate intervention if long-term developmental problems were to be prevented. The worker was particularly concerned about mental retardation resulting from the lack of stimulation and probable malnutrition.

Betsy was hospitalized for a short period, and a medical team evaluated her. Her height and weight were at the extreme low end of normal, but she showed no obvious signs of physical disability. She ate well and quickly gained weight from a high nutrition diet. Mrs. Walker was seen immediately at the mental health clinic, and was treated with antidepressant medication and weekly counseling sessions. She was also referred to a parents-of-infants support group run by the hospital. She was to bring Betsy each afternoon for two hours, during which time the nurses would teach her how to feed, care for, and stimulate Betsy. The program trained the mothers to talk to, play with, and handle their babies, and to involve them in activities. The nurses engaged the babies in exercises and activities to promote physical development, and encouraged the mothers to model their behavior. As Mrs. Walker's depression was alleviated, she showed more interest in both Betsy and Sherry, even though her parenting skills appeared to be very limited. The child welfare agency provided a homemaker, who worked with Mrs. Walker in the home and modeled appropriate child care practices. Betsy's health and progress were monitored at weekly visits to the hospital clinic.

Betsy's development, while slow, progressed along relatively normal lines. Within a month she was within the normal weight range for her age. She had begun to respond to interpersonal contact and would maintain eye contact with people who talked to her. It took several more months of intensive stimulation before she demonstrated interest and excitement in response to people or toys. Her physical development was also slow, but by one year she was sitting, and by 16 months she was walking holding on to objects. It was not clear whether her cognitive development would ultimately be within normal limits. There was the potential for mild mental retardation, but the hospital agreed to "graduate" Betsy to their preschool program when she was ready. This program offered intensive stimulation and individualized programming for children with disabilities. They indicated they had had considerable success with children like Betsy, whose developmental delays were the result of neglect, rather than from brain injury or other disabling conditions.

C. THE EFFECTS OF MALTREATMENT ON PRESCHOOL CHILDREN

1. Conceptual Framework

2. Application

3. Case Examples

Conceptual Framework

The primary developmental tasks and milestones in each of the four developmental domains for children age three to five are as follows:

PHYSICAL DEVELOPMENT OF THE PRESCHOOL CHILD

Physical growth of the preschool child occurs at a slower rate than the infant or toddler. The child gains approximately four to five pounds per year, and grows approximately three to four inches per year. A rule of thumb to help remember an average height and weight for a three–year-old child is to think of "threes": three years, three feet tall, 33 pounds. The preschool child also loses the swayed back and protruding abdomen that are typical of the toddler.

The rate of brain growth slows considerably. By early preschool, the brain will have reached approximately 4/5 of adult size.

The preschool child is very active, and cannot sit still for long periods of time. Preschoolers prefer to be busy and involved in activities. Physical games, drawing, painting, playing with more complicated toys, and learning to use playground equipment all promote the development and refinement of gross and fine motor skills, and eye–hand coordination.

Motor abilities may differ between boys and girls, and different cultural expectations can affect the nature of motor development. In cultures that reinforce "rough and tumble" play such as running and jumping, children will typically develop muscle strength and gross motor coordination; whereas, quieter play, with toys, crayons, and dolls, will generally promote the development of fine motor coordination.

COGNITIVE DEVELOPMENT OF THE PRESCHOOL CHILD

The cognition of preschool children has certain discernible characteristics. When considered together, these can help us to understand the world view of the preschool child.

Egocentric Thought

When we say that preschool children think egocentrically, we are not assigning a moral value to their behavior. We do not mean they are selfish or thoughtless, or that they only think about themselves.

Egocentrism describes the nature of their thought processes. Their universe is circumscribed; they, their family, and their homes are at the center. The scope of their awareness and understanding is limited to their immediate experience, and they view the world only from this perspective. They do not realize that other people have perspectives that might be different from theirs; their personal experiences have universal application. For example, Mike, age four, could see that his mom was upset because she was crying, so he gave her his teddy bear to make her feel better. Hilary believed the sun rose in her backyard, and set in her front yard.

Preschool children also think that everyone has the same information they do. When they describe an event, they often leave out important and obvious facts because they assume that everyone else already knows the details that they know.

The attribution of human characteristics to inanimate objects and animals is also typical. This is sometimes referred to as animism. For instance, three-year-old Kristin put a doll blanket over a chicken that her mother was thawing for dinner. When asked why, she said "because the chicken was cold, and I wanted to make it warm." Leigh, age four, had been very attached to a blanket since infancy. Leigh's mom had to launder the blanket when Leigh was asleep, because Leigh was convinced that the blanket would drown in the washer and would get dizzy in the dryer. When Leigh's mom accidently stepped on the blanket, Leigh insisted that she kiss it and apologize. Sarah told her mother the wind was blowing because it was happy, and, the flower opened its petals because it was getting a suntan.

Egocentricity does not mean that preschool children are oblivious or insensitive to other people's feelings. Even infants and toddlers become upset when other children cry. Preschoolers can also recognize visual cues of emotional states, and sometimes they can label them properly as mad, upset, happy, or sad. This is a precursor of empathy. They are, however, largely unaware of many feelings that generate visible behaviors in other people. Kelli, for instance, at age three and a half, was watching her aunt come up the front sidewalk. Aunt Judy, who had just ended a long, tiring, and frustrating day, was frowning as she approached the door. Kelli greeted her at the door with a concerned question, "Aunt Judy, why is your face mad?"

Illogical and Magical Thinking

It is inaccurate to say preschool children cannot think logically. The thought patterns of preschoolers appear illogical because preschoolers draw conclusions from the limited information that is derived from their circumscribed, often incomplete understanding of the world. Information for an egocentric preschooler comes from one source–the child's own experiences and perceptions.

Preschool children also have limited understanding of cause and effect. If two events are linked sequentially, or two attributes of an object coexist, one is often thought to have caused the other.

While preschool children's reasoning may be faulty by adult standards, their conclusions make perfect sense to them, and they will stubbornly cling to them when presented with more complicated and more rational explanations.

The following examples illustrate the typical logic of preschool-aged children.

It is not unusual for preschoolers to be afraid of being flushed down the toilet. In their experience, everything that gets thrown in the toilet disappears, never to be seen again. They cannot be talked out of their fear. Hilary told her mother that the sun comes up because it's yellow. Tommy said the moon shines at night because there's a man in it. Kelli was convinced that lightning caused the rain. Christopher's mother told him he couldn't go outside and play in the yard until the dew on the grass dried, so Christopher got a dish towel from the kitchen and brought it to his mother so she could dry off the grass. Andrew insisted that two pennies were more than a dime. They were larger, and there were more of them.

Preschool children have vivid imaginations and often engage in magical thinking. Fact and fantasy cannot always be differentiated. In describing an experience, the child will often embellish it to the point of fantasy. Mitchell, age four, went to the circus and saw horses in the center ring jump over low hurdles. When he later told his dad about the circus, he described the "beautiful horses that were flying in the air all around the circus tent." This should not be considered lying, as Mitchell was not deliberately fabricating. He was displaying the lively and expansive imagination of a healthy preschooler.

For Kelli, also age four, fact and fiction are easily interwoven in her imaginative play. One afternoon she came running into the kitchen and told her mom, "I need some porridge. I need some water. I need some poison. I'm going to mix them all together and make a dog." Kelli's mom said, "You don't want to use poison. You know what poison is, don't you?" Kelli said "No." Her mom said, "It's bad stuff. Poison can kill you!" Kelli thought for a moment, and then said, "All right, I'll make a dead dog."

The inability to separate fantasy from fact contributes to the development of preschool children's fears. At age four, Leigh fell and knocked out a front tooth. Her mom told her to put the tooth under her pillow and the tooth fairy would come and bring her money. Leigh became hysterical, thinking a stranger would be sneaking into her bedroom in the middle of the night.

In a similar example, Kelli woke up crying in the middle of the night. "There's something strange going on here," she told her dad. "There's a doggie with something in his hair." Her dad found a doll in a chair casting a shadow on the wall. Turning on the light and explaining that it was only the doll's shadow did nothing to calm Kelli's fear. The doll had to be moved, eliminating the shadow, before Kelli was assured that the threatening dog was no longer in the room.

Inability to Sequence Events in Proper Order

Preschoolers cannot relate events or ideas in their proper sequence. They do not have a well-developed understanding of time, particularly of long time periods. They may understand today, but yesterday and tomorrow are harder, and next week is incomprehensible. They confuse first, middle, and last, and cannot order events in time. They might be able to describe events, but the events are not likely to be in sequential order.

Role of Cognition in the Effects of Maltreatment

The preschool child's cognitive limitations are an important variable in understanding the potential effects of maltreatment.

A combination of drawing conclusions from very limited information, the tendency to attribute cause and effect to events that happen concurrently, and an inability to understand complex events contribute to the development of inaccurate and distorted perceptions. Abused preschool children almost universally believe that the abuse was punishment because they did something wrong. This thought pattern may persist into the school years. It is also typical for young children in foster care to believe they were sent away because they were bad. It makes no logical sense to them that they should have to leave home because someone else, their parents, did something wrong. If necessary, the child will invent or fantasize reasons for punishment to give a cognitive structure and a plausible explanation for the abuse.

Lisa, age six, had been placed in a foster home at age five and a half. Her step-father was a violent and dangerous man who once threw a cat through a plate glass window in a fit of temper. He and his wife had a violent argument during which time the police were called, and Lisa was removed to assure her safety. At the time of the argument, Lisa had been in the kitchen pouring a glass of milk, and she spilled it. Six months after her placement, she solemnly assured the social worker that she was bad, and that she had to live in a foster home because she spilled her milk all over the kitchen. When the worker told her she was placed in foster care so her daddy wouldn't hurt her, she indicated her daddy only hurt her mommy, not her, and that couldn't be the reason.

Understanding preschool-age cognition helps to explain the universal tendency for maltreated preschool children to develop a poor self-image and low self-esteem.

Language Development

During the second year of life, children enter the stage of cognitive development referred to by Piaget as preoperations. The ability to symbolize contributes to the development of language. Between the ages of three and five, the expansion and refinement of language are the most critical and most obvious cognitive advancements.

The preschool child quickly expands duos into full sentences by adding linking words, including prepositions, conjunctions, objects, and other components. Grammar also improves.

The child's spoken vocabulary increases exponentially. The greater the child's vocabulary, the better the child can express complete thoughts, which greatly enhances the ability to communicate. Thought and understanding (receptive language) are generally more well developed than spoken (expressive) language until the child is about four.

Preschool children use and repeat new words, even when they do not fully understand their meaning. They also make up words to suit the occasion, often with amusing results. For example, Hilary, three and a half, ran to help her mother answer a knock at the door. A minute later she was back. Her dad asked her who was at the door. Hilary assured him, "Don't worry, Dad. He's gone." Not satisfied, Dad asked again, "Hilary, who was at the door?" Hilary answered, "It was a peep. But he's gone now." "A what?" asked Dad. She replied, "A peep. But he went away." It was only after careful thought that Dad realized "a peep" was Hilary's singular of the word "people"; if many are called "people," one must be a "peep."

Most preschool children talk nonstop. They enjoy using language to communicate with others, but just as often, they talk just to talk. They are socially intrusive and will try to involve themselves in other peoples' conversations. They also talk to themselves. They are especially adept at asking questions, particularly "Why?" even though they are not always interested in the answer, and they seem to enjoy interjecting the "why" just to keep the conversation going.

Parents can promote their children's language development through conversation and reading. A parent can be taught to direct comments and questions to their child throughout the day and engage them in conversation. Parents who cannot read can be encouraged to look through a magazine or book with their children, talk about the pictures, or make up stories. Between 15 to 20 minutes of concentrated conversation each day can greatly promote children's language development.

Culture and Language

The development of language ability is universal. The nature of the language, the specific meanings of words, and rules for when and how people talk with one another are culturally determined.

When a caseworker assesses a child's language development, the assessment must be made within the child's cultural context. It is important not to confuse language or speech differences with language delays or speech deficits.

Words may have idiosyncratic meanings within cultures or subcultures, and the rules of grammar and syntax may not be the same as in standard English. If a four year old's language is not understandable, and if words are not used properly in context, it is certainly possible that the child may have language or speech delays. However, the worker should not automatically assume this is the case. It may be that the worker is unfamiliar with the use of language in the family, and the child's communication skills are appropriate within that cultural context. The worker should determine whether family members and others in the child's cultural reference group are able to fully understand the child's language.

Some cultures discourage children from approaching adults to begin conversations. These children are taught to remain silent in the presence of adults as a sign of deference and respect. The worker may need to observe a child in situations in which talking is encouraged, as when playing with other children, to determine the child's language ability. The worker may also need to gather data from the parents or other adults who know the child well. If the child's primary language is one that is unfamiliar to the worker, the worker should obtain assistance in any developmental assessment related to language.

SOCIAL DEVELOPMENT OF THE PRESCHOOL CHILD

There are two principal tasks of social development for the preschool child; the development of interactive play skills, and learning social roles and rules.

Interactive Play

Children do not develop interactive play until the preschool period. Toddlers engage in "parallel play," which is actually solitary play, with only incidental contact with other children likewise engaged in relatively private play.

The development of language, and the subsequent improvement in ability to communicate, promote the development of interactive play skills. Increasingly complex social interactions develop in stages throughout the preschool period.

For three year olds, toys are the focus of most play. Preschool children must learn basic social rules, such as sharing and taking turns, before they will be able to play cooperatively with other children. Frequent battles erupt while this is being learned, usually over who has possession of which toy. Few three year olds can cooperate toward accomplishment of a common goal, particularly if it means compromising their own wants and needs.

By age four and five, children increasingly form friendships with other children, and will ask to play with certain friends. Play is more cooperative, and is governed by rules. Each child may imitate a specific role in imaginative play, and children may direct each other's activities to complement their own. Joint involvement toward a common goal is more frequent. For example, Tonya and Leticia were playing "house" under the dining room table. Tonya could be overheard directing Leticia, "Now you be the mommy. You have to hold the baby so she won't cry, because I'm working. I can't be disturbed."

Kelli, age five, understood the rules about taking turns and confronted Brian, who had been monopolizing the paints and easel; "Can't you see that I'm sad because you've been painting for too long!" Robert and Billy were trying to build a city with snap–together building blocks. Their skyscraper wobbled precariously. Billy told Robert, "You hold the top and I'll make the bridge, so the building won't fall down when the cars go over the bridge."

Magical and imaginative thinking are frequently expressed in play. Preschool children will create fantasy characters and scenarios, including imaginary friends. Well-developed language allows them to talk to, and about, these friends. For example, they will weave elaborate scenarios about the life of a favorite stuffed animal, and will explain the animal's needs, feelings, and thoughts in detail to anyone who is willing to listen. Imaginative play also includes developing and telling stories, the events of which may seem unrelated, and in no logical sequence to the listening adult. Children may be overheard making up and telling stories to themselves.

The Functions of Play

Children engage in play for its own sake because it is pleasurable. However, psychologists believe that play serves several additional functions for the preschool child [Gardner 1978].

Play provides children with opportunities to practice and develop language skills by conversing with other children and adults about the play activities. Stories that are read to them, and those they make up both promote the development of language.

Through play the child learns and practices social skills. These include sharing, taking turns, cooperating, and controlling impulses. One of the goals of "free play" in preschool settings is to help children develop and internalize these skills.

Gross motor play, and activities and games that provide new challenges, help to develop gross motor abilities and promote refinements in balance and coordination. Toys with small parts, crayons, and other small objects encourage the development of eye–hand and fine motor coordination.

Children can experiment with social roles and different perspectives through imitation and imaginative play. They pretend to be someone, assume the perceived characteristics of the role, and model the person's behaviors. Jenny announced to Laurie that she was going to be the teacher, and Laurie had to be the student and sit still, because Jenny was going to write on the board and teach Laurie letters.

Children often discharge emotional tensions and anxieties through play. This affective function of play allows the child to safely discharge uncomfortable feelings. David used his "superheroes" to kill all the monsters that hid in the dark of night, waiting to attack unsuspecting victims.

Play can also help reduce fears. The imaginary companions of many children are wild animals who are made to be docile, cooperative, friendly, and totally under the child's control.

Erikson views play as a constructive means of helping children cope with stress and frustration [Gardner 1978]. Through play children can rehearse various coping strategies to help them deal with difficult situations. For example, four-year-old Joseph was scheduled to see the doctor. He engaged his younger sister in a game of "doctor," pretended to give her a shot, told her it wouldn't hurt very much, and reassured her that she would be all better soon.

These affective functions make play an excellent therapeutic tool, and a valuable casework strategy when working with preschool-age children.

Using play greatly increases the worker's ability to communicate with the child in a language the child understands. Observing play can also provide caseworkers with considerable information about children's feelings, perceptions, and needs.

Children are also more comfortable, and therefore more willing to communicate, in a play mode. The worker can use play to develop the casework relationship and gain the child's trust and confidence. Children really like adults who take the time to play with them. Further training in play diagnostics and play therapy are useful for caseworkers who work with young children on a regular basis.

THE EMOTIONAL DEVELOPMENT OF PRESCHOOL CHILDREN

The emotional development of preschool children can be examined from several perspectives.

The Development of Initiative

Erikson considers the development of initiative to be the preschool child's most important developmental task. The preschool years are a time of active discovery. Healthy children are exuberant, self-directed, and self-starters. They delight in orchestrating activities and being in charge. They take pleasure in "attack and conquest," and they experiment with new roles and skills.

Initiative has its risks. Children must have developed basic trust in themselves and in their environments to feel confident enough to initiate new activities. They must also have learned that they are capable of autonomous behavior. The healthy development of trust and autonomy during the infant and toddler stages contributes greatly to the preschool child's competence and sense of confidence. Self-starting and self-directed behaviors will be less well developed in children who are fearful, dependent, and unable to trust themselves or others.

The Development of Self–Control

Before the age of three, children react with noticeable emotional distress to frustrating situations. Infants cry when they are uncomfortable or unhappy. Toddlers become defiant and angry, cry, or have tantrums when they can't have their own way, or when confronted with a frustrating situation.

Infants and toddlers have not developed internalized self–control, referred to as "impulse control." Their behavior is managed and contained by the structure in their environment. For example, the presence of a parent saying "no" prevents the two year old from playing with a forbidden object. When the parent leaves the room, so goes the control, and the child will often approach the desired object. Controls on the child's behavior are, therefore, externally applied. Parents can avoid a confrontation by putting things out of the child's reach.

Preschool children are better able to control their emotions and behavior. Their improved cognitive ability, including more effective use of language, helps them think and talk about problems and solutions. Crying and temper tantrums in frustrating situations decrease during the preschool years, as children develop better self–control. Improved coping abilities enable them to withstand some frustration and discomfort without becoming so emotionally aroused that their behavior becomes disorganized, as is typical for an infant or toddler. Some parents notice that their preschool-age children can turn their tears on and off at will. This is another example of their increasing emotional control.

The preschool child is also better able to delay gratification. "You can have a cookie after dinner" does not lead to a tantrum; the child is now able to wait a short time for a reward. The child's previous experiences affect his ability to delay gratification; that is, whether he has received the reward as promised. The ability to delay gratification appears to be supported by predictability and consistency in the child's environment.

The Development of Conscience

During the preschool period, the development of conscience coincides with the development of self–control. By age five, most children understand the meaning of right and wrong. They don't need the parent to tell them "no" to prevent them from touching a forbidden object. They will avoid it because they know it is wrong to touch it, and that their parents will be angry with them if they do. The internalization of standards of right and wrong behavior form the rudiments of moral behavior, or conscience. Children feel guilty when they do something wrong.

The preschool child's understanding of right and wrong is fairly basic, however. The child cannot understand abstract moral principles. The concrete application of a moral principle is a "rule," and preschool children do understand rules. They tend to view rules concretely, in a "black and white" fashion. They have fairly strict interpretations of right and wrong.

Children who grow up in chaotic environments where the rules continually change, or where no rules exist, often show signs of anxiety and emotional disturbance. Clear and consistent rules provide the preschool child with a dependable structure and a sense of security.

The Development of Self–Esteem

By age three, the child has a rudimentary sense of self. She understands "I" and "me," and knows she is different from other people. With the development of conscience, she will also begin to evaluate her own behavior as good or bad. She feels pride when she is good, and guilt or shame when she is bad.

The preschool child's self-esteem is largely dependent upon other people's reactions to her. Normal expressions of initiative put her in continual contact with other people. If these people respond to her with praise and support, she is likely to feel positive about herself, and her initiatives will be reinforced. This, in turn, promotes learning and mastery of additional skills.

Conversely, if her creative initiatives result in criticism or punishment, she is likely to believe herself to be a bad child, and may experience guilt and shame. Low self-esteem and lack of confidence result, and the child will be less likely to initiate and engage in new activities. This can interfere with subsequent development in all domains.

Application

DEVELOPMENTAL CONSEQUENCES OF MALTREATMENT

The following are common effects of abuse and neglect on the development of preschool children.

Physical

- They may be small in stature, and show evidence of delayed physical growth.

- They may be sickly and susceptible to frequent illness, particularly upper respiratory illness (colds, flu) and digestive upset.

- They may have poor muscle tone, poor motor coordination, gross and fine motor clumsiness, awkward gait, and lack of muscle strength.

- Gross motor play skills may be delayed or absent.

Cognitive

- Speech may be absent, delayed, or hard to understand. The preschooler whose receptive language far exceeds expressive language may have speech delays. Some severely abused children do not talk, even though they are able.

- The child may have poor articulation and pronunciation, incomplete formation of sentences, or incorrect use of words.

- Cognitive skills may be at a level more typical of a younger child.

- The child may have an unusually short attention span, a lack of interest in objects, and an inability to concentrate.

Social

- The child may demonstrate insecure or absent attachment. Attachments may be indiscriminate, superficial, or clingy. The child may show little distress, or may overreact when separated from caregivers.

- The child may appear emotionally detached, isolated, and withdrawn from both adults and peers.

- The child may demonstrate social immaturity in peer relationships; may be unable to enter into reciprocal play relationships; may be unable to take turns, share, or negotiate with peers; may be overly aggressive, bossy, and competitive with peers.

- The child may prefer solitary or parallel play, or may lack age appropriate play skills. Imaginative and fantasy play may be absent. The child may lack normal interest and curiosity, and may not explore and experiment.

Emotional

- The child may be excessively fearful, easily traumatized, may have night terrors, and may seem to expect danger.

- The child may show signs of poor self–esteem and a lack of confidence.

- The child may lack impulse control and have little ability to delay gratification. The child may react to frustration with tantrums, aggression, or may give up in despair and withdraw from the frustrating situation.

- The child may have bland, flat affect, and be emotionally passive and detached.

- The child may show an absence of healthy initiative, and often must be drawn into activities; he may emotionally withdraw and avoid participating in activities.

- The child may show signs of emotional disturbance, including anxiety, depression, emotional volatility, self–stimulating behaviors such as rocking, or head banging, enuresis (wetting) or encopresis (soiling), or thumb sucking.

USING PLAY TO ENHANCE DEVELOPMENT

Caseworkers should also help parents to recognize the importance of play for preschool children. Many abusive or neglectful parents do not know how to promote or reinforce play with their children, and do not realize the opportunities for play that are available in their homes. Caseworkers can model ways that parents can play with their children. Expensive, complex, or purchased toys are not necessary. There are many resources for play in homes with very limited income that can be implemented by parents with limited parenting ability. Some possible activities that parents can do with their preschool children are:

- Cover empty cereal and cracker boxes, round oatmeal cartons, orange juice cans, and empty tin cans (no sharp edges) with contact or wrapping paper and use them to learn shapes, colors, and as building blocks.

- Cut pictures out of old magazines and paste or tape them onto large sheets of paper, including old newspaper, to make a "scrapbook," or a collage.

- Using a muffin tin or empty egg carton, sort buttons or various kinds of soup beans by kind, size, shape, or color.

- Draw pictures with pencils and crayons.

- Take turns singing songs. Form a "kitchen band" with pots, pans, spoons, and other noisemakers. Keep time to music from the radio.

- Toss pillows to one another to learn to throw and catch.

- Hide and find objects around the house, or play hide and seek.

- Put dishwashing soap and a little water in a bowl and beat them to frothy with a whisk or an egg beater. Pretend you're making clouds.

- Mix a flour and water paste, shred newspaper, and sculpt with papier mache around bottles or cans, or free form. Make a vase or pencil holder.

- Be creative.

Play is a universal activity. However, there are often differences among cultures in how people play. When teaching parents to play with their children, the worker should be familiar with culturally specific games, stories, activities, and play objects. This will prevent trying to teach play strategies that are not acceptable within the culture, and will also help to promote a positive cultural identity. For example, if a culture does not condone active physical play for girls, the worker should not try to teach a mother to play tag in the yard with her daughter. The worker can learn culturally specific play patterns by talking to and observing more functional families, as well as by accessing community-based service providers who specialize in working with families of a particular cultural group.

Case Examples

The following cases of Jenny and Leah illustrate the variable effects of maltreatment on the development and behavior of preschool-aged children.

The cases are presented in the format of a formal psychological and developmental assessment to provide workers with an example of what should typically be included in a comprehensive assessment for case planning purposes.

⅋ Jenny Billingsley, age four years, three months

Reason for Referral

Jenny was referred for psychological assessment by Marsha Ellis, social worker for the Adams County Department of Children's Services. Jenny is in the custody of the agency, and is currently living in a foster home. Ms. Ellis requested that an evaluation be performed to assist in adoptive planning, and to help the agency and prospective parents meet Jenny's continued emotional, social, and cognitive developmental needs.

History

Jenny has been in the custody of the Adams County Department of Children's Services as a result of abuse and neglect. Her biological parents have recently permanently surrendered Jenny to the department, and the agency plan is for permanent placement into an adoptive family. Jenny has been in her current foster home for approximately a year. She has adjusted well, and her foster mother reports that Jenny continues to progress steadily in her development.

Jenny was born in August, 1985. When Jenny was three years old, she was admitted to Children's Hospital. She was diagnosed at that time as physically abused, emotionally abused, and physically and emotionally neglected. No documentation is available regarding her early development, although the case record indicates one previous hospitalization in another state, when Jenny was an infant, for nonorganic failure to thrive.

Present Assessment

The following tests were administered: the Stanford–Binet Intelligence Scale and the Adaptive Behavior Scale for Infants and Early Childhood (ABSI). A clinical interview was also conducted.

With a chronological age (CA) of four years, three months, and a corrected mental age (MA) of four years, zero months, Jenny achieved an Intelligence Quotient of 94 on the Stanford–Binet. This places Jenny in the average range of intelligence and puts her in the 35th percentile. Jenny's first subtest failure was in general comprehension. Her highest pass was in a subtest strongly indicative of verbal ability.

Information on Jenny's adaptive behavior was provided by her foster mother during a clinical interview. Jenny's ABSI suggests she is functioning at an adaptive level lower than her cognitive performance level. Her adaptive functioning level was comparable to a child of Jenny's age who was mildly mentally retarded. Jenny's highest areas of adaptive behavior were in motor skills and communication. Her social skills, concept abilities, and independent functioning skills were uniformly lower. Jenny's most significant weakness in adaptive behavior was self-direction. Problems in this area included Jenny's inability to attend to task and her impulsivity. She is easily frustrated. There were significant emotional indicators on the ABSI, including a strong need for attention, some rebelliousness, and anti-social behaviors. Jenny was also noted to have problems socializing with peers; she was often jealous when other children received attention, was disruptive and demanding in peer group activities, and was physically aggressive with other children.

Jenny related to the clinician in a friendly manner, was easily engaged to participate in activities, and followed directions well. Jenny was not noticeably apprehensive, withdrawn, or anxious. She did require considerable encouragement to remain on task toward the end of the test period. Jenny's behaviors were essentially within normal limits, and typical of a four year old in a clinical situation.

General Impressions

Jenny exhibited age-appropriate behavior during the testing process. She achieved an I.Q. score of 94, placing her in the average range of intelligence. Her adaptive behaviors were below expectations, based upon her cognitive functioning. Jenny's lower adaptive behavior scores are likely the result of her early abusive and neglectful environment, and the lack of opportunities or stimulation to promote growth. Jenny's excessive dependency also appears to contribute to her delays in adaptive behavior. Her jealousy and anxiety when other children receive attention, her lack of self-direction, and other indicators of need for attention suggest a decreased ability to function independently. Jenny's intellectual and adaptive functioning should improve if she can benefit from a permanent, supportive, and nurturing family milieu.

Recommendations:

1) Jenny should be placed in a supportive and nurturing adoptive family. Ideally, for the first two years of placement, there should be no other young children in the family. Older siblings could provide Jenny with additional nurturance, and serve as role models for independent and self-reliant activities. An adoptive family should be aware of Jenny's dependency and should encourage age-appropriate independent and self-directed behavior.

2) After adoptive placement, Jenny would benefit from placement in a structured preschool program. Jenny needs this chance to develop socialization and peer interaction skills before she is enrolled in regular school programming.

3) Adoptive parents, teachers, and other caregiving adults can assist Jenny in the development of the following areas of adaptive behavior:

- Consistently meeting her own independent needs, such as dressing and undressing, toileting, bathing, and feeding;

- Developing gross motor skills such as jumping, hopping and running; and fine motor activities of grasping, holding and manipulating small objects, and drawing and coloring; and

- Continuing to learn and practice conceptual skills such as identifying shapes, colors, and size variations; sorting objects into groups; engaging in imaginative and pretend games and activities; and using art objects in play, including paint, paper, clay, play dough, etc.

4) Because of Jenny's separation history and her attachment to her current foster mother, adoptive placement should be carefully planned to include several preplacement home visits prior to the adoptive placement. Follow-up visits and contacts by phone or letter to the foster mother should be maintained for several months, and may be lessened as Jenny becomes more fully integrated into the adoptive family.

Discussion

Jenny is fortunate. Despite a history of consistent maltreatment, and a traumatic separation from her family, psychologically she is relatively healthy. Her measured I.Q. is currently within the normal range, although it is probably not reflective of her actual potential. The psychologist used the assessment to establish a developmental level for this child, which became the baseline from which to identify activities to stimulate continued development. The Adaptive Behavior Scale, which lists age-appropriate developmental tasks and abilities in increasing order of complexity, suggested logical next steps to help Jenny develop those adaptive areas in which she was delayed. Jenny also displayed behaviors suggesting early signs of emotional disturbance, but her responsiveness to the examiner, as well as her apparent positive attachment to the foster mother, suggest that she has the potential for healthy emotional development, provided her environment is secure, stable, and nurturing.

⋀ Leah Atherton, age five years, zero months

Reason for Referral

Leah was referred for psychological evaluation by her social worker. She is one of four Atherton children in the custody of the Department of Children's Services. The worker requested a development assessment of Leah to help in case planning, educational programing, and placement.

History

Leah is the youngest of four Atherton children. The family has been known to the Children's Service agency for several years, during which time they received intensive in-home protective and supportive services from the agency and other community providers. The family has a history of chronic family dysfunction, of domestic violence, and of serious neglect and abuse of the children. Mrs. Atherton is reported to have been mentally ill for many years. She has been hospitalized repeatedly. Two years ago she was placed in a psychiatric facility, and she remains there currently.

About four months ago, Leah's oldest sister, Patricia, disclosed having been sexually abused by Mr. Atherton, who is her stepfather and the biological father of the three younger children. All four children have been in the care of relatives since Mr. Atherton's incarceration for this offense.

According to the social worker, Leah was subjected to serious neglect while with her family. Her father was reported to often be away from home, leaving the care of the younger children to Patricia. The agency noted that the home was very poorly maintained, and that food was not always available. The social worker reported that Leah chronically wet the bed, that her bedding was rarely changed, and that the house often smelled of urine.

Initially, Leah was taken into agency custody at age two months, after having been diagnosed as failure to thrive. She was returned to the physical custody of her family at age four months. She received marginal but adequate care until a year later, when a domestic violence complaint was filed by the mother. Leah was again removed and placed in foster care. Leah was returned home four months later, and custody was terminated. She remained in the home for two additional years, when she was once again removed from the home and placed with relatives subsequent to her stepfather's arrest and incarceration. At the time of the present assessment, Leah is living with an aunt and uncle.

There is little information regarding Leah's early development. An assessment performed by the the county Head Start program when Leah was three years, four months old, showed developmental delays in most areas. At that time, her gross motor, cognitive, and prewriting skills were all assessed at two years; fine motor was at three years; and social was at three years, two months. Her areas of strength were language at three years, six months, and self-help at three years, 10 months.

Present Assessment

The Stanford-Binet Intelligence Scale and the Adaptive Behavior Scale for Infants and Early Childhood (ABSI) were administered. A clinical interview was also conducted.

Leah approached the test situation cautiously, but she was easily engaged into the test procedures, interacted well with the examiner, and complied with the examiner's requests and directions. She appeared to be comfortable and demonstrated no unusual behaviors. Her demeanor during the testing was somber; she did not smile. However, the examiner noted she did laugh and show positive affect for a brief period after the testing when playing with her sister. Leah's attention was easily maintained during the testing, and it is felt that the results are a valid indication of Leah's current abilities.

Leah's performance on the Stanford-Binet was in the low normal to borderline range of intelligence. With a cumulative age (CA) of five years, zero months, and a corrected mental age (MA) of four years, zero months, Leah's I.Q. score was 80. She passed all subtests at level III–6 (three years, six months) and no subtests at level VI (six years).

The ABSI was completed through an interview with her aunt, with whom Leah had been living. On the ABSI Leah exhibited mild deficits in all areas of adaptive behavior except in communication skills, which were in the average range. Leah had difficulty with fine motor tasks such as holding a pencil, and in gross motor tasks involving balance. She exhibited the greatest deficiencies on the ABSI in the areas of independent functioning and self–care skills such as feeding, dressing, bathing, and toileting, and in the area of personal/social behavior.

There were many indicators of maladaptive behavior on the ABSI, which reflect emotional disturbance. Leah was reported to tease and be physically aggressive against others, including pushing, kicking, slapping, scratching, biting, and grabbing at other people. She has frequent temper tantrums, throws objects, screams and cries excessively, refuses to talk to strangers, refuses to eat, will not pick up toys or do what she is told, plays with forbidden objects, and puts objects into her mouth, ears, and nose. Leah was also reported to exhibit an excessive need for attention, demand attention from caregivers, cling to adults, act silly to get attention, and pout or cry for long periods after being reprimanded. She was also described as behaving in an insecure and frightened manner in daily activities. Leah continues to wet the bed.

General Impressions

Leah is a five year old girl whose current cognitive functioning is in the low normal range with an I.Q. of 80, and who displays mild deficits in all areas of adaptive behavior except communication skills, which are in the average range. She has a history of neglect, and of disruption and discontinuous care. She was diagnosed as failure to thrive as an infant, and she has been removed from her home and placed into substitute care on three separate occasions. Leah shows many behavioral indicators of emotional disturbance, many of which may have been exacerbated by the current instability of her family and placement situation. She presented herself to the examiner as a compliant child who found no pleasure in the activities; she appeared to be weary and depressed.

Recommendations:

1) Leah's most critical need is for a consistent, stable, predictable, and nurturing family environment. Her need is immediate. Without such a family milieu, Leah's prognosis for healthy development is extremely poor.

2) Leah should receive ongoing therapy from a counselor who specializes in work with young children. Therapy should help Leah understand the reasons for her family disruption, and should provide consistent and nurturing support to Leah.

3) Leah should continue in her preschool program. Staff should stress the development of concept skills and social interaction skills. When Leah is in a secure home environment, her ability to benefit from school pro-

graming should improve, and improvements in her cognitive and adaptive functioning should be seen.

4) Leah's vision should be screened to determine whether visual problems may contribute to her difficulty with visual-motor tasks.

Discussion

Leah's development and behavior are fairly typical for a preschool child who has been subjected to chronic and serious maltreatment. She has pronounced developmental delays in all domains, and her I.Q. measures in the low normal range. However, her profile suggests the potential for normal cognitive development, since her verbal and communication skills, which are Leah's strengths, are one of the most prominent deficiencies in children who are mentally retarded.

Leah also shows many signs of emotional disturbance. Her behavior problems appear to be the result of low frustration tolerance and a limited ability to deal with the chronic anxiety and psychological stresses generated by her dysfunctional environment. She is also chronically depressed. Yet, she demonstrates some strengths. She played in an affectionate and interactive way with her sister, and she was able to appropriately control her behavior and respond in the structured test situation. A stable, nurturant, low stress home environment is critical, but not sufficient, to promote healthy development. Leah will probably need ongoing play therapy and a consistent, trusting relationship with her therapist to alleviate her emotional distress, and stabilize her before she will have the emotional energy to attend to other developmental issues.

Epilogue

The psychologist followed both of these children for several years after these assessments were done. Jenny was adopted by a close friend of her foster mother and is thriving. She continued to have frequent contact with her foster mother. Leah was also adopted. Despite significant early adjustment difficulties and behavior problems, she eventually integrated well into her new family, and was reported to be doing well.

D. THE EFFECTS OF MALTREATMENT ON SCHOOL–AGE CHILDREN

1. Conceptual Framework

2. Application

3. Case Example

Conceptual Framework

The primary developmental tasks and milestones in each of the four developmental domains for children age six to 12 are as follows:

PHYSICAL DEVELOPMENT OF THE SCHOOL–AGE CHILD

Physical growth in children between the ages of six and 12 is slow and steady. Growth spurts do not normally occur during this period. The child grows an average of three to four inches per year.

School–age children are active, energetic, and in perpetual motion. They rarely stand still or walk when they can run, jump, tumble, skip, hop, or climb.

School–age children can be easily involved in activities that promote the development and coordination of complex gross motor and perceptual–motor skills. Physical activity is directed into both formal and informal games and sports, such as soccer, basketball, softball, gymnastics, dancing, hopscotch, jumping rope, riding bikes, running, or turning cartwheels in the yard.

Fine motor skills are refined and practiced through painting and drawing, crafts, using tools, building models, playing musical instruments, and other activities that require the use of the hands.

Motor and perceptual–motor skills become increasingly well integrated during this period. School–age children can perform complex maneuvers with apparent ease, such as riding a bike without holding on, skate boarding, playing the piano, and balancing on a beam.

The development of motor skills may be influenced by cultural factors. Cultures that value physical strength and skill tend to reinforce activities that involve gross motor abilities. In some cultures, girls are discouraged from engaging in active, "rough and tumble" physical play. Cultures that place greater value on cognitive and social rather than physical skills may tend to discourage active physical play. American culture expects children to sit for long hours at a school desk. Combined with the prevalence of television as a primary recreational activity, many school–age children in this country are considered to be physically "unfit."

School–age children are naturally physical. If given the opportunity, they enjoy using their bodies in the performance of complex activities, and will create opportunities to do so.

COGNITIVE DEVELOPMENT OF THE SCHOOL–AGE CHILD

Dramatic changes in cognition occur between the ages of five and seven. The changes are so predictable and prevalent that they have been acknowledged by nearly all developmental investigators, and are referred to as the "five–to–seven shift" [Gardner 1978]. These changes are qualitative, not quantitative; there are distinct differences between the cognitive abilities of preschool and school-age children that cannot be accounted for solely by increased experience. These changes are thought to reflect a "developmental leap," in which new abilities emerge without obvious precursors.

Many theorists suggest that significant changes in the organization of the child's brain permit the appearance of these new skills, specifically, further development of the cerebral cortex, the portion of the brain that controls most higher cognitive functions [Gardner 1978]. Research has demonstrated that these changes occur in cultures that are markedly different from each other in values, norms, and educational practices, further suggesting a strong maturational component. These changes can be best illustrated by comparing the cognition of school-aged children with that of preschoolers in several cognitive skill areas.

Language

When compared with preschool-aged children, school-age children demonstrate major advances in their use of language. Preschoolers take pleasure simply in using language for its own sake; they enjoy learning, practicing, and perfecting words, and they often talk to themselves. They enter into conversations by posing seemingly irrelevant or "off the subject" verbalizations, and they may ask questions to maintain the conversation, without being particularly interested in the answers. Conversations between preschool children have often been referred to as collective monologues.

School-age children, by comparison, use language primarily as a tool to communicate, to promote mutual understanding, and to enhance interpersonal relationships. Their use of language is, therefore, interactive. They listen to what other people say, and consider these communications carefully. They also ask questions when they don't understand, and they continue asking questions until they are satisfied with the answer. They are also able to differentiate relevant from irrelevant information in a conversation.

School-age children also use language to guide their activities and to direct others. Their enhanced understanding of the relationships between objects and events enables them to describe events logically and sequentially. They can request instructions or directions, and they have the ability to carry them out precisely.

Conversations with school-age children are mutual, and school-age children are invested in the communication. They no longer engage adults in conversation just to provide themselves with an opportunity to talk and practice words. Subsequently, it is possible for an adult to have a discussion with the child, since the child is interested both in giving and receiving information, and in exchanging thoughts and opinions. The school-age child considers the needs of the listener in the conversation, and will try to provide information the listener will find useful or interesting. For the first time, parents can effectively use explanation and reasoning as a discipline strategy by engaging their children in a discussion of their actions, and the logical consequences of those actions.

The Emergence of Perspective Taking

Preschool children do not recognize that other people have perspectives which might be different from their own. School-age children have begun to develop the ability to understand other people's perspectives. This ability emerges in rudimentary form at the end of the preschool years, and develops in stages throughout childhood and adolescence.

Young school–age children can often understand how other people feel, but they will become confused if their own perspective conflicts with another person's. They cannot grasp that two contradictory perspectives can coexist, and that both may be valid.

By age eight to 10, children can recognize the difference between a person's behavior and intent. For example, if Dad accidentally steps on three–year–old Ted's hand, Ted will be angry at Dad for hurting him. When Ted is eight or nine, he'll understand that his father didn't mean to hurt him, and he won't be angry. He will understand that his father's intentions are different from his actions.

Caseworkers can help some school–aged abused and neglected children to accept, to a degree, that their parents didn't intend to harm them. Some children will be able to acknowledge that "My mom didn't take care of me because she is sick," or, "My dad got angry because he lost his job." The child can be helped to not blame herself. However, the school-age child cannot yet empathize with the parent's feelings, or fully understand the conditions that led to the maltreatment. The development of true insight occurs with the development of formal operational thinking, which is characteristic of adolescents and adults.

Throughout the school-age years, children become increasingly aware of and able to consider the needs and feelings of others. By the age of 10 or 11, children have the ability to listen to each other's points of view and discuss them, and when their views are in conflict, they can often identify solutions that consider what both children want. For example, when Sally wanted to play soccer, and Toni wanted to play in the tree house, they agreed to play soccer today and play in the tree house tomorrow.

Having the ability to understand others' perspectives does not guarantee that children will act in unselfish ways. It simply means they have developed cognitively to a level where they can accurately recognize, and consider, other peoples' points of view.

Development of Concrete Operations

Concrete operations is the name given by Jean Piaget to the stage of cognitive development that is characteristic of school–age children. The child has a relatively accurate perception of objects, events, and relationships between them, as long as these are concrete; that is, observable or touchable. Through observation the child learns about the nature of objects, and the causes and effects of events. For example, the child might observe that when a glass is dropped, it usually breaks. However, when a plastic cup is dropped, it bounces. The child would conclude, properly, that glass is more likely to break when dropped, than plastic. The child can generalize his knowledge about the fragility of glass to other forms, such as vases, picture frames, and eyeglasses, and can adapt his behavior to prevent breakage.

The school-age child's thinking is generally rational and logical. Magical and imaginative thinking are understood to be "pretend," and they are clearly differentiated in the child's mind from what is "real." School-age children no longer interweave fantasy and reality in their conversations or play, as do preschoolers. They no longer have imaginary friends.

The school–age child can recognize similarities and differences between objects and people, as long as the attributes are visible and concrete. For example, a younger school–age child might say an apple and an orange are similar because they are both round, or that you eat them. A child of this age might not understand that apples and oranges belong to an abstract class of objects called "fruit." Similarly, a dog and a lion might be considered alike because they have four legs and fur. The child might have difficulty recognizing the similarity between a tree and a fly, and might insist that they aren't alike, or suggest that they are both found outside. The concept of "living things" is too abstract for most school–age children.

The school–age child has also developed the ability to consider and reflect upon herself and her attributes. She will perceive herself in concrete terms, however, and would describe herself to others as, "I'm a girl, I have brown eyes, I play the piano, and I like school." She is less likely to consider abstract qualities, such as, "I'm friendly," or, "I'm artistic."

The school–age child is able to consider two thoughts simultaneously. A preschool child might think, "I'm hungry," and would request something to eat. The school–age child might think "I'm hungry," and at the same time think, "If I eat something now, Mom will be mad because I won't eat dinner," and consider both perspectives in making a decision of whether, and how much, to eat.

The child has a good understanding of concepts of space, time, and dimension. School–age children understand how to sequence events in time, that is, first, next, and last, and can relate the events in a story in their proper, logical order so others can understand.

The school–age child understands that the identity of an object or a person remains constant, regardless of outward visible changes. (When Mother puts on a scary mask, she is still Mother. She hasn't been transformed into a monster.) Young preschool children, by contrast, are not able to separate the mask from the person, which accounts for their common fear of masks.

The age at which children evolve from concrete operations to formal operations, characterized by abstract and hypothetical thinking, is variable. Elements of abstract thinking may emerge in children as young as nine or 10, particularly if they are of exceptional intelligence and have received a high quality education. In general, abstract thinking is associated with preadolescence and adolescence.

Memory

Children's memories improve as they grow. School-age children can remember events that happened weeks, months, or even years earlier. They also have an increasingly good short–term memory, which allows them to follow instructions, and, once they have learned the instructions, to repeat complex activities without assistance. These increased cognitive abilities promote the development of more effective coping skills, including the ability to behave in planful, goal–directed ways, and to control their behavior. For example, children at this age can think about past actions or events, and remember their consequences, and can use this information to plan strategies to solve problems and to meet needs.

School-age children also better understand how their own activities and behaviors affect other people and events. They learn, through observation, "When I do this, that happens," and can repeat a behavior to achieve a desired effect or goal.

Children's aptitude with language also increases their coping ability. They can "think to themselves," as well as better communicate with other people, both of which assist in solving problems and meeting their needs. Repeating rules to themselves also helps to direct their behavior. The availability of multiple strategies to solve problems provides school-age children with greater control over the environment. They are less apt to respond to frustration with emotional outbursts, because they can think through alternate strategies to solve a problem, and can mentally guide or "talk" themselves through the steps in carrying out their solutions.

SOCIAL DEVELOPMENT OF THE SCHOOL-AGE CHILD

The social environment of preschool children is generally limited to their homes, their immediate neighborhoods, and possibly a preschool or church. By contrast, the social world of the school-age child, while still focused largely on home and family, expands to include teachers, peers, and school mates, as well as the larger world learned about in school, through books, movies, or television, and through personal experiences.

School-age children's more sophisticated cognitive abilities and improved emotional control affect both the quality of their interpersonal relationships, and their behavior in social settings. School-age children are able to develop and maintain meaningful, mutual friendships with other children. School-age children may have a best friend and often belong to a peer group. Friends are often of the same gender. Many friendships between children develop through participation in common activities, or because of physical proximity. For example, a child might have a favorite playmate who lives next door, a different best friend in class, and yet another friend in church school or a scout troop. Friendships often do not cross settings.

Because many friendships are situation-specific, they may also be transitory. This is exemplified by the typical behavior of children leaving friends they met at a two-week summer camp. They claim undying friendship and promise faithfully to call or write, but they demonstrate little interest in maintaining the relationships once school and peer group activities resume at home.

Rules are important in guiding the school-age child's behavior. The child's ability to cope in a complex world depends upon how well the child understands and can adapt to rules. The child's understanding of the nature of rules and their utility becomes more sophisticated as the child gets older. Play, for example, is largely governed by rules. School-age children like board games, sports, and group or team play, all of which require that rules be followed.

The child's perception and understanding of the nature of rules changes as the child develops through the school-age period. At age five or six, children believe that rules can be changed to suit individual needs, and they will alter the rules of a game at whim to get what they want. This is a holdover from preschool egocentric thinking, in which the self is at the center of the world. By age seven or eight, the child is very conscious about obeying the rules, even though she will test limits and challenge authority. Rules are perceived as fixed, unchangeable, and handed down by an ultimate authority. This leads to strict interpretations of what is right and wrong. Issues of fairness are prevalent, and school-age children become angry, argue, and complain bitterly to adults if someone has broken an established rule or is not treating them fairly.

By age nine or 10, children begin to view rules as a useful means of regulating their activities, but they understand that not all rules are inflexible. Rules can be negotiated and constructed by equals to achieve an agreed-upon purpose. For example, if everyone in the group agrees that the rules of a game should be changed, so be it.

Rules provide the child with structure and security. Rules describe the laws of their world in concrete terms that they can understand. In a new or strange situation, the first thing a school-age child will do is observe and ask questions to determine what is permitted and what is not. Children respond with anxiety in situations where rules are ambiguous or absent. This is particularly important when considering the effects on a school-age child of moving into a new home setting.

The school-age child is beginning to understand social roles, and recognizes that certain behaviors can be associated with certain people, even though at this level of development, the traits and behaviors that define the role are concrete and observable. In response to the question, "What's a mother?" the child might say, "A mother takes care of you, she takes you to school." A father "goes to work and helps you with your homework." A teacher "helps you learn and starts games at recess."

In the cognitive context of the school-age child, roles are fixed, inflexible, and situation-specific. It is amusing to observe the surprise on an eight year old's face when she sees her teacher at the grocery store. Mothers shop for groceries—not teachers. The behavior does not fit within the child's conception of the role.

An understanding of roles, and the characteristics that define them, helps children adapt their behaviors to fit different situations. A child may be a dominant leader and give orders to others on the school playground, sit quietly and be an attentive listener in church, and be helpful to his mom by watching his younger brother at home.

Children at this age are also beginning to understand gender role differentiation. They realize that girls and boys are different, and are often expected to behave differently. Comments such as, "Don't be silly, boys don't play with dolls," exemplifies the rigid role expectations of many children this age. Most children will emulate those qualities that are valued for their gender in their culture. While some contemporary cultures tend to promote a less rigid delineation of roles by gender, the expectation that males and females are different is fairly universal. Culture strongly influences a person's values about acceptable behaviors for boys and girls.

EMOTIONAL DEVELOPMENT OF THE SCHOOL-AGE CHILD

Erikson considers "Industry versus Inferiority" to be the primary developmental task of school-age children [Erikson 1963]. "Industry" is derived from industriousness, or the ability to be self-directed, productive, and goal-oriented. Throughout the school years, children become increasingly decisive, responsible,

and dependable about making plans and following through with them.
They are productive and results–oriented, and experience pleasure and
feelings of accomplishment as a result. By contrast, children who fail at
being industrious are likely to experience feelings of inferiority, since
the self–esteem of school-age children is largely dependent upon their
ability to perform and produce.

The school–age child's increased awareness of other people's perspectives,
combined with adherence to a well–defined set of rules that govern good and
bad behavior, lead the child to be sensitive to other people's opinions. It is
important to gain the approval of important others, to do well, and to be liked.
The child is particularly sensitive to criticism, and feels personally inadequate
when performance falls short. To help school–age children develop positive self–
esteem, it is important to recognize their efforts, and commend them for their
intent or a good attempt, rather than to measure their success solely on out–
comes or final products.

Throughout the school years, children develop increasingly good self–control
and frustration tolerance. They develop alternative strategies to deal with frus–
tration, and are better able to control their emotions. They also develop ways to
express their impulses and emotions in safe, socially appropriate ways.
Emotional tension is often released through hard physical play. Older school–age
children are also better able to delay gratification.

Application

THE EFFECTS OF ABUSE AND NEGLECT ON THE SCHOOL–AGE CHILD

The chaotic, unpredictable, or explosive environment in an abusive family, or the absence of social and emotional structure in a neglectful family, can negatively affect both the behavior and development of a school–age child.

When the child's social environment lacks consistency and structure, the rules are rarely clear. Parents may impulsively change rules, or may respond differently and unpredictably to the child's behavior. In a neglectful home there may be no rules, leaving children without a clear structure to guide their activities, creating anxiety, and resulting in "out of control" behavior.

Abused and neglected children are also deprived of experiences that teach that their social behaviors can elicit reasonable and consistent responses from other people. This can interfere with the development of confidence in their ability to influence what happens to them, or how others relate to them. Similarly, when rewards are inconsistently given, or are absent, the child may learn that the only way to assure having something is to take it when you can. The child learns to behave impulsively and receives immediate reward, which counteracts development of responsibility, and the ability to delay gratification.

Maltreatment can have serious negative effects on children's relationships with their parents and other adults. Many maltreated children will not seek help or comfort from adults when in need. Experience has taught them that it will not be given, or that there may be painful consequences to help–seeking behavior. Many school-age children are emotionally insulated and communicate, through words and behaviors, that they are able to care for themselves. This "pseudo–independence" is a defensive response to a pervasive lack of trust in adults. Some maltreated children are overtly suspicious and mistrustful of adults, or conversely, overly solicitous, agreeable, and manipulative. Some children do not respond to positive praise and attention. All the above represent distortions in the child's ability to relate to others.

Yet, abused and neglected children generally talk in unrealistically glowing terms about their parents, perhaps in an attempt to convince themselves of the adequacy of persons on whom they must depend. Children also work hard to meet their parent's expectations for them, including, at times, assuming adult responsibilities in the family. Maltreated children often behave as little adults by regularly doing housework, assuming primary responsibility for the care of younger children, and at times, providing for the needs of their parents. This pattern of "role reversal" by a school-age child is often diagnostic of abuse in the family. (See related discussion in Section II–B, "Dynamics of Child Maltreatment.")

A child's ability to relate to peers is also damaged by abuse or neglect. Maltreated children often feel inferior, incapable, and unworthy around other children, especially if they lack age–appropriate social skills. They may be hyper-sensitive to other children's perceptions of them, and may be embarrassed and ashamed if they can't measure up to peer expectations.

Some children act out their feelings of inadequacy and helplessness by attempting to control, exploit, manipulate, or coerce other children. They may be bossy, a bully, or domineering with other children. They may blame others when things go wrong, or pick fights to legitimize the release of anxiety or aggression. The maltreated child's lack of social skills and inappropriate behaviors may also contribute to scapegoating by peers, which further damages children's self-esteem. Consequently, maltreated children often have difficulty making friends, may feel overwhelmed by peer expectations for performance, and may ulti-mately withdraw altogether from social contact.

School performance is almost always affected when children have been abused or neglected. The highly structured school setting, with its many demands and academic challenges, can be very threatening. The child who has developed few problem–solving skills may lack the confidence and perseverance necessary to learn and master academics. In addition, maltreated children are often unable to concentrate on schoolwork. They expend their emotional ener-gy trying to maintain self-control, worrying about what may happen when they go home, and coping with emotional distress. Frequent emotional outbursts, an inability to sit still or attend to task, and other inappropriate responses to frus-tration are typical.

A serious consequence of maltreatment in school–age children is the failure to develop industriousness, or self–directed and autonomous behavior. Children who are maltreated are often punished for autonomy and initiative. The abused child may learn that self–assertion is dangerous, and may assume a more depen-dent or compliant posture to avoid injury. These children may exhibit few opin-ions, and express no strong likes or dislikes. It may be hard to engage the child into productive, goal–directed activities, and he is often unable to initiate, par-ticipate in, or complete activities. He may give up quickly and appear to lose interest when activities become even mildly challenging. As a result, the child misses critical opportunities to develop and master age-appropriate skills, and the child may feel inferior when compared to other children.

Abuse and neglect deprive a child of the unconditional acceptance and nur-turance that should communicate the child's fundamental worth. Maltreated children often experience severe damage to self-esteem from the many deni-grating and punitive messages received from an abusive parent, or from the absence of positive attention and recognition in a neglectful environment. In addition, maltreated children are often scapegoated by other children. Maltreated children interpret these negative responses from other people to mean that they have done something wrong, that they have failed to figure out the right rule or formula for success, or that they are of little worth. Children's ability to trust can also be seriously damaged.

The absence of predictable outcomes in response to a child's acts or behaviors also interferes with the child's ability to learn coping strategies. The child may not develop constructive problem–solving skills. Maltreated children may have little impulse control, and often cannot prevent their feelings from being expressed in actions. The child may be easily frustrated, often feels help-less and out of control, and may behave explosively and inappropriate-ly in minimally stressful situations. Anxiety, anger, and frustration may be acted out in negative and antisocial behaviors, including hitting, fighting, breaking objects, swearing, verbal outbursts, lying, and steal-ing. Sometimes the term "SBH" (severely behaviorally handicapped) is used to describe these children.

Finally, abused and neglected children are at high risk of developing emo-tional disturbance as a result of maltreatment, particularly if chronic. A child's security is dependent upon a predictable and understandable world. When the world is erratic and incomprehensible, and when painful things happen rou-tinely and capriciously, the child often becomes chronically anxious or depressed. The emotional toll is significant.

Case Example

The following case example describes the negative developmental outcomes in a young, school-age child who has been seriously maltreated for much of her life. The case is presented in the format of the psychological assessment, which was sought by Chrissie's social worker to assist in case planning.

⊀ Chrissie Atherton, age six years, 11 months

Reason for Referral

Chrissie was referred for psychological assessment by her social worker. She is one of four Atherton children in the custody of the Department of Children's Services. Chrissie was exhibiting serious developmental delays and behavior problems, and a psychological evaluation was requested to assist in case planning, educational programming, and placement planning.

History

Chrissie is the third of four children. The Athertons have been known to the Children's Service agency for several years, during which time the family received intensive, in-home protective and supportive services from the agency.

The family has a history of chronic family dysfunction, domestic violence, and neglect and abuse of the children. Mrs. Atherton is reported to have been mentally ill for many years, and has been hospitalized several times. She was most recently hospitalized approximately two years ago in a psychiatric facility, and she remains there currently. About four months ago, Chrissie's oldest sister, Patricia, disclosed having been sexually abused by her stepfather, Mr. Atherton, who is the biological father of the three younger children. All four children have been in the care of relatives since Mr. Atherton's conviction and incarceration for this offense.

According to the social worker, Chrissie and her siblings were subjected to serious neglect while at home. Mr. Atherton was reported to often be away from home, leaving the care of the younger children to Patricia. The agency noted that the home was very poorly maintained, and that food was not always present for the children. The agency also reported that both Chrissie and her younger sister, Leah, were chronic bed wetters, that the bedding was rarely changed and laundered, and that the house often smelled of urine. Chrissie's brother, Shawn, has allegedly been physically abused by Mr. Atherton, and Mrs. Atherton filed several police reports regarding beatings she had been subjected to by Mr. Atherton. Chrissie had been removed from her home once previously, after having accidentally ingested an overdose of her mother's medication. She was returned to the family approximately a year later.

Chrissie was enrolled in Head Start classes, but her attendance was sporadic. Head Start staff reported her to be delayed in her development. She also exhibited behavior problems in the Head Start setting, alternating periods of stubbornness and defiance with periods of emotional withdrawal. In her school placement, begun in September of this year, Chrissie is reportedly exhibiting considerable disruptive behavior in the classroom.

More complete information regarding Chrissie's developmental history is not available. She has vision problems and must wear glasses. As noted earlier, she is also a chronic bed wetter. No other medical problems are known.

Present Assessment

The following tests were administered; Wechsler Intelligence Scale for Children/Third Edition (WISC–III); Bender Visual Motor Gestalt Test (Bender); Rorschach; Stanford Binet Intelligence Scale (Binet); and the Adaptive Behavior Scale (ABS). The initial test results on the Binet and the Adaptive Behavior Scale indicated potentially serious developmental and emotional problems. Follow-up testing using the WISC–III, the Bender, and the Rorschach were used to validate and confirm the initial impressions.

Chrissie approached the test situation with some hesitation, but she was appropriate in her behavior and in her responses to the examiner. On the WISC–III she achieved a verbal score of 84, a performance score of 75, and a full-scale score of 78, placing her in the borderline range. She shows comparative strengths in her concrete and abstract verbal reasoning abilities, as well as her ability to see relationships of parts to a whole. Both of these skills are within the average range of ability. No comparatively significant weaknesses are exhibited. The results of the Stanford–Binet support these conclusions.

Chrissie's score on the Bender places her below the range for a child of kindergarten age, suggesting significant perceptual–motor problems. This is supported by lower scores on the Coding and Mazes subtests of the WISC–III.

Psychological Data

Chrissie is currently struggling to contain volatile emotions. She exhibits poor emotional control when confronted with complex or emotionally laden situations. She is presently experiencing conflict between the expression or suppression of her emotions, and much of her energy is used in attempts to control or tone down her affect. The emotional pain she is feeling contributes to a tendency to withdraw.

The vacillation between containing and expressing emotions is closely tied to her lack of ability to see reality clearly. She is not able to organize her day-to-day world. Her test performance shows considerable reality distortion and psychopathology. She has learned to view her world as hostile, threatening, and harmful. She is particularly threatened by emotional situations, as when others are angry at her, and she is quick to view even commonplace events as threatening. She spends much energy withdrawing from these perceived threats. At times she seems to become so overwhelmed by the demands of her environment that she regresses to a safer haven of fantasy. She is better able to correctly interpret her environment when it is not highly charged with emotion. It is important to note that Chrissie is not always detached from reality.

Chrissie has an extremely poor self-image. She also exhibits considerable hopelessness and despair, and appears to have abandoned any hope of her needs being met. She denies the need for emotional closeness. Chrissie also expresses a rather morbid view of life and exhibits many depressive characteristics. When this occurs in a child of this age, it tends to be a rather durable characteristic.

Chrissie is a child who experiences significant reality distortions of considerable degree and duration. To what degree these are part of her inherent make-up, or a reaction to a series of severe traumas is unclear. However, since she is known to be a victim of an abusive environment, we believe that her perception of the world as a hostile and threatening place is at least partially in response to maltreatment. As a result of traumatic early experiences, she now views many nontraumatic events as scary and threatening, and may withdraw, act out, or distort reality in response. She has a damaged sense of self, and has discarded the need for emotional closeness.

Recommendations:

1) Chrissie needs a consistent, stable, predictable, nurturing family environment. Without the immediate provision of such a family milieu, Chrissie's prognosis for healthy emotional and psychological development is extremely poor.

2) A family for Chrissie should be consistently stable and nurturing, with no expectations for immediate reciprocal response from Chrissie. A family will need considerable ability to understand and tolerate Chrissie's inability to trust emotional closeness, while continuing to support and nurture her. A quiet, predictable, low-stress environment is essential.

3) Chrissie should receive intensive individual therapy with a therapist who specializes in the treatment of children with severe emotional problems. She should attend therapy weekly at a minimum, and preferably twice a week. It should be cautioned, however, that without implementation of recommendation #1, therapy will not be effective.

4) Chrissie's emotional outbursts, defiance, and aggressive behaviors should be handled in a firm, consistent, matter-of-fact manner. Expectations should be clearly stated and quietly reiterated whenever necessary. Negative behavior should be responded to with natural consequences as often as possible; for example, if she leaves her bicycle in the street, it should be put away. Chrissie should not be disciplined with physical punishment, or harsh verbal admonishment. The use of time-out should also be considered. She should also receive frequent positive reinforcement, praise, and reward for desirable behaviors.

5) Specialized educational programming should be provided for Chrissie, either within a special education class for emotionally disturbed children within the public school system, or in a specialized day treatment program. The school setting must also be highly supportive and encouraging. The local special education resource center should be contacted for assistance in specialized educational planning.

Discussion

Chrissie is at risk of serious emotional disturbance. While her family history of mental illness might suggest a predisposition to emotional problems, the abusive and neglectful environment in which she has been raised has certainly contributed to, if not caused, such serious emotional problems at such a young age. In a young child, the effects of chronic maltreatment are usually exhibited in generalized developmental delays. In school–age children, delays in emotional development may become fixed into more fundamental disturbances in personality development. Chrissie's denial of interpersonal need, and withdrawal from interpersonal contact is characteristic of a more enduring personality trait that will not be easily modified. In this sense, Chrissie is at a watershed. Immediate and intensive intervention are necessary, if there is to be hope for her normal and healthy development.

Epilogue

Chrissie was adopted by a single parent. The first few years were rocky at best. Chrissie received regular mental health services, and at one point was hospitalized for a brief period. Her adoptive mother "stuck it out," however, and after seven years the placement is intact. The agency also arranged with the adoptive families for periodic visits between Chrissie and her younger sister, Leah. While Chrissie still exhibits emotional problems, with therapy and support, she has continued to develop and function within a normal environment.

E. THE EFFECTS OF MALTREATMENT ON ADOLESCENTS

1. Conceptual Framework

2. Application

3. Case Examples

Conceptual Framework

Because adolescence is a period of extremely rapid change, and because it covers approximately eight years of a child's life, adolescence is usually subdivided into stages referred to as early, middle, and late adolescence. Individual and cultural differences may determine the exact age at which each child experiences particular changes; however, the sequence of stages is fairly consistent in normally developing adolescents.

Early adolescence refers to the period from about age 12 to 14. In this country, the 13–year–old eighth grader often epitomizes this group of children. Middle adolescence includes youth between the ages of 14 to 17. Most American high school students, grades 9 through 12, fall into this category. Late adolescence refers to youth between the ages of 18 and 21, and represents the final developmental step into adulthood. Recently graduated high school students and college students would be included in this category. Most adolescents served by child welfare agencies are 18 years old or younger. They may also be developmentally younger than is expected for their chronological age. We will, therefore, focus discussion on early and middle adolescence.

ADOLESCENCE AS A TRANSITION

Adolescence is an important transitional stage in human development. The adolescent period marks the end of childhood and the beginning of the transition into adulthood. There are abrupt and often dramatic changes in expectations for the child's behavior. Behaviors that were previously permitted or otherwise positively reinforced are no longer considered appropriate. "Stop that; you're too old to do that," is a common admonition from parents. What was once cute is now considered silly. Clothes that were once comfortable are now too revealing. Behaviors that were once prohibited are not only permitted, but are expected. In order to adopt new behaviors, old behaviors must be changed or relinquished. This is not an easy passage for youth.

When we compare the typical expected characteristics of children to the comparable characteristics normally expected of adults, it is easy to understand the magnitude of the expected changes. Children, for example, are understood to often be selfish and self-centered in thought and action. Adults, by comparison, are expected to be unselfish and thoughtful of others. Children are typically dependent upon adults for their survival; they are not expected to assume sole responsibility for themselves. Adults must not only be able to care for themselves, but must be responsible, dependable, and able to care for others.

There are other significant differences. Children's primary identity is with their family of origin, and what is considered right and wrong is generally dictated by the family values. An adult's identity and values may or may not diverge from those of his or her parents, but they are perceived as personal and independent.

Children are oblivious of problems and issues outside their immediate physical and social environments; they are not expected to make important decisions. Adults must be able to cope with family, community, and even world problems, and make important decisions on a daily basis. Finally, children are essentially nonsexual in interpersonal relationships. Adults are expected to be sexually competent and responsible.

In short, adolescence is a process wherein a generally self-centered, dependent, irresponsible child is expected to become a cooperative, dependable, independent, responsible, mature adult. In order to successfully transition into this new role, the adolescent must grapple with several key developmental issues, which represent the milestones of the adolescent period. Successful achievement of these milestones results in competence as an adult; failure to achieve them leaves the adult extremely vulnerable to social and emotional dysfunction.

PHYSICAL DEVELOPMENT OF ADOLESCENTS

The hormonal changes of puberty promote development in two critical areas.

First, there is rapid physical growth of bones, muscles, and other body tissues. Much of physical growth takes place during a growth spurt , wherein the adolescent adds several inches in height, and gains considerable weight in a relatively short period of time. Girls mature physically, on average, two years earlier than boys. Most girls experience a growth spurt between the ages of 11 and 14, boys between 13 and 17. There is a wide normal range of puberty in both sexes.

Hormonal changes also lead to the development of the sex organs and secondary sex characteristics. Hormonal changes in girls promote breast development, growth of pubic hair, maturation of the uterus and ovaries, and menstruation. The average age range for the onset of menstruation is between 11 and 14. Hormonal changes in boys lead to increased size of the genitals, and the production of semen by the testicles. Erections, which first occur in the infant, become more frequent, and ejaculations are now possible. Secondary sex characteristics include the development of pubic and body hair, facial hair, and changes in the tone and quality of the voice. The onset of puberty in boys ranges from about age 12 to 15.

Emotional responses to puberty are variable. Many adolescents are ambivalent about the physical changes. They may be concurrently proud or pleased, embarrassed and self-conscious, and at times, worried whether they are normal.

A girl's attitude about menstruation is largely determined by the attitude of family and friends. It may be experienced with pride and considered a rite of passage. It may also be perceived as an annoyance at best, and unpleasant and painful at worst. The onset of menstruation can be very traumatic for girls who have not been properly prepared and who neither expect, nor understand, the changes in their bodies. The bleeding may be felt to be a sign of internal injury or damage. It is particularly traumatic for a girl who has been sexually abused and who, as a result, is likely to believe that she has been physically harmed.

Unexpected and unexplained erections in adolescent boys can be the source of extreme embarrassment. To be called on in class to go to the board or stand up and recite at the time of an erection is a typical fear of many adolescent boys.

An adolescent's body image is rarely objective. Most teens exhibit anxiety about their physical appearance, and are likely to be very self-conscious of the changes. Minor physical features assume enormous significance, and considerable emotional energy is spent in scrutiny in the mirror, and trying to hide, or otherwise change, perceived flaws. This self–consciousness can lead to behaviors adults consider illogical and oppositional. Adults usually cannot see the perceived flaws, much less consider them worth worrying about.

It takes time to reacclimate to the rapid changes in body size and appearance. Boys who grow several inches in as many months are often awkward and clumsy until their physical coordination catches up with their physical growth. The changing voice is unpredictable for a period of time; the youth sounds like someone else to himself.

An early or late onset of puberty can have emotional and social significance for some youth. Research suggests that boys who mature early tend to be more self–confident and socially appropriate in their behavior than boys who mature late; late maturing boys are found to be less poised, and often perceive themselves to be less adequate. Differences in girls may be similar, but less marked. The following examples illustrate the effects on some youth of early or late puberty.

During junior high school, Bill had been a popular, active, and verbal student. He had many friends. He was 15 when he entered high school, and he was still very thin and very short. His voice had just begun to change, and it cracked with some regularity. Many of the other boys in his class were tall, strong, muscular, and in Bill's eyes, considerably more attractive than he. They were athletic; Bill was repeatedly "bowled over" by heavier boys during football practice in gym class. Many boys were shaving; Bill had only the barest beginnings of fine hairs growing on his upper lip. He was interested in girls, but he felt that they weren't that interested in him. Other boys seemed to talk to girls with ease; he was very embarrassed. He felt inadequate and unpopular.

Marjorie was an extremely pretty child. She was 11 years old when she began her menstrual periods, and she had fully developed breasts and body curves by the time she was 13. She began to attract considerable attention both in and out of school; boys flocked around her in the lunchroom and in the halls. Truck drivers and construction crews whistled at her as she walked by, and men often stopped on the street to stare at her. High school boys, and even a few college students, asked her for dates. Marjorie was initially thrilled by all the attention, and pleased that she was so popular. She begged her mother to let her date one of the high school boys, and then became very frightened when she was alone with him in the car and he tried to kiss and fondle her. She also became increasingly embarrassed by all the attention she received from adult men, and felt increasingly alienated from her girlfriends, who did not receive such attention, and who appeared to be jealous and resentful of her. She eventually began to wear sloppy sweatshirts and baggy jeans to hide her body.

In both situations, a gap existed between the child's emotional and physical development. Bill, at age 15, is emotionally ready for more mature relationships, but his body is still that of a preadolescent. Marjorie, at age 13, is psychologically a very young adolescent with a body of an adult woman. The greater the discrepancy between physical and emotional maturity, the more conflict the youth experiences.

Generally, youth are most self-conscious about their bodies during early adolescence. By middle to late adolescence, physical and emotional development have usually caught up, and youths become more comfortable with their physical self. However, while less extreme, some degree of self-consciousness is still the norm in late adolescence.

The adolescent's body image can also be affected by emotional factors, including emotional responses to maltreatment. Youth, most often girls, who have high or perfectionist expectations for themselves, may perceive themselves as fat and unattractive, even when they are very normal in build. Eating disorders in adolescents, such as anorexia and bulimia, indicate serious psychological problems.

Sexual abuse can have a pervasive negative effect on a youth's body image. Sexually abused adolescents are commonly embarrassed and ashamed of their bodies, and are certain that they have been permanently physically damaged. They often describe themselves in derogatory terms such as "fat," "ugly," and "ruined."

Youth who have sustained permanent physical injuries from abuse, including scarring and physical malformation, are also likely to have low self-esteem, and be ashamed and embarrassed by their physical deficits.

COGNITIVE DEVELOPMENT OF ADOLESCENTS

Piaget refers to the stage of cognition that emerges during adolescence as formal operations. Not everyone achieves formal operational thinking. A combination of factors, including level of education, the presence of emotional problems, cultural influences, and innate ability may affect the emergence, and the ultimate degree of sophistication, of these cognitive skills. It is believed that while the ability for formal operational thought has a maturational component, these cognitive skills can be greatly improved and perfected by the formal education found in a college or advanced technical school setting. Therefore, these highly developed cognitive abilities are greatly affected by environment and culture.

Formal operational cognition includes several new abilities. The youth can think hypothetically. This means being able to consider and calculate the consequences of thoughts, actions, events, or behaviors without ever actually performing them. Hypothetical reasoning is often referred to as "if-then" reasoning; for example, "If I were to do X, then Y would probably happen." It allows the youth to consider a large number of possibilities and plan behavior accordingly. The youth with formal operational cognition is better able to think in logical terms, and can use logic in abstract thought. This means the youth can identify and reject hypotheses or possible outcomes based upon their logic.

The youth is now able to think about thought. Preoccupation with thought itself, and especially with thoughts about oneself, is characteristic of adolescent cognition. Introspection and self-analysis are common.

Perspective-taking ability assumes its most advanced form during late adolescence. The youth is able to understand and consider not only the perspectives and views of other people, but the collective perspectives of entire social systems (such as the attitude of conservationists about environmental pollution). The youth has developed insight, and is now able to consider and understand his or her own and other people's feelings and motivations, as well as how personal behaviors affect other people, and how their behaviors affect the youth.

The ability to cognitively manipulate abstract concepts, to hypothesize possible outcomes, and to understand logical relationships greatly facilitates planning and problem solving. The youth can now attack a problem and think about it in detail, weighing all information and possibilities in order to choose the best solution. The youth can also evaluate the success or failure of a solution, and make adaptations as needed.

SOCIAL DEVELOPMENT OF ADOLESCENTS

Adolescent social development does not occur independently of cognitive and emotional development. The youth's improved insight and perspective-taking ability lead to changed expectations for interpersonal relationships, and an increased ability for self-disclosure and intimacy. The development of identity and independence also have strong influences on how youth relate to other people. Young adolescents (age 12 to 14) are very different from older adolescents (age 16 to 18) in their social interests, the nature and quality of their social interactions, and their level of interpersonal skill.

Adolescent social development occurs in a progression of steps. The first step for a youth in the development of an independent self is often to psychologically distance himself or herself from family, and particularly from parents. In early adolescence, parents' attitudes are often summarily rejected, and parents are accused of being out of touch, old fashioned, and not understanding (in whatever colloquialisms are "in" for describing parents who are "out.")

Concurrently, the youth establishes a strong identification with peers. The peer group provides teens with strong support and clear standards of behavior. Young adolescents form many kinds of peer groups, usually composed of same-sex youth. Members conform to the group's standards of conduct, dress, language, and demeanor. Acceptance by the group depends upon adopting the group's norms. Standards are explicit and often unforgiving.

Social status is largely related to group membership. Youths who belong to groups with high social status are popular, and may be envied by youths who are not part of the group. Youths who are highly visible, and who have "desirable" attributes usually comprise these groups. What is considered "desirable" varies between settings and cultures, but the standards are fairly rigidly applied within a group. Youths who view themselves as less adequate or popular may try to emulate the values and standards of the "in" group.

Social acceptance in young adolescents depends upon conformity to observable traits or to roles that group members value. The social worth of other people is rarely based upon an insightful assessment of their personal attributes. In this regard, young adolescents may be fickle and hypocritical. They may greatly alter their behavior, compromise their beliefs, and even reject childhood friends to gain acceptance into the clique or group that provides them the most social status.

The young adolescent's need to be independent from parents is generalized to adults outside the family, particularly adults in authority positions. Teachers, police, and the parents of friends are commonly the target of criticism. Yet, these same youth may develop "crushes" on adults or older youths, and they may try to emulate these adults' mannerisms, dress, or behavior. This role modeling is superficial; rarely are these adults personally well known or understood by the youth.

Young adolescents are typically ambivalent about sexual relationships. They are often very shy, embarrassed, and self-conscious. Early sexual relationships usually involve group dating and activities, or just "hanging out." In this manner, the youth can test out their social skills within the security and support of their same-sex peer group.

During middle adolescence, youths continue to associate with their peer groups; however, one-on-one friendships with same and opposite sex peers become increasingly important. These relationships are often based upon criteria that were absent from their previous relationships, including mutual understanding, loyalty, and intimacy. Increased insight and perspective-taking ability enable youth to understand that others have feelings and experiences both similar to and different from their own. The recognition of similarities promotes mutual understanding and support. The recognition of differences provides opportunities for self-assessment and to try out different styles of thinking and acting. Middle adolescents commonly talk to each other with great intensity and conviction about very personal feelings and issues.

Self-revelation is a first step toward the development of interpersonal intimacy. Intimacy requires self-understanding and the communication of feelings and thoughts to others. The development of intimacy is a difficult and gradual process, and is partly dependent upon the youth's experiences with intimacy within the family. Youths who are raised in families where intimacy is absent, or in which interpersonal relationships are distorted, may have considerable difficulty becoming comfortable with self-disclosure and self-expression.

Intimacy has its risks. As a result, youths develop expectations for loyalty, confidence, and trust in their close relationships. Good friends are expected not to disclose personal information to others, and to remain loyal and understanding, regardless of the information that is shared.

During this time, youths develop similar expectations for relationships with adults. The middle to late adolescent is less likely to think that no adult can be trusted. The youth is able to discriminate individual differences, which allows the youth to consciously choose adults that he or she likes and wants to know better. During middle adolescence, many youths are intensely curious about how adults feel, think, and perceive the world. They see adults as possibly having answers to some of their questions and concerns. If adults, including parents, can share their thoughts openly without lecturing or behaving in an authoritarian manner, youth will often listen and will consider their opinions.

Youths who are capable of self-disclosure also expect the same from adults. They respect people who are honest and straightforward. They are also quick to point out hypocrisy and dishonesty in adults.

During middle adolescence, many youths become sexually active. However, there are significant differences between individual youths in the expression of sexual behavior, depending upon several factors, among them personal readiness, family values and standards, peer pressure, cultural or religious affiliation, internalized moral standards, and opportunity.

Early expressions of sexuality are largely exploratory, and may involve considerable experimentation, including self–exploration and masturbation. Motivation to engage in sexual behavior may include biological and hormonal pressure, curiosity, practice, a desire for social acceptance, and an attempt to increase self–esteem. Being pushed into sexual activity before an adolescent is emotionally ready, either by peer pressure or a need for acceptance, can contribute to significant emotional distress.

Sexual development in adolescence for both boys and girls is almost universally negatively affected by sexual abuse. Porter, Blick, and Sgroi [1985] describe the tendency for sexually abused youths to view themselves as "damaged goods," that is, mysteriously altered and somehow permanently damaged physically and socially from their sexual experiences. The authors suggest that other people's emotional responses to a child they perceive to now be "sexually experienced" can also contribute to the child's negative self–perception and a poor sexual self–image. The authors cite cases in which sexually abused girls are propositioned by both adolescent and adult males who believe that because of their backgrounds, they are desirous of, capable of, and a proper focus of sexual activity. Intense guilt, shame, poor body image, lack of self–esteem, and lack of trust in sexual relationships are frequent developmental outcomes of sexual abuse. All these can pose serious obstacles to a youth's ability to enter into mutually satisfying and intimate interpersonal and sexual relationships as adults.

MORAL DEVELOPMENT OF ADOLESCENTS

Moral development is a component of social development that deserves special attention in any discussion of adolescence. Lawrence Kohlberg has conducted much of the research that has identified predictable stages of moral development in youth [Damon 1977; Gardner 1978].

The moral development of most children under the age of 11 is at the preconventional level. Preconventional morality is largely "rules driven." For most preschool children, morality is based upon a "punishment/obedience" perspective. The child recognizes the superior power of an authority, and conforms to rules (is obedient) simply to avoid punishment. Later in childhood, children begin to understand that rules can be useful in promoting "self–interested exchanges." Specifically, children obey the rules in order to get what they want.

Significant changes in moral thought are brought about by advancements in abstract thinking, perspective taking and insight. Adolescents are often able to understand that moral principles have social utility; rules exist for the betterment of society and the benefit of its members. This perspective is called conventional morality. There are two stages in conventional moral thought. The first is epitomized by the Golden Rule–ethical behavior is behaving in ways that benefit, and do not harm, other people; the reciprocal being that others will also behave so as not to harm or take advantage of you. A second level of conventional morality is called the "law and order" perspective, which holds that rules exist for the good of society, and citizens must uphold the law because the system could not function without considerable conformity and cooperation.

The standards of conventional morality, whether interpersonal or legalistic in origin, are internalized. The person does not need a strong external authority present at all times to enforce the rules. Youths who have developed to the conventional level experience shame, guilt, and other self-blame when they fail to live up to internalized moral standards or the expectations of important others.

In assessing the moral development of youths, it is important to differentiate between moral thought and moral behavior. Young adolescents, particularly, may espouse certain moral principles but behave in ways that are in direct contradiction to their expressed values. Lack of self-control or lack of strong positive reinforcement are powerful stimuli to act in ways that are not consistent with espoused values. By middle to late adolescence, most youth are better able to control their own behavior to coincide with internalized values and beliefs.

EMOTIONAL DEVELOPMENT OF ADOLESCENTS

The principal task of emotional development during adolescence is the development of an individual identity. This is not a task that is easily achieved. In actuality, identity formation may continue well into early adulthood. Life-span developmental psychologists also believe that while certain components of identity are established during the adolescent years and remain relatively stable, identity continues to be redefined throughout the life cycle, with intermittent "life crises" that promote a self-reassessment and a reformulation of values and directions. Adolescence, however, is the first time in the life cycle that the development of identity is of central importance and a key developmental task.

A primary impetus for identity formation is the need for youth to psychologically, and often physically, separate from their parents and to prepare themselves to live independently. To do this, they must develop an internalized set of standards, values, beliefs, and rules that can provide them with the structure and guidance previously provided by the family.

Prior to adolescence, the child's attitudes and behaviors are largely determined by the values and expectations of the family and culture in which the child is raised. The adolescent's transition from being a member of a family to being on his or her own in the larger society challenges the youth to develop a sense of self that is more individualized, and to redefine one's relationship with one's family of origin.

Blatant rejections of parental standards by young adolescents can be seen as primitive attempts at independence and individuality. Individuality is expressed by adopting attitudes and values that at least, on the surface, appear to be in contradiction to those of parents. Conflicts between early adolescents and their parents generally occur in arenas where the expression of values is very concrete, such as hair style, manner of dress, friends, lifestyle choices, preferences in music, and doing homework versus going out. Youths at this age lack both the cognitive ability and the experience to evaluate parental values and standards on their own merit.

Young adolescents may substitute the structure of the peer group for the structure of the family. Youths often consider themselves to be independent simply because they are behaving differently from their families. However, they often fail to recognize that their excessive conformity to group standards does not reflect greater independence; it simply reflects dependence on a different group of people to provide self-definition. The peer group does serve a function, however. It encourages youths to try out different ideas and behaviors in a generally accepting and supportive setting. It is a first step in validating the development of independent ideas.

Early adolescence can be an emotionally chaotic period, and the young adolescent is often more emotionally labile than at any other time during development. The early adolescent period is inherently stressful because of rapid changes and difficult challenges. Youths are more aware of their feelings and emotional states, and they recognize their feelings to be an inherent part of themselves. The degree to which they experience feelings is new, and they are open to examination and experimentation.

Young adolescents often engage in activities that promote intense emotional experience. Listening to loud music, attending concerts and other group activities where emotions are at a peak, going to horror movies, riding amusement park rides, and reading about intimate interpersonal or sexual experiences all serve to activate intense and new feelings. Young adolescents typically lack the ability or experience to modulate or control their intense emotions. For some youths, experimentation with drugs and alcohol are attempts to magnify emotional experiences, as are driving at excessive speeds, performing "daredevil" stunts, or otherwise taking risks. However, the combination of volatile emotion, experiential innocence, lack of judgment, and dangerous activity can have devastating and even life-threatening consequences.

Negative parental reactions to the youth's volatility and mood swings may promote explosive behavior, pouting, withdrawal, or intense arguments. Probing questions by the parent such as, "Why are you acting this way?" only increase the youth's confusion, since the youth is generally not able to answer the question. The young adolescent is truly at the mercy of his or her emotions.

Perspective-taking ability during middle adolescence enables the youth to recognize differences in people's values and beliefs, which stimulates more intensive examination of other people's values. Youths begin to wonder about the validity of teachings that were previously accepted without question, and they are also more introspective, often questioning their own values. This awareness of inconsistencies in values creates ambiguity, and may be very threatening.

Formulation and definition of a personal identity is the focal point of middle adolescent emotional development. According to Erik Erikson [1959, 1967] identity formation includes both cognitive and affective (feeling) components. "Self" is an abstract cognitive concept. The ability to objectively view the elements of "self" requires perspective-taking ability and insight. The development of identity includes organizing perceptions about personal attitudes, values, behaviors, and beliefs into a coherent whole. Personal identity, or conception of self, remains generally stable and consistent across changing environmental conditions.

The affective component of self refers to feelings of self-worth and self-esteem. A positive self-image is a person's belief that he or she has inherent value, and that the person is acceptable to himself or herself and to others. Healthy self-esteem helps people to be objectively critical of their own shortcomings, and gives them the confidence to attempt changes.

Identity confusion, according to Erikson, is the negative outcome of failure to develop a positive identity. He suggests that identity-related psychopathology is the most common clinical disturbance in the first two decades of life. Some degree of identity confusion is a normal developmental problem, and should be expected. For most individuals, however, the confusion is generally resolved by late adolescence or early adulthood.

According to Erikson, identity confusion can manifest itself in a number of ways, and can be affected by a lack of resolution of earlier developmental tasks. Failure to achieve basic trust in childhood has the most severe consequences on the development of identity in adolescents. These youths exhibit what Erikson calls an almost "catatonic immobility." They fail to understand that changes in their lives are possible, much less understand their own role in promoting these changes. These youths cannot tolerate momentary delays in gratification; they have no confidence that the passage of time will provide a remedy, or that their needs will eventually be met. They feel impotent to change things, and cannot look with any confidence toward the future. They are truly lost. Typical expressions by these youth include, "I don't know," "I give up," and "I quit," all of which may reflect serious depression and despair.

Similarly, failure to achieve autonomy, initiative, and industry during earlier developmental stages can affect the adolescent's ability to develop a stable, positive identity. Youths who have not positively resolved the earlier stages may exhibit feelings of self-doubt and shame, pervasive guilt, self-criticism, poor perceptions of self-worth, overly rigid expectations for their own behavior, and a sense of inadequacy concerning task-related competence, which reflects futility and feelings of inferiority.

Youths may try to deal with these negative outcomes by overcompensating, including becoming narcissistic and unrealistically self-complimentary; or harboring grandiose ideas of their capability, and having high expectations for their performance in the future. They can also give up and behave in self-defeating ways, or fail to even try to master the challenges of developing an independent self. These youths appear to be lost and directionless, without the motivation to try.

The failure to achieve identity can interfere with development in the next of Erikson's stages, the development of mature intimacy. According to Erikson, to be comfortable in intimate relationships, the individual must have a well-developed and positive sense of self. The experience of emotional and sexual intimacy can be threatening to persons without a strong identity. Erikson suggests that during the development of identity, adolescents may avoid intimacy out of fear of "losing themselves in the other person." At its most pathological, adults without a firm sense of identity avoid all intimate relationships and maintain a state of personal isolation, or are dependent upon other people to define who and what they are.

By the end of middle adolescence, most youth have developed a concept of themselves that offers enough structure and stability to allow them to pursue new activities, such as entering the work force, continuing their education, or starting their own families. Their ability to function in the world will continue to improve as they grow and their identity becomes more stable.

Application

Most adolescents who are served by child welfare agencies have a history of maltreatment, or have been raised in dysfunctional families. The developmental outcomes of maltreatment in adolescents may vary considerably, depending upon a variety of factors.

The age of onset of the maltreatment

Since the effects of maltreatment are cumulative, the earlier in the child's life the maltreatment began, the more pervasive the developmental problems are likely to be. Residual effects of early maltreatment on subsequent development are common, especially if proper intervention is not provided. The failure to master early tasks makes the mastery of later tasks all the more difficult. The normal stresses and challenges that confront the child at adolescence may be over-whelming and insurmountable, if the youth has not mastered critical early coping skills.

The frequency of the maltreatment

Generally, the more frequently the child has been maltreated, the more perva-sive will be the detrimental effects. An adolescent who has been chronically mal-treated is likely to have more developmental problems than a child who was maltreated only sporadically, with generally good care provided otherwise.

The severity of the maltreatment

The more severe, painful, and debilitating the maltreatment, the more severe and extensive the developmental problems are likely to be.

The nature of the child's relationship to the maltreating adult

Maltreatment by parents is very traumatic, and is likely to result in more serious long-term problems for the child. Maltreatment by strangers is also traumatic. However, supportive and nurturing parents can help a child cope with the trau-ma of maltreatment that is perpetrated by someone outside the immediate fam-ily. This can help to minimize the likelihood of serious developmental conse-quences.

Constitutional factors of the child

Some children are inherently more resilient, and others are more sensitive and vulnerable. This does not suggest that resilient children are invulnerable to the effects of maltreatment. However, it does suggest that the same degree of mal-treatment may affect different children in different ways.

The family context of maltreatment

Maltreatment is "situational" when it is precipitated in a generally functional family by excessive and unusual family stress. Situational maltreatment in a family that normally provides adequate care will generally not be as traumatic for the child as chronic maltreatment in a seriously dysfunctional family. Disturbed family interactions can, by themselves, create developmental problems for a child.

At times, child welfare workers will encounter youths who have been maltreated for the first time during adolescence. The normal stresses of adolescence can create crisis situations for some families that were previously capable of more appropriate management. An adolescent's rebelliousness, thrust for independence, critical and judgmental attitudes toward parents, and emerging sexuality can be difficult to manage and very threatening to some parents. Also, changes in family composition, including changing family structures subsequent to divorce, remarriage, or death of a parent, may alter the family dynamics, precipitating an excessive response by parents to an adolescent's behavior.

Youths who are maltreated for the first time during adolescence typically display very different developmental outcomes than do children who have been subjected to maltreatment for most of their lives. They are often "healthier" and more accessible to short-term services or crisis intervention counseling. However, their behavior may at first glance appear to be as dysfunctional as that of a chronically maltreated child. It is therefore critical that the caseworker make a thorough and accurate assessment of the child's developmental level and strengths before formulating a treatment plan. For some adolescents, the problematic or acting-out behaviors are an adaptive response, designed to protect themselves from very dysfunctional family situations.

A significant percentage of both boys and girls who become truant, or who develop unruly or acting out behaviors, are reacting to sexual abuse. For this reason, the presence of sexual abuse should always be considered and carefully assessed for every adolescent served. Truancy and acting-out behavior, combined with depression, are common responses to sexual abuse in the family.

It is important to consider the implications of chronic maltreatment for adolescents, since many adolescents served by the child welfare agency typically have long histories of abuse and neglect. Maltreatment potentially affects development at all the stages in Erikson's typology. Maltreatment in infancy promotes insecure attachment, which interferes with the development of basic trust; maltreatment of toddlers can interfere with the healthy development of autonomy and can create pervasive feelings of shame and doubt; maltreatment of preschool-age children interferes with the development of initiative and generates guilt; and finally, school-age children who have been maltreated are subject to pervasive feelings of inferiority, and are often unable to compete in the performance of even basic skills and abilities. Identity diffusion in adolescents, and its accompanying cognitive, emotional, and social problems, can be considered one of the most distressing and serious long-term consequences of maltreatment in children.

We can use case examples to illustrate differences in the developmental levels of adolescents who have been chronically and seriously maltreated, and those for whom maltreatment has been more recent or less serious.

Case Examples

The following case examples illustrate some of the potential outcomes of maltreatment on adolescent development. Francie and Shawn, the two children who were most severely and chronically maltreated, exhibit the most pervasive developmental and emotional problems. Lee, who was primarily neglected, shows some significant developmental delays, but he is not emotionally disturbed. Leslie demonstrates the responses of a generally healthy youth to an acute situation of maltreatment.

Francie Woods, age 16

History

Francie lives with her mother and two younger sisters, ages 10 and 12, in a poorly maintained apartment in a low-income neighborhood. Francie's mother has never had a stable marital relationship; she has lived with several different men since Francie's birth, and has been occasionally battered by them. She has also been arrested for prostitution. The family has lived on public assistance since Francie's birth. All three girls have different fathers, and Francie never knew her father. Ms. Woods abandoned the children and moved to California with a man she met in a bar when Francie was five, and then returned a year later. The children were placed in foster care for the year she was gone. Ms. Woods has frequently left the children in the care of neighbors and relatives for short periods. Francie's early years were characterized by profound neglect, family disorganization, and emotional deprivation. One of her mother's boyfriends was suspected of sexually fondling Francie when she was 10, but there was never any proof, and the boyfriend disappeared shortly after the allegation was made. Francie has been chronically truant from school.

Developmental Assessment

Francie's emotional and cognitive development are egocentric, typical of a preschool child. She has no awareness of other people's perspectives. There is only one perspective from which to assess any event: her own simplistic view. Her ability to understand the world is, therefore, grossly deficient. She has no awareness of cause and effect in her environment or in relationships, and she is largely unaware that she has any control over her circumstances. Things happen "out there" arbitrarily and at whim. In her own mind, she's always a victim of unpredictable circumstance.

Francie has not progressed developmentally to understanding rules, so there is no consistent structure in her world. She is not mentally retarded, although her measured I.Q. on a standardized test would probably be depressed due to social and environmental deprivation. Her social perception is extremely deficient, as are her social skills. Her behavior is focused on meeting her own needs, and as such, she is generally perceived by others as selfish and inconsiderate. This perception is valid, as Francie views people only as resources to meet her needs, in much the same manner as would a very young child.

Francie's emotional development is very disturbed. She has no reciprocal attachments. She exhibits a kind of "bottomless pit" dependency, and a pervasive lack of trust, and she has significant deficiencies in autonomy, initiative, and industry. Concepts of "self" or "identity" are meaningless to her.

Francie is very impulsive; she takes what she wants, fights when she's mad, runs away when she's afraid, and has a tantrum when she's cornered. She has no frustration tolerance, no ability to delay gratification, and she is easily thwarted and upset. She has not developed the ability to use language or other more mature coping skills to manage stressful situations. She goes immediately to "emotional overload" in even minimally stressful situations.

Her relationships with people are very shallow and entirely lacking in continuity. Her "best friend" could be someone she met three days (or three hours) earlier. As long as people are nice to her, they are "friends." If they withhold what she wants, they are "mean." It is very possible for Francie to like a person one minute and hate them 30 seconds later, depending upon whether they have been nice or mean to her. If people are mean enough she'll abandon them, until they're nice to her again. She is oblivious to other people's perspectives, and she is unaware that other people have feelings, much less an understanding of what those feelings are. Therefore, she interprets other peoples' actions in a very concrete and egocentric fashion. Francie also uses relationships for gratification of her immediate needs, and she behaves in transparently insincere and clumsy ways in an attempt to flatter or please other people in order to get what she wants. She exhibits no evidence of recognizing other people as human beings with intrinsic worth.

Francie only superficially understands how her behavior affects other people, or what happens to her. When unpleasant or painful things happen, she blames others or general bad luck. She is genuinely baffled, and feels unfairly attacked when others try to assign part of the responsibility to her. Without awareness of rules or structure to relationships, she interprets the actions of other people as totally arbitrary. If things go her way, she feels good. If things don't go her way, she gets mad. The sum total of life revolves around how she feels, what she wants, her concerns and needs.

Because she has no awareness either of social rules or the feelings of others, she doesn't understand what other people expect of her, unless it is spelled out in crystal clear, concrete, behavioral terms. "Please be considerate" is meaningless to her. "Pick up your clothes and put them in the basket" is understood.

Francie has no ability to think about or plan for the future. Her life exists in the present moment and is dominated by getting her own immediate needs met. She feels other people should take care of her. In spite of feeling a victim, she has grandiose ideas about how wonderful things will be when she's 18 and "on her own." She has no conception of how this will happen, however.

Treatment Recommendations

Francie's pervasive personality disorganization is likely the result of her very chaotic and disorganized early environment. Because of the scope of Francie's developmental deficiencies, treatment would need to be structured at a very basic level. Insight therapy or verbal counseling are not appropriate. Francie doesn't have the ability to begin to understand her own or other peoples' feelings, or to understand the dynamics of her behavior.

Francie must be provided with opportunities to learn, at a very basic level, that she *can* have an effect on what happens to her. Her environment must be highly structured and concrete, with positive reinforcement liberally given for very specific tasks. She must be taught that she has the power to get what she wants by performing specific behaviors. This will take a lot of time. A very highly structured treatment foster home or group placement is probably the best placement resource for her. Caregivers should have no expectation of reciprocal attachment or emotional response from Francie. She will be impulsive and emotionally volatile. Caregivers will need to respond to Francie in a constant, consistent, warm and nurturing manner, while setting easily understandable, firm, and consistent limits. Continuity in caregivers is also essential to help Francie learn trust and reciprocal attachment. The prognosis for change is limited.

⚐ Lee Thomas, age 15

History

Lee was the fourth of six children born and raised on a farm. A seventh child was stillborn. Lee lived with his parents, three brothers, two sisters, his grandmother, an elderly aunt, and a cousin. His father was 50 when Lee was born, his mother 22. His family had enough money to get by, but they rarely had extra. Lee's father was alcoholic and often drank to a stupor. He would occasionally be verbally abusive toward his wife and the children, but there was no evidence of physical abuse. Lee's grandmother and his aunt provided some nurturance and attention, although not much structure or direction. Lee's mother had great difficulty coping with the farm and six children, and while basic needs were generally met, the children were often left to fend for themselves. Two years ago, Lee's father died of alcohol-related illness. Lee's mother couldn't manage the farm, and moved with Lee and two younger siblings into the city. She survives on public assistance payments.

Developmental Assessment

Lee is a quiet, generally cooperative youth. He is easy to get along with, almost to the point of overcompliance and passivity. He readily agrees with others, and conforms quickly to their demands, particularly when he views them to be in power. He typically overestimates other people's power, and sees himself as having almost none. He has very poor self-esteem, and he feels entirely inadequate in comparison to people around him. To adults, he appears helpless and in need of protection.

Lee is dependent on others to meet his needs. He craves social approval and acceptance. He yields quickly to peer group pressure when with peers, and to adult authority when with adults. He will comply with whomever is in control at the moment, in order to be accepted and viewed in a positive light.

His cognitive development is to the level of concrete operations; he views the world in simplistic, "black and white" terms. He has limited perspective–taking ability. He knows that people are different, but has no insight into other people's feelings or behaviors. He describes differences in concrete, observable terms. For example, he views his mother as "nice, she cooks good meals." His father "was a drunk and worked a farm." He describes himself as "friendly, not so good in school."

His lack of awareness of other people's needs and feelings, and his low self-esteem contribute to deficiencies in social skills. His peer relationships are poor. More socially competent peers see him as inept, and do not include him in their activities. He is not given equal status. This makes him vulnerable to develop exaggerated attachments to anyone who relates to him in a marginally positive way. For example, he really likes to be with a 20–year–old friend he met once while "hanging out" in town. He says, "Tom is cool–he has his own car and rents a neat apartment."

Lee's moral development is at a preconventional level, with unquestioning compliance to rules, if they are backed by authority. Lee thinks it's wrong to skip school, and it's good to go to church and sit quietly. He believes he shouldn't fail in school, and he should get a good job when he grows up. He believes it's wrong to hurt other people, and important to be nice. He doesn't like "being in trouble" at all.

Lee also understands his own feelings in concrete terms. He knows he gets mad, and that sometimes he's happy, sometimes he's sad. He doesn't think it bothers anyone when he gets mad. He is impulsive. He knows he shouldn't run away, that he should be in school, and that he should get better grades. But none of this changes his behavior. He follows other youths, and he models their behavior without consideration of the consequences. He is viewed by peers as a "tag–along," and is often used by peers. He will do whatever he's told, because he craves social acceptance. He is only marginally accepted, however, and at times is scapegoated.

Lee understands that there is a system to getting along in the world. However, he believes this system exists outside of himself. His success is determined by aligning with the right people–adults or peers who have power and therefore, have the "key to success."

His emotional development has been thwarted, but his general trust is intact. It is this same overall trust that makes him vulnerable to being helped, or exploited, by others. He lacks autonomy and exhibits little self-direction. His opinions and actions are determined by whoever is in proximity and is per-ceived as having power and authority. He lacks insight into himself and others, and he cannot describe what makes him different from other people. He would have considerable difficulty establishing a stable sense of identity.

Treatment Recommendations

Treatment goals are to develop Lee's self–esteem, and his awareness of himself as a capable, important individual. To do this, he will need to learn how his behavior affects others, learn to recognize his own feelings and what generates them, and begin to think about his likes, dislikes, and wants, apart from the opinions of other people.

Lee has potentially good relationship ability. He looks to others for help, and would not be difficult to engage. He would not participate as an equal member of a relationship, but would behave much as a younger child would with an esteemed adult. Positive, consistent, and nurturant relationships with caring adults in therapeutic roles can be very effective treatment strategies. The caseworker or therapist should work with Lee individually, perhaps using activities as a focus, to promote social and emotional development.

A structured, therapeutic peer group would be useful in teaching social skills, and helping Lee assert himself in a group setting. This would also provide Lee with an opportunity to identify with accepting, competent peers. If Lee needs placement, a treatment–oriented foster home is recommended. He should not be placed in a group or residential treatment setting.

Lee would not benefit from insight–oriented therapy. Reality therapy, positive reinforcement for appropriate behaviors, and the use of positive relationships to model appropriate behaviors would be recommended. Differential reinforcement is preferred to punishment. Natural and logical consequences should be used as discipline to reinforce the concept that his behavior affects what happens to him. Adult attention should be made contingent upon desirable behaviors. This child should not be lectured for hours about what he did wrong.

🚶 Leslie Johnson, age 16

History

Leslie is 16 years old. She lives with her mother, her two younger brothers, and her mother's new husband, Jerry. Leslie's early years were relatively uneventful. She was an average student and showed no serious problems. Her parents both worked blue collar jobs and made a good living. The children were well cared for. When Leslie was 12, her father had his first heart attack; he died six months later from another heart attack. Leslie's mother had been able to hold the family together with help from Leslie's grandmother, who lived with them, during the rough time. About a year after her husband's death, Leslie's mother met Jerry. They were married six months later, and Jerry moved in with the family.

Leslie liked Jerry at first, but after a few months, she began telling her friends that he was "weird," and "wouldn't leave her alone." Leslie confided to her best friend's mother that Jerry "felt me up," "pinched my butt," and "came into my room at night and put his hands all over me." Leslie expressed interest in living with her friend's family. The friend's mother called Leslie's mother, who ordered Leslie home, and forbade Leslie from seeing her girlfriend again. Her mother threatened to file charges against Leslie for lying and grounded her for a month. Shortly after, Leslie's truant behavior began.

Leslie definitely feels that what Jerry was doing to her was wrong. She says he is her mother's husband, and he shouldn't be messing with other women, especially his own daughter, even though she is only a stepdaughter. She had told him she didn't like it and wanted him to stop, and was mad because he just laughed at her. She said she felt as if "what I felt and wanted didn't matter to him at all! He's a selfish jerk. I really like–liked–my mom. But I think she's gone nuts. Something must have happened to her when Dad died."

In the past several months, Leslie's school work has deteriorated, and she has been chronically truant. She has stopped seeing her old friends; they think she's changed. She's been hanging out with a group from another school, and has been living with the emancipated 18-year-old sister of one of her new friends in a one-bedroom apartment above a store. Leslie has been sleeping on the floor. She says she tried drugs, but quit because they scare her. She does drink. She thinks that drinking too much is wrong, but all the other kids were doing it, and it kind of felt good. When she's drunk she doesn't have to think about home. She doesn't like "being in trouble," and feels bad that she can't live a "normal life." "I wish things were different," she says. She's afraid of embarrassing her mother, although she's not sure that she wants to ever see her mother again.

Developmental Assessment

Leslie's maltreatment is of fairly recent origin. Her early development, in a healthy family, was normal. As a result, her current dysfunction is less pervasive than is usually seen in many maltreated children. Her healthy personality development will be a strength in helping her cope with the current situation.

Leslie is a fairly typical adolescent with normal development in all domains. She has achieved formal operational cognition. She is capable of hypothetical and abstract reasoning. She has also developed insight into other people's feelings and needs, and is capable of abstract problem solving.

Her social skills appear to be appropriate for her age. She evaluates people as individuals based upon their personal characteristics, and she chooses relationships with people she likes and respects. She sees herself as a moral person, and she has well-developed values. Her moral development is at the conventional level.

Leslie is appropriately trusting, and she exhibits normal autonomy and initiative. She has a prior history of productivity, both in school and in other activities. She appears to be developing an independent identity, with no more than the usual amount of adolescent conflict and uncertainty. She has adequate self-esteem, considering the typical adolescent "ups and downs" in self-perception. She is likely to suffer some esteem problems directly as a result of her recent treatment by her stepfather and her mother.

Leslie's emotional and behavioral problems are reactions to anxiety and depression directly related to her current situation, rather than resulting from any developmental delays or internalized personality problems. Her truancy is a rational attempt to cope with an untenable home situation. At 16, however, she does not have the ability to fully manage her own life without the help of adults she can trust.

Treatment Recommendations

Involving Leslie and her family in therapy is very important. Leslie's mother and siblings should be helped to believe the abuse occurred, to support Leslie, and to develop strategies to protect her from further abuse. Therapy can also help the family cope with the consequences of the abuse, including the likely disruption in the parents' relationship. An alternative placement should be considered for Leslie, if her mother cannot, or will not, prevent Jerry from having access to Leslie. If Leslie cannot be returned home, placement in a relative's or friend's home should be considered.

Leslie could also benefit from individual counseling and crisis intervention. She will be easily engaged into a therapeutic relationship by a warm, supportive, and accepting adult. She has the capacity to participate in problem solving, and to continue to develop coping skills. Her insight can help her explore and differentiate her problems from those of her family.

She should also be helped to identify her feelings of anxiety and depression related to the sexual abuse, the rejection by her mother, and her recent behavior. Supportive and clarifying interventions can help her to resolve the issues around the sexual abuse, and promote a healthy striving toward independence.

Whether, and when, Leslie's stepfather should be included in therapy with the family should be based upon his diagnosis, his motivation to pursue treatment, and the prognosis for reuniting the family. (See Chapter III, Sexual Abuse, for more detailed discussion of treatment interventions for family members in situations of sexual abuse.)

🚶 Shawn Atherton, age 13– Psychological Assessment

Referral

Shawn was referred for psychological evaluation by his social worker, who was concerned about possible emotional problems. Shawn was exhibiting both academic and behavioral problems in school. He and his three sisters have been removed from their home by the Department of Human Services subsequent to physical and sexual abuse and neglect.

History

Shawn is the second of four Atherton children. The family has been known to the Children's Service agency for several years, during which time they received intensive in-home protective and supportive services from the agency. The family has a history of chronic family dysfunction, of domestic violence, and of neglect and abuse of the children. Mrs. Atherton is reported to have been mentally ill for many years, and has been hospitalized several times. She was most recently hospitalized approximately two years ago in a psychiatric facility, and she remains there currently. About four months ago, the oldest child, Patricia, disclosed having been sexually abused by her stepfather, Mr. Atherton, who is the biological father of Shawn and his two younger sisters. All four children have been in the care of relatives since Mr. Atherton's conviction and incarceration for this offense.

According to the social worker, Shawn was believed to have been physically abused by his father. In addition, Mr. Atherton was reported to often be away from the home, leaving the care of the younger children to Patricia. The agency noted that the home was very poorly maintained, and that food was not always present for the children.

Shawn has a history of considerable absenteeism from school as a result of many alleged acute illnesses. The social worker states that his absenteeism may have been the result of Shawn's parents not sending him to school for reasons other than illness.

Present Assessment

Bender Visual Motor Gestalt Test (Bender); Draw–A–Person (DAP); Peabody Individual Achievement Test (PIAT); Wechsler Intelligence Scale for Children–Third Edition (WISC–III); Thematic Aperception Test (TAT).

Shawn scored in the low–average range on the WISC–R with a full scale I.Q. of 84. Shawn's performance on several subtests would suggest he possibly has learning disabilities, including short–term visual memory deficits, general attention deficit, or visual–motor coordination problems. His achievement test scores indicate an overall grade percentile rank of 18%. He exhibited his highest achievement in General Information at the 36th percentile rank. All other scores were between the 20th and 30th percentiles. His PIAT performance was very consistent across the subtests, and consistent with his performance on the WISC–III.

Shawn's Bender performance indicated significant problems in distortion of shape, integration, and spatial interrelations. Tests suggest that he has visual–motor coordination difficulties. Shawn's Bender performance also showed several indicators of emotional distress, including confused order, distortion of size, dot substitution, and wavy and overworked lines.

Shawn's Draw–A–Person performance was developmentally immature with indicators of low self–esteem, feelings of victimization, and overconcern with self–image.

There were significant recurrent themes and needs reflected in Shawn's TAT performance. Recurrent themes were of battles and confrontations in various social and physical settings, ultimately ending in the "hero's" morbid demise by losing, succumbing, or dying. Shawn's responses indicated strong and recurrent needs for control and dominance, and a perception of the environment as fraught with physical danger, capricious, and unpredictable.

General Impressions

Shawn's present cognitive performance is in the low–average range of intelligence. His achievement is consistent with his present ability. He has visual–motor coordination problems, which will interfere with certain school activities that require copying or drawing. There is some indication of attention problems, which do not appear to be a result of an attention deficit disorder, but rather from his emotional problems. His cognitive potential probably exceeds his present abilities and performance. If Shawn's social environment becomes more nurturing, consistent, and stimulating, and facilitates normal emotional growth, it could be expected that his WISC–III and academic performance would also improve.

Shawn's projective test performance indicates possibly serious emotional problems, the developmental outcomes of which would likely be a personality disorder rather than psychosis or neurosis. Shawn may be at a "watershed" point in his emotional development. With the immediate establishment of a nurturing, consistent, stable and permanent family environment, Shawn's prognosis for normal emotional development is good. Without such a supportive milieu, his prognosis is very guarded.

Treatment Recommendations

1) Shawn immediately needs a consistent, stable, predictable, nurturing family environment.

2) As much as possible, Shawn should be mainstreamed in his academic activities. Any academic programming should consider strategies to enhance his self–esteem, and to avoid programming which he or his peers could construe to be punitive, or an indication of his inadequacy. At the same time, he would benefit from general remedial education programming, which includes tutoring. Remedial programming may be inherently difficult, especially if negative or esteem–threatening connotations are to be avoided, but every attempt should be made to provide these activities.

3) Shawn should receive regular individual counseling therapy with a skilled therapist.

Discussion

Shawn displays evidence of developmental problems in all domains. His poor cognitive and academic performances are likely the result of multiple school absences, complicated by an inability to concentrate or attend to task because of emotional factors. The negative effects of long–standing maltreatment on his emotional development are pervasive. His perception is that the world is a dangerous, hostile place where a selfish and preemptive approach is a necessity for survival. There is an inherent despair and hopelessness communicated by this world view that will affect healthy autonomy and self-direction. Shawn needs both a consistent, nurturant family, and regular therapy, but he will probably be difficult to reach. He has strong needs for control and dominance, probably as self-protection, and these will likely promote considerable testing in any relationship with an adult. He is also an early adolescent, and typical adolescent testing and emotional volatility can be expected, which will complicate the picture. He can potentially be expected to be ambivalent about living in a family at a time when his developmental need is to begin to emancipate and develop independence, particularly because he is threatened by intimacy. A family will have to be consistently firm and nurturant, without expecting any immediate reciprocal emotional involvement. A treatment–oriented adoptive or permanent foster family would be a good placement option for Shawn.

Epilogue

Shawn was adopted shortly after this assessment was completed. A flexible and supportive family placement was developed for him, and he was placed in regular individual counseling. His adoptive family also attended counseling to help in their adjustment and to learn how to best help Shawn. Shawn adjusted well to his new home, and while he exhibited considerable testing, he eventually became an integral part of the family. His placement continues to be stable.

VII. CHILD WELFARE SERVICES FOR CHILDREN WITH DEVELOPMENTAL DISABILITIES

A. Understanding Developmental Disabilities

B. Myths and Misconceptions About Developmental Disabilities

C. The Primary Developmental Disabilities: Identification and Early Intervention

D. Services for Children with Developmental Disabilities and Their Families

E. Child Welfare Services for the Catastrophically Ill Neonate

A. Understanding Developmental Disabilities

1. Conceptual Framework

2. Application

Conceptual Framework

It is likely that all of us have one or more developmental disorders. The processes of gestation and birth expose the fetus to many potentially hazardous complications. Thus, gestation and birth form an inexorable leveling mechanism. All of us have a touch of cerebral palsy and mental retardation, some more, some less–the pathological endowment of gestation and birth.

Most of us develop strategies to compensate for our developmental shortcomings. For most persons with poor eyesight, for example, a pair of eyeglasses adequately corrects the problem. A competent assistant likewise helps the absent-minded executive to remember names and numbers, and also corrects the boss's spelling. Similarly, the clumsy person develops ways to keep from bumping into and breaking things.

When, then, should we begin to view developmental problems as developmental disabilities? It becomes clear that we are talking about degrees of dysfunction across a continuum that includes, at one end, a disorder that is limited and merely a nuisance, and on the other end, a disorder that is pervasive and potentially life-threatening. Functional definitions were developed in efforts to delineate at what point along this continuum a disorder would be severe enough to be termed a disability.

The term "developmental disability" was first used by the federal government in the late 1970s in a move to expand the range of developmental conditions eligible to receive federal funding and services. Previously, funding and services had been provided "categorically," that is, only to persons with particular diagnosed conditions, generally, mental retardation. The initial change in federal law was the expansion of eligible conditions to include cerebral palsy, epilepsy, and autism. However, this definition still excluded persons with other developmental conditions who were equally in need of developmental and remedial services. A functional definition eventually replaced the earlier categorical definitions. A functional definition formulates criteria for eligibility based upon the effects of a developmental condition on the person's adaptive ability, or capacity to function independently, appropriate for the person's age, in a typical life environment.

The following summarizes the components of the functional definition adopted in federal legislation in 1978. This definition has been adapted and incorporated into most legislated definitions at the state level as well. In this definition, a developmental disability is a severe, chronic condition which:

- Is caused by a mental or physical impairment, or a combination of such impairments;

- Shows signs of affecting the person before age 22;

- Is likely to last for a very long time, perhaps a lifetime; and

- Makes it most difficult to do things in the following areas:

1) Self-care (to feed and dress and to take care of one's health);

2) Receptive and expressive language (to hear and understand what is being said, and to be understood by others);

3) Learning (in both day-to-day and formal educational environments);

4) Mobility (to get around inside and outside of home, school, work, and community);

5) Self-direction (to make decisions about relationships with others, and about jobs, education, money, and other important things);

6) Capacity for independent living (to live safely without assistance for at least half the time); and

7) Capacity for self-sufficiency (to work at a job and earn a living).

While this definition attempts to measure where developmental disability begins, the incorporation of words and phrases such as "severe," "chronic," "likely to," and "most likely" into the definition renders its interpretation somewhat ambiguous. This is not necessarily bad. Some ambiguity may be necessary to allow the professional diagnostician the latitude to weigh the variables given in this functional definition, or to consider other variables, in determining eligibility for services and support.

An important variable in this definition is the age of onset. Most definitions state that, to be considered developmental, the disability must be manifest before a certain age. The upper limit in many definitions is age 22. In viewing human life as a continuing developmental process, however, any age limit may appear arbitrary. Brain trauma causing epilepsy at age 17 may not appear significantly different from the same accident at age 23. Huntington's Chorea, a progressive central nervous system disease that usually appears in the fifth decade of life, is a genetic disease–a developmental part of the individual's future, destined from conception. It is not considered a developmental disability, however, when its symptoms are first manifested later in life.

Still, there are significant reasons for recognizing an upper age limit of 18 to 21 years, other than fiscal or administrative utility. Although development continues throughout most of life, an important number of normal maturational milestones are typically attained by age 22 or earlier. In relation to cognitive development, Piaget suggests that formal operations, the most highly developed cognitive activities, are attained by late adolescence, if they are attained at all. Structural growth of the brain is completed by early adolescence, and most other physical maturation is completed by age 22. The emotional growth necessary for the achievement of a personal identity and a sense of an adequate and capable self, essential for adult activity, is typically formed by age 22, although modifications may take place throughout the life cycle. And by that time most persons achieve a social maturity that allows them to accept and maintain a social role as a functional adult member of society.

The concentrated development during the first two decades of life, its maturational culmination, and the potentially pervasive destructive effects of disorders during this time can, in some respects, justify an upper age limit of 22. We will therefore use the following broad definition in our discussion of developmental disabilities and related child welfare issues:

> A developmental disability is a condition or disorder, physical, cognitive, or emotional in nature, that has the potential to significantly interfere with the normal process of a child's growth and development. To be a developmental disability, the disorder must be present and affect the child before the age of 22.

Conditions and disorders that may be included in the category of developmental disabilities are mental retardation, cerebral palsy, epilepsy, autism, learning disabilities, speech and language disorders, spina bifida, hearing loss and deafness, visual disorders and blindness, orthopedic disorders, and congenital malformations. These developmental disabilities are often seen in children being served by the child welfare system. Many other developmental disabilities occur less frequently, and are not discussed here.

Application

CONTRIBUTING FACTORS TO DEVELOPMENTAL DISABILITIES

At times, it is possible to identify the specific factors that have caused a developmental disability. For example, children with Down Syndrome have an identifiable and common chromosome aberration. Epilepsy and cerebral palsy are, at times, caused by brain damage resulting from a severe blow to the head. However, the specific causes of most developmental disabilities cannot be determined with certainty, although many factors have been correlated with the presence of developmental disabilities. These factors may themselves cause the disability, or they may contribute to a sequence of events that ultimately results in a disability. The following describes some of these contributing factors. (More extensive information on many of the conditions listed below follow in Section VII-C, "The Primary Developmental Disabilities: Identification and Early Intervention.")

Genetic Inheritance

Our genes are the "blueprints" for our development. These genetic plans are transmitted through the reproductive cells of our parents and are present in every cell in our bodies. Disabilities that result from genetic governance are usually of three types: gene inheritance, chromosomal abnormality, and spontaneous mutations. Conditions such as phenylketonuria (PKU) and Tay–Sachs syndrome result from the inheritance of genes or combinations of genes that dictate the development of a disabling condition. Conditions such as Down's, Turner's, fragile–X and Klinefelter's syndromes result from accidents in reproductive cell division that lead to abnormalities in chromosomes.

Although popularly believed to be a major cause of developmental disabilities, such genetic problems account for only a small percentage. Many genetic abnormalities preclude fetal viability; the pregnancy often terminates by miscarriage.

The contribution of genetics to disabling conditions is not, however, always clear. Some conditions are thought to be caused by a genetic predisposition combined with exposure to an "environmental trigger." If persons with a certain genetic make–up are exposed to some other condition–a virus, an environmental toxin, another illness, or trauma, they are more likely to develop the disabling condition. Without the trigger event, however, the genetically predisposed person does not develop the condition. Conversely, persons who lack the genetic predisposition will not develop the condition, even with exposure to the trigger event.

Trauma

Traumatic injury to a child through a direct blow or assault can cause severe disability. This is especially dangerous when the brain or central nervous system is affected. The area of the brain that is injured and the extent of the brain damage together determine the nature and severity of the resulting disability.

Auto accidents and falls onto hard surfaces such as concrete are common causes of head injury in children. Child abuse is also a frequent cause of head and central nervous system injury in infants and young children, as is "shaken baby syndrome." Mental retardation, cerebral palsy, and epilepsy are some of the possible outcomes of child abuse, including shaking an infant or young child.

Exposure to Toxic Substances

The ingestion of toxic chemicals and substances by a pregnant woman can seriously interfere with normal fetal growth and development. Alcohol, tobacco, some prescription medications, street drugs, and fumes from materials such as paint, glue, and varnish are all toxic substances that can be harmful to the fetus. Exposure to radiation, such as X-rays, is also in this category. Ingestion of poisonous substances by children may also result in developmental disabilities.

Fetal alcohol syndrome (FAS) is a common disability in infants of women who consume large amounts of alcohol while pregnant. Alcohol destroys and damages cells in the central nervous system, and widespread destruction of brain cells in early fetal development results in malformations in the developing brain structures. Fetal alcohol syndrome includes both prenatal and postnatal growth deficiency, mental retardation, microcephaly, behavior disorders, and problems in motor control. Fetal alcohol effects (FAE), a less serious form of the disorder, can occur with a moderate amount of alcohol consumption during pregnancy.

Prenatal exposure to crack cocaine and other drugs can also have a destructive effect on fetal development. Low birth weight, growth retardation, a high rate of perinatal complications, and neurological problems are all associated with crack cocaine abuse.

Maternal Age and Health

A higher risk of developmental disabilities may be associated with a maternal age below 15 or over 35. Poor health of the mother during pregnancy is also associated with disabilities in the fetus. Chronic illnesses, such as diabetes, high blood pressure, severe anemia, hypothyroidism, kidney disease, and congenital heart disease can negatively affect fetal development, but are much less likely to have adverse effects if well-monitored and treated during the pregnancy. Extreme obesity of the mother has also been associated with disabilities. Malnutrition of the mother before and/or during the pregnancy increases risk of disability in newborns.

Complications During Pregnancy and Birth

At one time, Rh-incompatibility was a major cause of infant morbidity. The Rh factor refers to the presence or absence of a particular substance in the blood (hence, Rh+ or Rh–). Rh incompatibility occurs when a mother with an Rh– factor carries a fetus with an Rh+ factor. With this condition the mother's immune system develops antibodies that attack and destroy the red blood cells of the fetus. This can cause brain damage in the developing fetus. A first child usually is not seriously affected. The first pregnancy sensitizes the mother's immune system, which results in increased problems in subsequent pregnancies and a higher risk of brain damage in later-born children. The development of a special injection therapy is successful in desensitizing the mother's immune system, allowing the fetus to develop normally. Prenatal identification of the Rh incompatibility, and proper medical treatment are critical to prevent brain damage in the infant.

Complications during labor and delivery, such as prolonged and difficult labor, premature separation of the placenta, or a knotted or prolapsed umbilical cord, can cause brain and central nervous system damage from anoxia, or deprivation of oxygen to the brain. A high percentage of infants born with cerebral palsy are thought to have sustained birth injury.

Improper use of forceps during delivery can sometimes result in brain damage from direct trauma. Overuse of anesthesia for the mother may lead to asphyxia in the newborn. Careful fetal monitoring, the use of cesarean section delivery during high-risk childbirth, and sophisticated infant intensive care units have reduced the occurrence of birth-related injury and disability.

Minimizing complications of pregnancy and birth, however, depends upon access to and use of appropriate health care. Many children and families served by the child welfare system do not have access to proper health care, or do not utilize available services.

Prematurity

Neither the premature infant nor its mother is prepared for the birth process, and the infant is not fully developed for survival in the postnatal environment. These factors increase the risk of developmental disabilities. Contractions that push the undeveloped child against an undilated and uneffaced cervix can cause central nervous system damage. The lungs of a premature infant may not be sufficiently developed to allow normal breathing. An excess of oxygen, such as may be found in poorly controlled isolettes and incubators, has been associated with infant blindness and brain damage.

Viral and Bacterial Infections

Rubella, or German measles, is a common and relatively mild viral infection. Symptoms are flu-like and generally last only a few days. If a pregnant mother contracts rubella, however, there are significant risks to the fetus, particularly during the first trimester of pregnancy when the fetus's brain and vital organs are developing. Rubella can cause blindness, deafness, congenital heart defects, and mental retardation. A high percentage of children who are both blind and deaf were exposed to rubella early in pregnancy. Immunization therapy has made it possible to eliminate rubella as a cause of developmental disabilities. Yet, there are still children being born whose mothers have not been properly immunized.

Several venereal diseases are associated with developmental disabilities. Syphilis, a bacterial disease, attacks and destroys brain and central nervous system tissue in its later stages. It is usually responsive to antibiotic therapy; however, if undetected or left untreated in an infected mother, it presents a risk of brain damage to the fetus. Gonorrhea, also a bacteria, can lead to infant blindness when present in the birth canal during childbirth. Routine application of antibiotics to infants' eyes immediately after birth is a precautionary measure against gonorrhea. In recent years, strains of both syphilis and gonorrhea have become resistant to previously effective antibiotic therapy.

Variations of the herpes virus are common infective agents in humans. Chicken pox and shingles are caused by a herpes virus. Another variation of the virus, herpes simplex I, is the common cause of cold sores of the mouth, and may occasionally be associated with genital lesions. The common cause of herpes-related venereal disease is herpes simplex II. This disease typically causes recurring painful blisters and sores in and around the genitals, anus, or mouth. If active sores are present in the genital area during childbirth, the infant may contract the virus from the mother. Infection of the infant may lead to severe neurological damage or death. Developmental problems may be avoided through cesarean section delivery when active herpes is present.

Meningitis, encephalitis, and other viral and bacterial illnesses can directly affect the central nervous system, and are associated with subsequent brain damage. Excessively high fever associated with severe viral or bacterial infections is also at times associated with brain damage. The human immunodeficiency virus (HIV) can also be transmitted from pregnant women to their babies.

Toxoplasmosis, a parasitic organism that may be found in cat litter boxes, has been associated with central nervous system damage and mental retardation. Pregnant women should avoid contact with cat feces.

Nutrition

Numerous research studies have demonstrated the negative effects of poor nutrition on children's growth and development. The prenatal period and the first two years of life are characterized by extensive and rapid brain and central nervous system growth. Good nutrition is required during these periods to promote healthy cell development. Malnutrition of the mother during pregnancy, and of the young child, can interfere with healthy development. Malnutrition is thought to be a probable contributor in many milder cases of mental retardation.

SUMMARY OF THE EFFECTS OF CONTRIBUTING FACTORS

Exposure of a fetus or an infant to deleterious prenatal, perinatal, and postnatal factors will not always result in a disability. Mediating variables include the amount of exposure to the contributing condition (large amounts of exposure and extended exposures constitute higher risk); the genetic and constitutional predispositions of the mother and the fetus; and the age of the fetus or child when the exposure takes place (some exposures are more likely to cause problems during the first trimester of pregnancy, when the fetus's vital organ systems are developing; on the other hand, younger children are more likely to recover from serious neurological trauma than are older children). It can be concluded, however, that infants who have been exposed to any of the contributing factors will have a higher risk of developing disabilities than children who have not been so exposed.

Many of the factors that may contribute to disabling conditions can be avoided or prevented through education and preventive health care.

CHILD ABUSE AND NEGLECT, AND DEVELOPMENTAL DISABILITIES: A COMPLEMENTARY RELATIONSHIP

There is considerable evidence to suggest a significant interrelationship between child abuse and neglect, and developmental disabilities. Many factors that are common in situations of abuse and neglect are also common correlates of developmental disabilities: poor diet and nutrition; lack of regular and adequate medical care, including poor prenatal care; an unsanitary and unhealthy environment, with higher risk of exposure to harmful and toxic substances; high incidence of drug and alcohol abuse; poor supervision of children and resultant higher risk of injury; and lack of nurturance and stimulation. It appears that developmental disability is both a cause and an effect of child abuse and neglect.

Many studies have suggested a direct link between physical abuse and developmental disability or delay. Studies of physically abused children have documented significant neuromotor handicaps, including central nervous system damage, physical defects, growth and mental retardation, and serious speech problems. Cognitive and language deficits have also been noted in abused children [National Research Council 1993]. A study of 42 abused children by Martin [1972] conducted over a three–year period, found:

- 43% of the study group had neurological abnormality on follow–up examination. Martin concludes that "permanent damage to the brain is a frequent sequela of physical abuse."

- 33% of the study group were functioning at a retarded level, with a measured I.Q. of less than 80. Martin states, "It is clear that there is an intimate relationship between central nervous system insult and residual retardation."

- A large number of the abused children demonstrated "absent, minimal or impaired speech and language." Martin notes that 75% of the children with language delays were of normal intelligence. It can be inferred that abuse interfered with the acquisition and use of language in children." .

Environmental factors common in neglectful situations are thought to contribute to developmental problems. Martin refers to the work of Harlow and Spitz, Provence, and Lipton, among others, who report that environmental deprivation, such as that experienced by institutionalized infants, can result in retardation. Martin also stresses the role of undernutrition in subsequent developmental delay. In an earlier study, Chase and Martin [1970] concluded that permanent retardation can result from undernutrition in the first year of life. Helfer, McKinney, and Kempe [1976] assert, "The most disturbing and consistent finding in observation of young children who have been abused and neglected is the delay, or arrest, of their development." They have noted a variety of developmental problems in abused and neglected children, including difficulty in feeding; delay in motor development with poor muscle tone; delay in social development and social responses, such as smiling and vocalization; a lack of activity; a generalized apathy toward objects and people; a consistent and considerable delay in speech; and the absence of reaction when separated from parents. Problematic school performance such as low grades, poor test scores, and frequent grade retention, is a fairly consistent finding in studies of physically abused and neglected children, with neglected children appearing the most adversely affected [National Research Council 1993].

A developmentally disabled child is also at a high risk of being abused or neglected. Steele [1987] refers to the three major criteria found to be highly correlated with child abuse:

- The parents must have the potential to abuse; a particular set of personal parent factors predisposes a parent to be abusive;

- The child is viewed by the parent as somehow special; the child who is different, who requires special care, or who is perceived as unlike other children is at potentially higher risk of abuse; and

- A crisis, or series of crises, including high stress and accompanying inability to cope, tends to precipitate the abuse.

Children with disabilities may indeed be different from other children, or may be perceived as different by their parents. They may differ in physical appearance or capability; they may require specialized care and treatment; they may not be able to respond socially or emotionally to the parents' expectations. Parents of developmentally disabled children frequently mourn the loss of a "normal" child. Anger is part of the mourning process, and it can sometimes be turned outward by abusive parents toward the disabled child. Additionally, the presence of a disabled child creates numerous emotional and environmental stresses for the family, and the resulting emotional turmoil can reach crisis proportions. Therefore, if parents have the psychological potential to abuse, a disabled child is often at higher risk of abuse than are other children.

Children with disabilities may also be subject to a special type of neglect. The child's exceptional needs for care and treatment may create a situation of neglect through no fault of the parents. A family that can manage adequately under normal circumstances may not have the personal or financial resources to meet the exceptional medical, nutritional, social, and educational needs of a child with a disability, thereby creating a situation of inadequate and insufficient care of the child.

The strong correlation between abuse or neglect and developmental disabilities is further illustrated by the numbers of children with disabilities who are served by the public child welfare system. A study completed by the Ohio Department of Human Services reported that approximately 20% of all children in out-of-home care were mentally retarded or developmentally disabled [Institute For Child Advocacy 1987]. Another study, conducted in Hennepin County, Minnesota, suggested that 40% of all children receiving services from child welfare agencies had developmental problems [Richardson et al. 1989].

The escalating numbers of abused and neglected children, and the potentiating relationship between child maltreatment and developmental disabilities support the need for an approach to serving children that actively considers both areas. Yet, in spite of this, public social services systems continue to provide categorical, or separate services for child maltreatment, and for developmental disabilities. Many factors contribute to this problem, including a serious lack of coordination between community social agencies that serve children with developmental disabilities and their families [Richardson, West, Day, & Stuart 1989], and a widespread lack of knowledge and skill regarding disabilities among professional staff in most social service systems [Martin & Laidlow 1989; Falconer 1982].

Child welfare services, and services to children with developmental disabilities, are frequently separated at the federal, state, and local levels. They are funded from different sources, administered by different bodies, and delivered by separate local agencies. Service delivery objectives often appear to be quite different, each focused on the remediation of different conditions, and defined by a perception of quite different presenting problems. And, while services are available, they remain inaccessible due, in large part, to barriers erected out of philosophical and legislative differences among agencies and programs. A survey by Richardson and associates also suggested that ignorance on the part of staff members in one agency about how to access or use services in another agency created barriers to the accessibility of services for children with developmental disabilities [Richardson et al. 1989].

A review of the literature suggests that a lack of training of child welfare workers is a common contributor to poor services to children with developmental disabilities. Kurtz [1979] strongly suggests that lack of knowledge and skill in child welfare workers is a serious impediment to the identification of children with disabilities and to the provision of early intervention services. Kurtz believes that many child welfare workers have a general understanding of child development, but lack sufficient knowledge and skill related to disabilities. Therefore, they do not recognize or cannot make accurate judgments about early signs of disabling conditions. He suggests that lack of training may explain why children with disabilities are often underrepresented in child welfare statistics.

Schilling, Kirkham, and Schinke [1986] concur that the child protection system may not recognize and document children in the child welfare system who have disabilities. The authors claim that the lack of training is a significant contributor, as "few social workers, even those with graduate degrees, have had developmental disabilities courses," and cannot assess these conditions, particularly when mild in nature. Finally, Coyne and Brown [1985 1986] suggest that caseworkers' lack of accurate information about developmental disabilities interferes with proper placement of children with disabilities in adoptive families.

The child welfare field is evolving toward a developmental, family–centered orientation to services that is concerned with prevention, as well as remedy. As such, we must develop our system's ability to identify maltreated children who have, or are at risk of, developmental disabilities. Their needs must be properly assessed, and early coordinated and integrated services must be provided. The following sections of this chapter were designed to assist child welfare professionals in their efforts to become more knowledgeable about developmental disabilities, and to emphasize the central role of the child welfare field in serving children with developmental disabilities and their families.

B. MYTHS AND MISCONCEPTIONS ABOUT DEVELOPMENTAL DISABILITIES

1. Conceptual Framework

2. Application

Conceptual Framework

Myths and misconceptions regarding developmental disabilities have been prevalent in most cultures, and persons with disabilities have commonly been viewed with fear, suspicion, and pity.

These attitudes and misconceptions are reflected in our language. The word "handicap" is an epithet derived from the practice of holding cap in hand, i.e., begging [Handicapism 1976]. Begging was institutionalized by English law, and was a regulated entitlement of the disabled. The word "seizure," which refers to the random spasmodic motor activity associated with some epilepsies, was born of the belief that affected persons were "seized" or possessed by the devil. Children born deformed or disabled were called changelings; it was believed that, before birth, they had been changed or substituted by the devil for the normal children of God. Midwives attending such births, or priests who had blessed the pregnant mothers, were often suspect. These unfortunate persons sometimes lost their lives because of their suspected collusion with the devil. Such "children of the devil" were often allowed to die, or were even put to death within an obligatory ethic. Infanticide for children with developmental disabilities has been sanctioned in many cultures throughout history [Rosen, Clark, & Kivitz 1976].

Today, science enlightens us. The etiologies of developmental disabilities are no longer considered diabolical. What was once righteous intercession has become benign neglect in hospital delivery rooms. The results are often the same: misinformed decisions are made to allow children with developmental disabilities to die at birth. Some persons with disabilities still beg, and most people still expect this, and respond with pity. Persons with grand mal epilepsy are still often viewed as possessed by something foreign and beyond their control, in spite of the fact that approximately half are seizure-free with medication, and seizures are significantly reduced for many others. We have forgotten the roots of the words we use to label and describe people with disabilities. The harmful stereotypic and prejudicial attitudes have become less blatant and more subtle, but they are equally entrenched. The words no longer scream their prejudice, but instead, propound subtly, not arousing us to reflect.

Application

Child welfare professionals will regularly encounter negative stereotypes, attitudes, and misconceptions in the community; in some families of children with disabilities; among professional groups, including physicians, educators, and social workers; and probably within themselves. Such attitudes can seriously interfere with case management, and the adequate delivery of services to persons with disabilities and their families. It is the purpose of this section to help workers to become aware of these attitudes and misconceptions, and to develop an awareness of our own misconceptions and harmful stereotypic attitudes.

> **Myth: Developmental disabilities are clearly defined, visible conditions that are permanent and constant disabling factors in a child's life, and will therefore prevent active involvement in much of life's normal activities.**

The term developmental disability is not easily defined, and, since its inception, has included a changing variety of conditions. Federal legislation originally designated four conditions as developmental disabilities: epilepsy, autism, cerebral palsy, and mental retardation. More recent federal law does not refer to particular conditions, but rather to the effects of any condition on growth and adaptation.

All disabling conditions have the potential to interfere with, retard, or alter the course of a child's physical, cognitive, social, and emotional development, but the degree and nature of such effects depend upon a number of social and environmental factors.

Developmental disabilities are varied and complicated phenomena, and the degree to which a condition presents adaptive problems is different for different persons. Two factors can influence the degree to which any condition will be disabling: 1) the extent and severity of the condition, and 2) the availability of corrective, supportive, or rehabilitative help.

Most disabling conditions can range in severity from very mild to very severe. The greater the severity of a condition, the greater the potential for interference with a child's growth and development. However, once the means and technology are available to remedy or correct a condition so that it no longer significantly interferes with adaptation, the condition ceases to be disabling. Prior to the invention of corrective lenses, vision problems could significantly interfere with daily living. Anyone who is severely nearsighted can attest to the pervasive problems he or she would have in mobility, employment, and general survival without eyeglasses.

Many other potentially disabling conditions have become correctable or made less debilitating through advances in science and technology. Congenital heart problems can be remedied by corrective surgery; braces and other orthopedic apparatuses enable many children with spina bifida and cerebral palsy to sit, stand, or walk; motorized wheelchairs, specially equipped vans, ramps, and wheelchair-accessible curbs allow independent mobility and transportation; anticonvulsant medication can prevent or significantly reduce the incidence of epileptic seizures; and sign language provides a complete, rich means of communication for persons who are hearing impaired. As technology develops, and science unravels the mysteries of many disabilities, one may expect fewer and fewer conditions to be disabling. Brain pacemakers to regulate neural impulses, bionic replacement of limbs, drugs to correct biochemical and enzyme imbalances, and computerized boxes that talk at the push of a button are some of the new technological advances that could revolutionize our thinking about disabilities.

Supportive interventions can also help minimize the effects of a condition on adaptive functioning. For example, a personal assistant, who provides assistance with dressing, feeding, bathing, laundry, meal preparation, transportation, cognitive and life management activities, and/or infant and child care can facilitate a person with a disabling condition to participate fully in work, community, and social environments.

Early Intervention

A child's development is a dynamic process. The general nature of development is determined in large part by genes. A common heredity predisposes most children to perform various developmental tasks in an order and time frame similar to other children, as part of typical maturation. The particular outcomes of development for any child, however, will be ultimately determined by the child's interaction with the environment, and the child's success or failure in mastering the challenges presented by social and environmental pressures.

The process of development is cumulative. Early successes in mastering age-appropriate tasks build a foundation for mastering later, more complex skills. Conversely, failure to master early tasks can interfere with later development. When a disabling condition prevents a child from becoming involved in the activities and experiences that stimulate normal growth, the child's development may be delayed and perhaps altered, and the negative effects of the disability may be compounded over time. Physical, social, cognitive, and emotional development all affect and are affected by each other. An undiagnosed or untreated disability in one area can have negative effects on other areas as well.

Early recognition of disabilities, and timely remedial and supportive services are essential to maximize a child's potential for more healthy growth and development. Early intervention can often correct or help compensate for disabling conditions, prevent the cumulative negative effects of the condition on normal growth, and guard against deterioration. Even for children whose disabilities are so severe that they cannot be expected to exhibit typical development with even the most timely and appropriate intervention, early recognition and intervention can help prevent deterioration, and enhance continuing adaptation.

> *Myth: Developmental disabilities are unfortunate accidents of nature, and there is little that can be done to avoid or prevent them.*

VII. B. Myths and Misconceptions About Developmental Disabilities

The earlier discussion (See Section VII–A, "Understanding Developmental Disabilities") of causal and contributing factors to disabilities illustrated that many of these factors are environmentally determined, and therefore, may be modifiable. A knowledge of these factors, and a commitment to providing a safe and healthy environment for a developing child can often prevent disabilities. Prevention includes, for example, avoiding drug and alcohol use during pregnancy; rearing children in environments free of abuse or neglect; accessing timely prenatal care; assuring adequate nutrition of pregnant women and young children; avoiding toxic fumes and substances; treating maternal health conditions; vaccinating all children against diseases; and others.

The concept of prevention cannot be limited, however, to the prevention of the occurrence of a disabling condition. Despite our best efforts, some children will continue to be born with or will develop disabling conditions. The concept of prevention must also include limiting the negative effects of a condition, and preventing subsequent physical, social, cognitive, and emotional deterioration.

Leland and Smith [1974] discuss three additional important aspects of prevention. These include:

- *Preventing the growth or extension of a condition.* When disabling conditions do occur, further exacerbation of the condition can often be avoided. For example, the timely insertion of a shunt can arrest progressive brain damage from hydrocephalus, and careful dietary control will prevent the mental retardation associated with untreated phenylketonuria. (Phenylketonuria, or PKU, is a metabolic disorder in which the child lacks an enzyme to break down a protein commonly found in most foods. The toxic accumulation of this protein causes progressive brain damage and retardation. Avoidance of this protein in food while the brain is growing can prevent retardation, even though the child will always have PKU.)

- *Prevention of negative social effects.* Negative stereotypes, misconceptions, and prejudices can compound the social problems experienced by persons with disabilities. With proper education, individuals, families, and professionals can become more aware of the negative effects such attitudes can have on the social adjustment of persons with disabilities. Such awareness also promotes a more realistic assessment of the disability and appropriate professional intervention.

- *Prevention of later deterioration.* An individual who is limited in adaptive skills or who lacks resources will generally have more difficulty managing life tasks. The consequences may be a deterioration in all areas of the individual's functioning. A variety of readily available supportive and developmental services for persons with disabilities can enhance the development of adaptive skills, contribute to coping resources, and thereby prevent deterioration in functioning.

Myth: Developmentally disabled children have very different service needs than other children. Services to these children must be provided by personnel highly trained in work with the developmentally disabled if they are to effectively meet the disabled child's needs.

Viewing a child with a developmental disability as distinctly different from other children is misleading. A focus on specific presenting problems fosters this misconception. Most specialized children's services are remedial in nature, designed to confront and resolve any one of a number of conditions and problems. For example, children might be denoted as abused, neglected, developmentally disabled, physically ill, economically deprived, or needing special education. Services are then developed to address the particular presenting problem.

Specialized fields of practice ensure that difficult problems can be addressed with a depth of knowledge and expertise not often found in a generic setting. However, an awareness of the child's other basic needs, and the interrelationships among all areas of the child's development, is often missing in this categorical approach to services. Disabilities, for example, often become the focus of attention, and their significance is exaggerated; or the importance of other factors in the child's life, including those shared with typical children, are discounted. A case example illustrates this point. It was presented by a foster care caseworker in a workshop on developmental disabilities.

⚕ Case Example: Sally

Sally was a five-year-old child with severe cerebral palsy and an undetermined degree of mental retardation. She had been in several foster homes since being permanently surrendered by her biological mother at age two. Her most recent foster family had moved out of state, and because of limited foster home resources, the agency resorted to placing Sally in a nursing home facility until a more appropriate placement could be found.

Jean A, age 23, met Sally while doing volunteer work at the nursing home during her last year of college. After graduating, Ms. A was employed as a nurse's aide in a hospital, and she hoped to return to school to pursue an advanced degree in nursing. She had been assigned to work with Sally during her field experience, and afterwards she continued to visit Sally several times a week. She brought Sally toys and books, talked to her, fed her, sang to her, and developed an affection for and commitment to the child. After more than a year, she asked to adopt Sally.

The foster care worker was at a loss. She had limited experience with children with developmental disabilities, and even less experience with their adoption. She brought the case up for discussion during the workshop, in hopes that the trainer could tell her how to proceed.

The group discussion focused on the basic principles of adoption practice. The group considered Ms. A's level of personal maturity despite her youth; the degree of her demonstrated commitment to Sally; her experience with and ability to tolerate stress; her expectations for the child over time; her own emotional support systems–friends and family–since she would be a single parent; her ability to support herself and a child; her plan for the care of Sally while she was in school; and her willingness to undergo the changes in her life that would result from the responsibility of caring for a young child.

Sally's needs were also discussed: the agency's preference for a permanent home for her rather than foster or nursing home care; evidence that a close relationship had developed between Sally and Ms. A; and how to plan and effect a move that would be the least traumatic for Sally. Increased visiting, including visits to Ms. A's home, and thorough planning by Ms. A in preparation for bringing Sally home, would have to be encouraged before approving the adoption plan.

Much of the case discussion took place without reference to Sally's disabling condition, since it was not relevant. Because Sally had the universal needs of all children, her adoption was viewed from the perspective of all older–child adoptions. The disability was an important factor, but only to document Ms. A's ability to provide the special medical care and rehabilitative services Sally needed. Her nursing background and an available adoption subsidy quickly resolved these issues in her favor. The worker became more comfortable with her role when she realized that Sally's disability did not change the fundamentals of adoption planning.

Most children with disabilities are more similar than dissimilar to other children, and trained child welfare workers can generally be effective in providing case management services to them. Special services pertinent to the disability can be provided by specialized service systems in much the same way as services are provided to meet the special needs of any child. Training workers in competencies from other service systems, such as mental retardation and developmental disabilities, and in skills for interagency collaboration greatly increases the effectiveness of child welfare casework and case management activities for children with special needs.

> *Myth: Children with disabilities can be helped best to learn and grow in specialized settings where they can be with children similar to themselves. They should not have to compete with children who do not have disabilities, nor be exposed to the cruel remarks of such children.*

This belief often reflects a well–meaning attempt to serve the best interests of children with disabilities. Proponents feel that specialized programs ensure that their special needs are better met, and that the children are protected from feelings of inadequacy and inferiority. In practice, however, this attitude can reinforce segregation, promote stereotyping and prejudice, and may even deny many children a place as contributing members of society.

Segregationist attitudes can be institutionalized through such programs and activities as special recreation programs for persons with mental retardation, or "the handicapped children's day at the zoo." These programs and practices draw attention to children with disabilities as a group who are identified primarily by their common developmental conditions–a group more similar to each other than to children without disabilities. Children with disabilities are thus perceived as so different that we must educate and entertain them in their own separate group, guarding and protecting them from the larger society. There is also an implicit assumption that children with disabilities cannot function in the larger society.

Special programming may, at times, be valuable and beneficial for children with developmental disabilities. In some respects, IEPs (Individual Education Plans) and IFSPs (Individual Family Service Plans) formalize the development of special interventions that directly address a child's and his or her family's unique needs. However, if special programs are intended to replace integrated programs, there are significant liabilities for children both with and without disabilities.

Segregation may interfere with the healthy growth and development of children with disabilities. Throughout childhood, considerable learning takes place through identification and modeling of the behaviors of other children. When a child is deprived of routine involvement with typical children, his or her environment is an inaccurate representation of social reality. The child who is raised in segregated environments is denied the opportunity to explore, experience, and learn in the larger social environment. He or she may be sentenced to a life of overprotection and segregation; or, if expected to enter society as a productive adult, will be at a serious disadvantage.

Healthy and optimal growth for any child is best facilitated in a healthy and typical environment that provides for both general and exceptional needs, but which does not place the child outside of everyday social realities. Any program that segregates its recipients has an inherently negative effect on the population it is attempting to serve. The logistic requirements for, and benefits of, such a program must clearly and substantially outweigh its negative aspects before it can be considered valid.

Segregation of persons with disabilities is also a disservice to society, as it promotes and perpetuates stereotyping, misconceptions, and prejudice. Segregation denies most people day-to-day exposure to persons with disabilities, and there is no opportunity for myth to be replaced by fact learned from direct experience. Additionally, without interpersonal contact in typical everyday environments, society may not recognize the individual differences and competencies among persons with disabilities, and may not benefit from their potential contributions.

An extension of this myth is that people with disabilities prefer life and activities with "their own kind." It is true that years of segregation can contribute to feelings of anxiety and fear when a person with a disability is confronted with an integrated environment. When he or she withdraws to the safety of a more familiar environment, it is then interpreted as the cause and justification for segregation practices, rather than their effect. This myth is often a rationalization to cover and reinforce our own discomfort in the presence of persons with disabilities.

Children who are reared in everyday interaction with disabled children relate to the disability as a matter of course; the disability becomes a single, and not always relevant, characteristic in understanding the nature of the person.

> *Myth: But many children with disabilities need special services if they are to grow and develop to their fullest potential, and often these can be best provided in special settings: treatment facilities, group homes, and schools.*

It is not our intent to deny the necessity for, or the effectiveness of, specialized services. The problem is not with the existence of these services when used judiciously, but rather with assigning an individual to special or segregated services that far exceed their domain of efficacy, thus depriving people with disabilities of integrated services when they are adequate and appropriate. This can be illustrated by the concept of educational mainstreaming, or inclusion. Inclusion should not be interpreted as "dumping" all children, regardless of need or handicap, into a regular public classroom setting without appropriate support.

The primary federal legislation affecting the education of children with disabilities is P.L. 94–142, the Education of All Handicapped Children Act, which was passed in 1975. The legislation was amended in 1986, and again in 1990–91, and is now known as the Individuals with Disabilities Education Act (IDEA). This legislation stresses the importance of early intervention and individualized educational planning for children in the least restrictive environment. This means that child who can learn in a regular classroom should not be in a special class. A child who needs individualized attention and can receive it in a regular classroom with individualized instruction, or in a special education group in a public school, should not attend a segregated school. And finally, a child who can learn and grow in a specially structured school program should not be limited to a home tutor. The least restrictive environment is the most integrated social and educational environment in which the child can function. For example, it may not be appropriate to insist that an adolescent with cerebral palsy or other orthopedic conditions, and who has normal intelligence but is confined to a wheelchair, be sent to a special school. With ramps and elevators, a tape recorder, and perhaps occasional note–taking assistance from other students, (all referred to as "reasonable accommodation"), the regular high school classroom may well be managed, and offers a more normal adolescent educational and social experience.

Individualized health, educational, and social services are essential components of a total approach to growth and development for children with disabilities. However, when assignment to special programs is not clearly determined to be the best possible approach based upon the child's needs, it must be viewed as segregationist, limiting, and damaging to the child's potential development. The fact is, what the child misses in socialization, communication, and education in the integrated environment usually far exceeds the potential benefits of the specialized attention presumed available only in the special environment.

Myth: Persons with developmental disabilities are . . .

Any number of descriptive words or phrases could complete this potentially misleading statement. Although certain descriptive characteristics might provide some information about certain people, persons with developmental disabilities are not a homogeneous group. Disabling conditions vary widely; even the nature, severity, and effects of a particular disabling condition may be different for different persons.

Persons with developmental disabilities are unique individuals whose needs, skills, strengths, and personal traits span the continuum of possible human characteristics. The fact that many individuals may have the same disabling condition does not make them any more alike than does having other traits in common, such as short stature, blue eyes, or a hobby of stamp collecting. Yet the myths surrounding developmental disabilities include many stereotyped images.

Stereotyping usually results from misinformation. For example, it is commonly believed that people with epilepsy have no control over their seizures. This belief persists in spite of the fact that anticonvulsant medication renders nearly 50% seizure free, and helps another 30% significantly.

Stereotyping may also result from overgeneralizing basically valid information. For example, it is true that people with cerebral palsy may also be mentally retarded. But it is also true that people with cerebral palsy are often intellectually typical of the general population. Persons who have cerebral palsy and mental retardation have two disabilities, involving different areas of the brain. The disabilities might both have resulted from the same insult or trauma; however, the presence of one condition in no way assures the presence of the other.

Stereotypes regarding persons who are mentally retarded are particularly misleading. Some common beliefs are that they are generally ignorant, socially inept, and usually incapable of responsible action and self-support. The truth is quite different. Mental retardation ranges from mild to profound. Eighty to ninety percent of all persons with mental retardation fall within the mild category, and are variously capable in decision making, responsible action, social understanding, and self-sufficiency.

Stereotypes exist regarding families that have children with developmental disabilities. Consider the following:

a) Most families of children with disabilities resent the special needs of the child, and are often happier if their children are placed in substitute care.

b) Parents of children with disabilities are strong people who will do anything to ensure their child has the best possible care, and are committed to keeping the child at home if at all possible.

Both views are polarizations on a continuum of possible responses. Families fitting both descriptions exist, but families of children with disabilities do not have a special style, or configuration of personalities, or responses to their children. Regardless of what valid general information we possess regarding developmental disabilities, each case must be assessed individually and objectively.

When working with families of children with disabilities, we must be consistently aware of the potentially harmful effects of stereotyping. While we often use generalized information to help us better understand a particular condition, we should never apply any assumption drawn from general information to an individual child, without first assessing its validity for that child. Individualized assessment and treatment planning are as critical for children with disabilities, and their families, as in all other aspects of child welfare practice.

Myth: Diagnostic labels are always useful tools in assessing and understanding an individual's developmental disability.

Diagnostic labels are, very simply, tools that can facilitate precise and concise communication. But any tool may be inadequate, or the person using it may not understand its proper use. The overinclusive nature of some labels lim-its their diagnostic utility. For example, the label mental retardation, even with subcategories of mild, moderate, severe, and profound, does not sufficiently differentiate the subtleties found in intellectual capabil-ity and adaptive functioning of persons with mental retardation. In another example, a label of pervasive developmental disorder, autism, or child-hood schizophrenia may be given to similar presenting symptoms. We may assume different etiologies, and plan different treatment strategies based upon which label is assigned, yet the only significant factor for a differential diagnosis may be the age of onset.

One must be alert to the possibilities of misdiagnosis or misuse of a label. Child welfare professionals should have a basic understanding of diagnostic principles and categories. Good case management includes knowing the creden-tials and abilities of the professionals who are sought for diagnostic consultation.

Negative expectations that are often derived from a diagnostic label can become self-fulfilling. A research study has demonstrated, for example, that when children were arbitrarily labeled "academic spurters," classroom teachers developed high expectations for them, and they progressed better than children not so labeled, even when there were no significant differences between the groups. [Rosenthal & Jacobson 1968]. Labels that connote negative expectations similarly can have a negative effect on the ensuing behavior of the persons so labeled.

While diagnostic labels are useful tools of communication, professionals must be constantly aware of the potentially harmful effects that can result from mis-understanding and misusing them.

C. THE PRIMARY DEVELOPMENTAL DISABILITIES: IDENTIFICATION AND EARLY INTERVENTION

1. Conceptual Framework

2. Application

Conceptual Framework

The developmental disabilities most likely to occur in young children, particularly if they have been abused or neglected, are cerebral palsy, epilepsy, and mental retardation. Child welfare workers may also encounter several other conditions in their work, including autism, spina bifida, Down's syndrome, fetal alcohol syndrome, fragile–X syndrome, and several genetic conditions.

Children with developmental disabilities are at higher risk of both abuse and neglect by their caregivers. They may be medically neglected, if their parents do not provide them with necessary medical care and treatment for their disabling condition. The quality of care they receive may also be poor, especially if their caregivers are not properly trained to meet their special needs.

For many disabling conditions, the provision of proper medical, social, educational, and supportive services can greatly maximize the child's potential, and may even influence the eventual extent of the disability. Early intervention can both stimulate healthy development, and minimize the effects of a disabling condition on the child's growth.

The purpose of this section is to review the conditions most commonly seen by child welfare workers; to describe their signs and symptoms to promote recognition and early identification; and to describe the most appropriate interventions. The child welfare caseworker will often assume a case management and advocacy role in assuring that these children and their families receive comprehensive specialized services.

Application

CEREBRAL PALSY

Cerebral palsy refers to a group of conditions in which damage to the brain causes problems in movement and motor functioning. According to the United Cerebral Palsy Research and Educational Foundation, cerebral palsy may be defined as:

> ...a group of conditions, usually originating in childhood, characterized by paralysis, weakness, incoordination, or any other aberration of motor function caused by pathology of the motor control center of the brain [Thain 1980].

There are multiple potential causes of cerebral palsy, including prenatal and postnatal abuse and neglect. Most often, cerebral palsy is present at birth and is thought to be the result of some prenatal insult from illness, injury, or the presence of toxic substances. Mothers who have no prenatal care or who abuse alcohol or drugs increase the risk of cerebral palsy in their infants.

The incidence of cerebral palsy is generally estimated to be between 1 and 2 per 1,000 births. Approximately 7,000–9,000 children are born annually with some form of cerebral palsy. Another 1,500 preschool-age children acquire it, often as the result of head injury from abuse or accident. Incidence figures are sometimes difficult to ascertain, because many very mild cases go undiagnosed, or are unreported.

The range of disability for persons with cerebral palsy varies greatly, and is dependent upon the extent of brain dysfunction. Persons may have mild, moderate, or severe degrees of involvement with all types of cerebral palsy. Early symptoms of cerebral palsy are variable. In milder cases, the condition may not be diagnosed until the child reaches school age. Generally, the more severe the condition, the earlier it can be detected.

Many different conditions fall within the broad terminology of "cerebral palsy," and there are considerable differences in descriptive terminology in the literature. The types of cerebral palsy can, however, be broadly divided into three major categories.

Spastic cerebral palsy results from dysfunction primarily in the portion of the brain where voluntary motor activities originate. When this motor area of the cerebral cortex is injured, or when it is improperly developed, it cannot regulate or coordinate neural stimulation to the muscles of the body. The result is hypertonia, or abnormally increased muscle tone in the affected muscles. Nerves in the motor areas of the cerebral cortex stimulate or inhibit contractions of muscles in very specific areas of the body. The particular sites of brain damage, and the extent of damage account for the differences seen in the portions of the body affected by spastic cerebral palsy. Increased spasticity can significantly reduce muscle efficiency, and can make both simple and complex motor tasks very difficult or impossible.

With mild to moderate spastic cerebral palsy, the person's gait is often awkward and balance is impaired. Spasticity in the muscles of the legs and feet may lead to toe-walking, or walking with the toes and knees turned inward. In severe cases, certain muscle groups may be entirely dysfunctional, and the person may not be able to stand or walk at all.

Both gross motor and fine motor activities can be affected. Gross motor activities such as walking, sitting, standing, and simply maintaining head control, are impaired. A person with spastic cerebral palsy may also have considerable difficulty using the hands and fingers, may have difficulty in using the mouth and tongue to formulate speech, and may have vision problems due to muscle weakness and lack of control of muscles of the eyes.

The presence of primitive reflexes, such as the ATNR (Asymmetric Tonic Neck Reflex) and other strong infantile reflexes, is common in cerebral palsy. The persistence of such reflexes over long periods of time may interfere with many normal activities, and may produce scoliosis, a malformation of the spine.

Weakness of the diaphragm muscle makes the production of sounds difficult. An inability to force air out of the lungs can also lead to frequent respiratory infections. This is particularly problematic when food is inhaled while eating, and cannot be coughed out. Impairment of the muscles used in chewing and swallowing also make eating or feeding very difficult. Tightness of the bowel may lead to chronic constipation, with a risk of bowel impaction.

Athetoid cerebral palsy is thought to be caused by damage to the basal ganglia, located toward the center of the brain and related structures, causing involuntary muscle movements, varying degrees of muscle weakness, and hypotonia (lack of muscle tone). It is estimated that 20 to 40% of persons with cerebral palsy have the athetoid type.

Athetoid cerebral palsy is characterized by slow, writhing, involuntary and uncontrolled muscle movements accompanied by muscle weakness. Movements are often irregular and unpredictable, and include spasmodic contractions of individual muscles, such as jerks and twitches, or slow, smooth, writhing and undulating movements. Persons with athetoid cerebral palsy often have severe difficulty with head control, and many cannot sit without being supported or propped.

In mild to moderate cases of athetoid cerebral palsy, the person may walk with a stumbling, lurching, uncoordinated gait. Pervasive muscle weakness may interfere with and, at times, totally prevent many motor activities.

Persons with spastic and athetoid types of cerebral palsy together comprise between 75 to 80% of all cases. Many persons with cerebral palsy exhibit characteristics of both types.

Ataxic cerebral palsy may occur when there is damage to the cerebellum, the large area at the base of the brain that controls balance and coordination. Ataxic cerebral palsy is characterized by disturbances in balance and depth perception. People with ataxia may display varying degrees of imbalance and lack of coordination. They may stumble, fall, or walk into objects or furniture, and may have difficulty with eye coordination and depth perception. Their motor behaviors may be similar in appearance to symptoms of being intoxicated, and many persons with ataxic cerebral palsy are unfairly accused, and even at times arrested, for intoxication. In very severe cases, people cannot maneuver their bodies through space, and therefore, cannot walk. Approximately 10% of persons with cerebral palsy have the ataxic type.

While the term cerebral palsy broadly identifies a group of conditions, other medical terminology is often used to more specifically describe individual conditions. For example, the prefixes "hemi", "di", "para", "bi", and "quadra" describe the involved portions of the body. The term "plegia," which translates as "paralysis," refers to the severe motor limitations of some persons with cerebral palsy. The term "paresis" is also used. It means weakness, and refers to the characteristic muscle weakness found in most types of cerebral palsy. Abroms [1980] defines some common diagnostic categories:

- *Spastic Hemiplegia* refers to cerebral palsy of the spastic type affecting one side of the body only, with the arm generally more involved than the leg, and affecting the right side about twice as often as the left. "Hemi" literally means half.

- *Diplegia* refers to cerebral palsy in both legs, with little or no involvement of the arms or upper body. This may also be referred to as "paraplegia." (This is not the same as the paralysis in the lower half of the body that results from spinal cord injury.)

- *Spastic Quadraplegia* refers to cerebral palsy of the spastic type, with all four limbs affected, but the legs generally more affected than the arms. Spastic quadraplegia is among the most commonly diagnosed types of cerebral palsy.

- *Dyskinesis* is a term that is often used synonymously with "athetoid" or "athetosis," as defined above.

Cerebral palsy is most often congenital, or present at birth. The specific cause cannot generally be determined. Many factors are thought to be common contributors to cerebral palsy, including prenatal infection such as rubella or cytomegalovirus (CMV), RH incompatibility, deprivation of oxygen, or head injury during birth. Cerebral palsy can also result from trauma during a long, difficult birth process, although it has also been suggested that difficulty in birthing may be a result of the cerebral palsy rather than the cause of it. Cerebral palsy may also be acquired by young children as a result of head injury from abuse or accident, from infections such as meningitis or encephalitis, or as a result of severe convulsions associated with high fever.

Children with cerebral palsy frequently have speech disorders due to poor control of the muscles involved in talking. Speech may be slurred, slowed, and difficult to understand. In the most severe cases, the child may be unable to speak. Alternative communication systems, such as signing, symbolic communications systems, or electronic speech devices, may provide a means of communication for the nonspeaking individual.

Associated Complications

Cerebral palsy is a disorder of motor functions. However, some persons with cerebral palsy have other disabilities as well, usually as a result of insult or damage to other areas of the brain. While the following conditions may be present in persons with cerebral palsy, they are not symptoms of cerebral palsy, but are indicators of a separate disabling condition.

- *Mental retardation.* It is estimated that from 35 to 50% of persons with cerebral palsy are also mentally retarded to some degree. However, it is incorrect to assume that someone with cerebral palsy is also retarded, even if they are very severely affected with cerebral palsy. At least 50% of persons with cerebral palsy are within the normal and above average ranges of intelligence. Unfortunately, the sometimes unusual looking behaviors and contorted speech patterns of persons with severe cerebral palsy have, in the past, led to their being misdiagnosed as mentally retarded, and subsequently institutionalized.

- *Epilepsy.* Studies have indicated that approximately 30% of persons with cerebral palsy also have some form of epilepsy. Persons with hemiplegia have been found to be the most vulnerable to seizure conditions.

- *Visual and hearing deficits.* Some individuals with cerebral palsy have hearing and visual disorders. Persons with cerebral palsy should be routinely screened for these problems. Strabismus, or a crossing of the eyes caused by involvement of the muscles in the eyes, is fairly common in individuals with spastic cerebral palsy.

Early Identification

In most cases, cerebral palsy is present at birth. It should, therefore, be detected and diagnosed as early as possible to insure optimum intervention. The early symptoms of cerebral palsy are variable. In milder cases, the effects are minimal, and the condition may not become apparent until the child is school age. Generally, the more severe the condition, the earlier it can be detected.

Child welfare workers must be skilled at recognizing the early indicators of cerebral palsy in populations of abused and neglected infants and children. This can insure optimum early intervention. The following conditions might indicate cerebral palsy, and would warrant a referral for assessment and diagnosis.

ABNORMAL MUSCLE TONE

Infants with cerebral palsy may exhibit either *hypotonia*, a significant lack of muscle tone characterized by loose, flaccid muscles and extremities; or, *hypertonia*, an excessive degree of muscle tone characterized by tightness, stiffness, rigidity of limbs, and constricted movement.

Infants with cerebral palsy of both the spastic and athetoid types are typically hypotonic, lacking muscle tone, for the first few months of life. Spasticity will become evident around four to five months, or around two to three months in very severe cases. Typical signs of hypertonia in infants related to spastic cerebral palsy might include:

- Keeping one or both hands tightly fisted, or keeping the thumb clenched inside the closed fist, if the child is over four to five months old.

- Tightness of the hips, making it difficult to separate the infant's legs to change a diaper.

- Keeping the legs in a fully extended position, or crossing the legs or ankles; kicking both legs in unison by bringing both knees up to the chest together, rather than the more normal alternating–leg, bicycle–style kicking.

- Evidence of lack of vision, inability to focus, or to track moving objects in an infant over two months.

- Tongue thrust, moving the tongue in and out of the mouth, excessive drooling.

- After the age of three, child does not talk, or child's speech is slurred and garbled, and cannot be understood. Child appears to lack the physical ability to form and produce sounds.

- A persistent strabismus, or crossing of the eyes.

The most typical signs of hypotonia, or lack of muscle tone, are delayed motor development, and a generalized "heaviness" or "floppiness" of the body. Signs include:

- Infant slumps, wobbles, lurches; cannot hold own body steadily in position, if over four months. Appears to have no strength.

- Infant may not be able to suck or swallow; chokes on food or formula; may not have strong sucking reflex.

- Infant or young child's movements may be jerky and uncontrolled; child may reach for things and either under- or overshoot an object, or the arm will appear to "fly out of control" and knock over the object the child is reaching for.

ABNORMAL PATTERNS OR DELAYED MOTOR DEVELOPMENT

Delayed motor development may exhibit itself in numerous ways:

- Inability of a newborn, placed face down, to lift and turn its head to the side to avoid suffocation; failure to achieve head control by three months; by five months, failure to lift head and chest from a prone position when the child is on his stomach; persistence of a head lag if the child is more than five months (when pulling the child by the arms from a position lying on his back, the head falls or "lags" back toward the floor, rather than being held in line with the rest of the body).

- Inability to bear weight on legs when held in a standing position, if older than five months.

- Failure to reach for objects, or to transfer objects from one hand to the other, if older than seven months.

- Collapsing forward when placed in a sitting position, or a rounded back when seated, if older than eight months.

- Inability to roll from back to front, if older than six months;

- Inability to stand holding on to objects or furniture, if older than 10 months.

Abnormal patterns of motor development can refer to developmental milestones that are only partially reached, or to differences in the infant's skill in mastering motor tasks using various parts of the body. For example:

- Persistent use of only one hand when playing with a toy, including reaching across the body to retrieve an object, rather than reaching with the arm that is on the same side of midline as the object. Infants typically use both hands equally for the first 15 to 18 months of life, and they rarely reach across the midline.

- Good use of hands and arms, but drags legs. While many infants go through a stage of crawling on their stomachs, failure to progress to more advanced use of the legs might be indicative of cerebral palsy.

- Trembling or inaccurate aim when reaching for an object may indicate athetoid cerebral palsy.

- Child walks and runs at age-appropriate time, but is always very clumsy, has very poor balance, falls all the time, runs into walls and door frames, or trips, after the child has been walking long enough that he should exhibit good balance and coordination. This may be symptomatic of ataxic cerebral palsy.

- Persistent walking on toes, with the heels not touching the ground, in a child over two years.

PERSISTENT REFLEXES

- Persistence of the Asymmetric Tonic Neck Reflex (ATNR), also known as the "fencing posture." This reflexive posture results in one arm bent at the elbow and raised to the level of the ear, with the head turned toward the opposite arm, which is stretched straight out from the shoulder, as if the infant were involved in a fencing match. This normal reflex in infants generally disappears within the first few months of life. The persistence of this reflex after a few months may indicate cerebral palsy. Many older children with cerebral palsy cannot turn their heads toward center-front without the reflex taking over and being repeated in the opposite direction. The presence of the reflex makes it impossible for these children to bring their hands together at the midline, to face directly forward, or to roll over back to front. This also clearly interferes with self-feeding and object manipulation.

- Persistence of a strong reflex to arch the head and upper torso may also suggest cerebral palsy. If an infant develops a bald spot on the back of his head from lying on his back, this may be indicative of a strong tendency to arch backward.

- Young infants typically stand on their tip-toes when held in an upright position in an adult's lap. By the time children learn to walk, they should be able to put their feet flat on the floor with the heels down. If toe-walking persists, the child may have an exaggerated toe-walking reflex, indicative of cerebral palsy. If this condition is not corrected, the muscles and tendons of the lower legs may permanently constrict and shorten, interfering with normal walking.

Treatment and Prognosis

Cerebral palsy is not a degenerative disorder. In other words, there is no progressive worsening of the brain damage. The symptoms and effects of the condition can, however, worsen if proper medical management is not provided. The degree to which cerebral palsy will disable an individual is related to the provision of prompt, effective, and lifelong intervention.

Physical therapy is essential to help the individual learn to compensate for and control primitive reflexes; to maintain muscle strength and flexibility; to develop coordination and control; and, ultimately, to permit optimal development in other developmental domains as well. When physical therapy is not provided, the tendency in spastic cerebral palsy is for the muscles to constrict, tendons and ligaments to shorten, and eventually for the joints to "freeze," seriously restricting the range of movement. With athetoid cerebral palsy, muscles that are not regularly exercised will further weaken and atrophy, reducing their efficiency even more.

For some individuals, drug therapy can help spastic muscles relax. Even though the spastic condition is caused by brain dysfunction, stress in the environment, and a state of emotional tension in the individual, can exacerbate the degree of spasticity in the muscles. Many persons with spastic cerebral palsy may be taught relaxation techniques to lessen muscle spasm related to environmental stress.

Vision and hearing should be routinely screened and monitored. Many persons with cerebral palsy need glasses to assure proper vision.

Speech therapy is an important intervention for persons whose ability to form speech is affected. Many people with cerebral palsy are fully capable of language, but because of poor muscle control of the mouth, lips, and tongue, and the inability to push air from the diaphragm through the larynx, speech is exceedingly difficult. For persons who are severely involved, alternate communication systems such as Bliss Boards (symbolic communication systems), signing, or computerized "voice boxes" can provide them a means of communicating with other people. The individual's ability to make his or her needs known, and to communicate with other people is essential to healthy psychological and social development. The person with cerebral palsy should be provided with a means of communicating with others.

Daily care of persons with cerebral palsy requires specialized training and knowledge. Feeding may be difficult and time consuming. Persons with cerebral palsy may have extreme difficulty chewing and swallowing, and there is a danger of aspirating food during eating. Caregivers must be taught proper feeding procedures, and must recognize symptoms of upper respiratory distress.

Many people with cerebral palsy want to feed themselves, and need assistance or special equipment in order to manage utensils. Even with assistance, eating may take a long time. However, self-sufficiency should be encouraged to whatever degree possible.

Because of the difficulty in eating, many people with cerebral palsy may not get adequate nutrition, and may be underweight for body size. Foods should be prepared with high nutritional value and should be easy to eat.

Caregivers should also be taught physical play activities that encourage the proper use of the child's muscles, which increase flexibility and strength, and which maintain a wide range of motion. Specialized leisure time, play, and educational activities should be provided which are appropriate for each individual's physical ability, and which take into consideration the level of cognitive ability, to assure sufficient cognitive stimulation.

🚶 Case Example: Maria Hernandez

Maria was four months old. Her mother, Lydia Hernandez, had been referred to the child welfare agency several months before she delivered Maria because of questionable care of her two-year-old daughter, Stella. With the worker's help, Lydia had improved her care of Stella, and managed reasonably well when the baby arrived.

Maria was a happy baby who seldom cried unless she was very hungry or upset. Yet, she flopped around when anyone picked her up, and at two months, she couldn't hold her head up unassisted. When the worker saw the baby at four months, she was lying on her back on a blanket on the floor. Both legs were straight and rigid, and Maria's hands were tightly fisted, with the thumbs clenched inside. When excited, she flailed her tightly fisted hands on rigid arms in a jerky and exaggerated manner in front of her face. She kicked as if her legs were tied together at the knees and ankles, drawing both knees to her chest and then straightening the legs, digging her heels into the floor. Her smile was large and infectious, and she responded to interpersonal contact with expressive smiles and vigorous excited flailing of her arms and legs. She became very excited whenever her mother appeared, or when people talked to her. Her mother said she had a good appetite, but feeding her was difficult; she had trouble sucking and her thrusting tongue often got in the way of the spoon.

The caseworker recognized Maria's symptoms as typical of cerebral palsy, and referred her for diagnostic assessment. The attending physician confirmed spastic quadriplegia, and referred Maria immediately for physical therapy and infant stimulation. The baby's responsiveness to other people, direct eye contact, and interactive nature suggested that despite her considerable physical disability, she could potentially have normal intelligence, even though it was still too early to know. However, the caseworker's early recognition of Maria's condition assured that the baby would receive the necessary services to help her to develop to her potential.

EPILEPSY

Epilepsy, or more appropriately, "the epilepsies," refers to a group of disorders whose symptoms usually include seizures, which are symptoms of abnormal chemical/electrical phenomena in the brain [Abroms 1980].

Before the role of the brain in seizure conditions was understood, it was thought that persons with epilepsy had been "seized" or possessed by the devil or other spirits; hence, the word seizure was used. Many people with seizure disorders were put to death or ostracized. It is now known that epilepsy can be hereditary or may be acquired through various insults or trauma to the brain. It is generally estimated that approximately 1 in 100 persons have some type of seizure disorder.

Many factors are known to contribute to acquired (nonhereditary) epilepsy. The most common are prenatal infections, alcohol or drug use during pregnancy, radiation during pregnancy, complications in labor and delivery with anoxia (deprivation of oxygen), direct head trauma, metabolic disorders, infections, diseases with high fever, and direct head injury from accidents or child abuse.

Generally, a seizure disorder results when some metabolic or structural abnormality temporarily or permanently changes the electrical stability of a group of neurons in the brain. The affected tissue is called the "focus." A seizure results when this area of instability spreads electrical stimulation inappropriately to other nearby neurons in the brain. The uncontrolled, abnormal firings of the neurons creates symptoms which are related to the particular area of the brain affected. With damage to different areas of the brain, different patterns and types of seizures are seen.

Epileptic seizures may be characterized by a broad range of symptoms, including alteration of consciousness, feelings, behavior, autonomic function (sweating, paleness, redness), somatic sensations (tingling hands), and motor activity. There are dozens of different types of seizure disorders. The most common are described below.

Generalized Tonic–Clonic Seizures

The generalized tonic–clonic seizure (previously known or referred to as grand mal) is also referred to as a major motor seizure. Tonic–clonic epilepsy may either be genetic or acquired. One type of tonic–clonic epilepsy is inherited as an autosomal dominant, and is therefore present to some degree in nearly half of the members of an affected family. In a percentage of these persons, on an EEG (electroencephalogram) an abnormality will be present, but the patient will have no seizures. Tonic–clonic epilepsy is also thought to be acquired by any of the contributing factors listed above.

A generalized tonic–clonic seizure normally occurs in two phases. During the tonic phase, the individual will suddenly lose consciousness, fall, or slump over. Air rushes from the lungs and a scream or cry may be emitted. The motor centers of the brain send a bombardment of electrical stimuli to the muscles of the body, which become very rigid and stiff. Contraction of the muscles of the bowel and bladder may produce incontinence. The diaphragm muscles may also be contracted, and the individual may cease breathing, perhaps becoming cyanotic (blue from lack of oxygen).

During the second phase, called the clonic phase of the seizure, the muscles alternately contract and relax. This produces the jerking, sometimes violent thrashing that is often associated with tonic–clonic seizures. "Frothing" or excess salivating may occur as the individual begins to breathe again. A tonic–clonic seizure usually lasts from three to five minutes, and then the individual will regain consciousness. The after–effects of a seizure may include headache, drowsiness, and a period of prolonged sleep.

Once a tonic–clonic seizure begins, it must run its course. The person should not be restrained, nor should anything be forced between the person' teeth. Well–meaning but untrained individuals can actually tear ligaments and break the bones of the person they are trying to help by trying to restrain them during a seizure. Objects placed in the mouth have, at times, been inhaled, causing strangulation. Statistics show that the potential of harm far outweighs the efficacy of putting something between the person's teeth.

Appropriate interventions include loosening clothing, and putting something soft under the person's head. Turning the person on his side or stomach will facilitate the flow of saliva from the mouth, and will prevent blockage of the air passage by the relaxed tongue. Sharp objects and furniture should be removed from the area to prevent injury. Medical attention should generally be sought. If the seizure lasts more than a few minutes, or if one seizure is followed immediately by another, it should be considered a medical emergency. Unabated seizures of this type can lead to brain damage. Finally, having the person regain consciousness to a large group of staring spectators should always be avoided.

Most tonic–clonic epilepsy can be controlled by medication. Well–controlled childhood seizures may be outgrown by late adolescence, and the individual can maintain a seizure–free state without medication. In some cases, however, the biological changes during puberty may bring about a seizure condition for the first time in predisposed individuals.

Absence Seizures

There are several types of absence seizures with differing symptoms and prognoses. The most common was previously called petit mal. During this type of absence seizure the individual has a momentary lapse of consciousness. He may blankly stare straight ahead and cease all movement and speech. There may be a rhythmical fluttering of eyelids and, at times, some finger or facial movements. If the individual is standing or sitting up, he will generally remain so and will not fall or slump over. At times, the person will just "stop what she's doing," with her body in position, until the seizure is over. One mother noted her daughter had a seizure while brushing her hair–she stopped, stared off into space with the brush in hand, high above her head, poised and ready to use. She remained this way for several seconds, then resumed her brushing. The seizure generally lasts for 10 seconds or less; however, some persons with absence seizures may have between 50 and 200 seizures per day.

Absence seizures are often mistaken for day dreaming or inattentiveness. This type of epilepsy usually begins after age three and is most commonly seen in girls in the five to nine year age range. Occasionally, seizures may begin during adolescence. In over 70% of the cases, absence seizures cease by the time the child is 18 years old. If other types of seizures are present as well, it is less likely the absence seizures will be outgrown. Other types of absence seizures may be present in adults.

No intervention is possible during the seizure. However, if you are with a person for long periods of time, the frequency and duration of the absence seizures should be noted and reported. Often the physician or psychologist with case management responsibility will never witness a seizure, and must rely on others for a description of the condition. This information, sometimes combined with abnormal EEG findings, will confirm the diagnosis of absence seizures. The most typical symptoms are repeated short "daydreaming" spells, a seeming inability to hear complete sentences or to follow directions, and repeated blank stares.

Some types of absence seizures can be well controlled by medication. However, if undiagnosed and untreated, the repeated lapses of consciousness may have significant effects. Untreated individuals may miss a significant amount of what goes on around them, and as a result, their ability to attend and learn may be negatively affected. In addition, emotional problems may result from a caregiver's anger at what appears to be an individual's inattentiveness, unresponsiveness, and apparent refusal to listen.

Psychomotor Seizures (Complex–Partial Seizures)

This type of seizure varies a great deal in appearance. It is often mistaken for emotional disturbance or other psychological disorders. While the symptoms of the seizure vary significantly from person to person, a single individual will display similar symptoms and behaviors during all seizures. These behaviors are often referred to as "stereotyped" behaviors.

There are both psychological and motor components related to this seizure condition. The seizure often begins with a sudden arrest of activity, with staring and a blank, dazed facial expression. The individual does not lose consciousness, but there is a "clouding of consciousness." The person seems "foggy," and does not appear to be clearly in touch with his environment.

Repetitive, automatic, and purposeless behaviors are frequent. These include inappropriate motor behaviors such as pacing, foot tapping, lip smacking, chewing movements, playing with nearby objects, and incoherent or irrelevant speech. Physical symptoms of stomach distress including vomiting, and headache may at times accompany seizure.

The seizure may also be accompanied by strong emotional outbursts of anger or fear. The individual may swear, yell, physically strike out, and display an anger that does not seem to be appropriate for the situation. At other times the individual becomes very fearful and anxious. It is for these reasons that psychomotor seizures are sometimes misdiagnosed as psychological or behavioral problems.

A psychomotor seizure may last anywhere from minutes to hours. When the seizure is over, the person generally remains lethargic, and may sleep for a long period of time. The individual may have a partial, clouded memory of the seizure and of his behavior, and generally will be confused. Youths with psychomotor seizures may have some awareness of their behavior, and may apologize later, suggesting "I don't know why I do that."

Psychomotor seizures are less well controlled by medication than many other types of epilepsy. Individuals having the seizure should be monitored to ensure that they do not harm themselves or other people. It is most important that other people not respond to their angry outbursts with reciprocal anger; individuals with psychomotor seizures are not in control of their actions. Behavior outbursts must be viewed as a symptom of the seizure, and the individuals should be dealt with in a calm, reassuring, supportive fashion.

A substantial number of people with psychomotor epilepsy remain undiagnosed. They may develop secondary behavior problems resulting from the negative responses generated by other people in response to inappropriate behaviors displayed during seizures. They may be referred to as "crazy," "uncontrollable," or "dangerous,"–labels which do not build positive self-esteem.

大 Case Example: Steve Daniels, age 13

Steve was 13 years old when the child welfare worker was assigned his case. Steve's family had received services from the agency when Steve and his younger sister, Mindy, were in preschool. At the time, the children were found to be neglected. Steve's mother had remarried shortly afterward, the care of the children had improved, and the case was closed. The current case opening was a referral from the juvenile court. Steve was reported to be "out of his parents' control," was truant from home and school, and had reported to court officials that his parents "beat the crap out of me." While there was no evidence of current or past bruises or scars, the court referred the case to the child welfare agency for assessment. Steve later admitted that his parents yelled a lot, but they had never beat him, and he must have been mad when he said it.

When the worker met with the family, they reported that at about age nine, Steve had developed "an attitude," which had gotten worse over time. The family asked whether Steve could be placed in a special school where he could be controlled and "taught some manners." The worker asked the family to describe Steve's behavior. They said he had "moods," and had violent temper tantrums, often over nothing at all. When he was like that, there was no talking to him, and no settling him down. He would storm around the house, shout at them, scream at them, insult them, swear at the top of his lungs, kick things, and stomp his feet. They said he looked like he was possessed. At first, his family tried to talk to him and find out what was bothering him, but he wouldn't listen. They said he acted like he didn't even hear them. He said very cruel things to them, and they were afraid he would hurt his younger sister. The worker asked if he ever had these moods anywhere else but home. The mother said he'd had several in school, enough to get him suspended several times. She also said that Steve was so angry at the school for punishing him that he now refused to go at all.

The worker asked about Steve's history. The family said that up until the age of nine, Steve had been a good child. The worker asked about his medical history, and the family couldn't remember his having any special problems. The worker asked whether there had been any stresses or problems in the family when Steve was nine. Again, they couldn't think of any.

The worker asked how long Steve's "moods" lasted. The mother said usually anywhere from an hour to half a day. She then said, "It just seems like he wears himself out. He winds down, and when it's over, he almost always goes to sleep for a good while." His mother then said, "Don't get me wrong; I think Steve's still a pretty good boy. When he's not in a mood, he's helpful and can be very pleasant. And I suppose he still has some of the morals we taught him, because he always acts real sorry later for cussing and acting up. But it must not stick, because it doesn't keep him from doing it the next time."

The worker recognized the pattern of Steve's behavior as possibly being psychomotor epilepsy. She asked the family if they could think of anything else Steve did during his moods, any repetitive motor behaviors with his feet, his hands, or his mouth. The family said he always stomped his feet. His mother also said that he drummed his fingers on the table top–enough that it almost drove her crazy.

The caseworker suggested to the family that a medical problem could be contributing to Steve's behavior, and asked the family's permission to make a referral to a pediatric neurologist. Steve was diagnosed with psychomotor seizures. They were partially controlled with medication. Steve's parents and school personnel were counseled to deal with Steve's condition, and Steve was referred to a developmentally oriented youth group at the mental health center.

Other Seizure Conditions

In addition to these three major types of seizure conditions, two others should be mentioned because of their frequency in young children.

Infant myoclonic epilepsy is characterized by the sudden flexion of the infant's neck, trunk, and thighs with forward extension of the upper limbs. Myoclonic seizures look very much like the sudden full-body jerks that often occur just as we begin to drift off to sleep. The onset of infantile myoclonic seizures is usually between 6–12 months of age, but they may appear as early as two months. Myoclonic seizures may be frequent (several times a minute) and last for long periods of time (up to many weeks). These seizures in infants are usually a symptom of some neurological disease, and most infants exhibit subsequent symptoms of brain damage with mental retardation. Many affected infants have a shortened life span.

Finally, febrile seizures occur in conjunction with high fever in young children. This generalized seizure condition is usually limited to the duration of the fever, but may occasionally progress to other forms of epilepsy. It is important to refer a child who has had a febrile seizure to a physician for examination and possible treatment. The physician may prescribe anticonvulsant medication for a period of time to prevent additional seizures, and to reduce the likelihood of having seizures later in life.

Treatment Interventions

Several drugs are used to control seizures. They include Dilantin, Tegretol, Depekane, Zarontin, Valium, phenobarbital, and others. Most anticonvulsant medications are central nervous system depressants, and therefore, may produce drowsiness, lethargy, and difficulties in concentration.

There are other more serious complications which are sometimes produced by anticonvulsant drugs, including digestive disorders, anemia, hyperactivity and irritability, skin eruptions, kidney and liver dysfunction, loss of motor coordination, double vision, slurred speech, sleep disturbances, and loss of appetite. The adjustment of drug levels in persons with epilepsy is an ongoing process, and the objective is to produce the greatest degree of seizure control with the fewest negative side effects. The efficacy of medications and their toxicity may also change over time. Drug intervention must be very closely monitored by a physician.

Approximately 50% of persons with epilepsy can expect to be seizure free with proper medication. For another 30%, the frequency and/or duration of their seizures are significantly reduced. For approximately 20%, drug intervention does not significantly affect the duration or frequency of the seizures.

It has also been noted that learning disabilities are more common among children with epilepsy than in the general population. Special educational interventions should be provided.

Despite the advances in medical knowledge, there remains a stigma about seizure conditions. Persons with epilepsy are sometimes discriminated against unnecessarily in job selection; a well-controlled seizure condition will usually not affect job performance or ability. However, some persons with seizure conditions cannot drive without posing a risk to themselves and others; and, some occupations, such as construction on high rise buildings or operation of certain machinery, can be dangerous for persons with epilepsy.

The stigma that often surrounds epilepsy may also contribute to psychological problems for persons with seizure disorders. Seizures may be frightening to the individual, and are often very frightening to people who witness them. With many seizures, a person may display erratic or embarrassing behaviors and a loss of control. Negative and inappropriate responses from people who witness a seizure can contribute to self-consciousness and lowered self-esteem. Caseworkers should be very conscious of the sometimes frightening nature of seizures, and of the social stigma and prejudice that often surround seizure conditions. They should be supportive and reassuring to the affected children and their families, and should not overreact with inappropriate fear or anxiety.

The child welfare worker should recognize the following symptoms of epilepsy, and should refer children suspected of having seizure conditions for medical evaluation:

- Children may have absence seizures if caregivers report that they often stare into space; don't hear half of what they are told; never listen; daydream continually; can't follow directions; seem to be in a fog or "spaced out;" or stop what they are doing for several seconds in a "freeze frame," and then spontaneously resume where they left off.

- Children who are reported to have episodes of either emotional or behavioral outbursts accompanied by "strange" motor movements should be screened for psychomotor epilepsy. These seizures differ from other behavior or emotional problems in that there may not appear to be a logical precipitant for the emotional outburst, and the symptoms of the disturbance are stereotypic.

- If caregivers report that their infants' bodies "jerk" hard, the infants should be evaluated for evidence of myoclonic seizures.

MENTAL RETARDATION

The term "mental retardation" comes from the Latin word *retardare*, which means to be delayed or late. Mental retardation refers to the significant delays in cognitive, social, emotional, and physical development that are symptomatic of a wide variety of underlying conditions and syndromes.

Syndromes in which mental retardation is common include fragile-X syndrome, Down's syndrome (Trisomy 21) and many other genetic abnormalities, hydrocephalus, microcephaly, phenylketonuria (PKU), metabolic disorders, and others. Most often, however, a specific condition causing the mental retardation cannot be identified. Therefore, the term mental retardation is generally used as a broad diagnostic classification when significantly delayed development in all domains is the only symptom that can be clearly identified.

It is misleading to presume that persons who have mental retardation are a homogeneous group. There is wide variation in the degrees of developmental delay included under the broad classification of mental retardation. Mental retardation is generally subdivided into four categories to assist in classification: mild, moderate, severe, and profound. Each classification represents an increasing degree of delay in development and adaptive ability.

Hundreds of possible contributing factors have been associated with mental retardation. Some of these are more likely to result in severe or profound mental retardation: they include genetic factors, metabolic disorders, severe birth injury and trauma, severe prenatal infections, anoxia (lack of oxygen), head injury from an accident or abuse, and Rh incompatibility. However, only about 10% of persons with mental retardation fall into the severe and profound ranges.

In approximately 70% of cases, the cause of retardation cannot be determined. This is particularly true for persons with mild mental retardation. Environmental factors such as inadequate nutrition, lack of environmental stimulation, and prenatal exposure to drugs and alcohol are thought to be important contributing factors to mild mental retardation.

Approximately 3 in 100 individuals, or 3% of the total population, have some degree of mental retardation. Of these, approximately 90% fall into the mild range; 7% in the moderate range; and 3% in the severe and profound ranges.

Clinical Description

Mental retardation is defined by the American Association of Mental Retardation (AAMR) as follows:

> Mental retardation refers to substantial limitations in present functioning. It is characterized by significantly subaverage intellectual functioning, existing concurrently with related limitations in two or more of the following applicable adaptive skill areas: communication, self-care, home living, social skills, community use, self-direction, health and safety, functional academics,

leisure and work. Mental retardation manifests before age 18 [American Association of Mental Retardation 1992].

"Substantial limitations" is further defined as scoring a minimum of two standard deviations below the mean on I.Q. tests and adaptive behavior assessments.

Intelligence

Intelligence is cognitive capacity. However, cognitive capacity is not a simple construct. Our cognitive capabilities are determined by the interaction of many different functions, including memory, analytic ability, perspective–taking ability, ability to synthesize information, symbolic reasoning, visual–spatial conceptualization, and others. Different strengths and weaknesses within the various cognitive functions are the basis for assessing cognitive capacity, or intelligence. Variability of individual strengths and weaknesses in different areas of cognition also gives us a rich diversity of cognitive styles. When a person has pervasive limitations in most of the cognitive functions, however, problems in adaptive behavior are more likely, including limited social judgment, difficulty adapting to changing circumstances, poor self–care and protection, deficits in practical reasoning, and limited vocational performance.

Clearly, it is very difficult to measure something as complex and fluid as human intelligence. Yet, standardized intelligence tests are useful tools to measure cognitive capability, and they have proven to be highly correlated with a person's ability to learn and use new information, particularly in an educational or school setting. However, I.Q. tests by themselves cannot always supply enough reliable information about a person's capacity to function in day–to–day living. This additional information is essential for proper assessment, accurate diagnosis, and relevant case planning. Measures of adaptive behavior provide additional tools to assess a person's life skills.

Adaptive Behavior

The addition of adaptive behavior assessment in the diagnosis of mental retardation is relatively recent. Previously, mental retardation was diagnosed solely on the basis of performance on standardized intelligence tests, which do not assess a person's mastery of daily living. Such a measure is important, since mental retardation typically results in developmental deficits in many areas of functioning. Utilizing standardized measures of adaptive behavior decreases the likelihood of misdiagnosis. For example, many children with learning disabilities perform poorly on standardized intelligence tests, often because of reading or auditory processing problems. However, they are quite normal in most areas of functioning. In the past, such children were often misdiagnosed as mentally retarded based on their I.Q. test scores. With the addition of adaptive behavior inventories as a required part of the diagnosis for mental retardation, such misdiagnosis is less likely to occur.

Adaptive behavior is broadly defined as "the effectiveness or the degree with which the individual meets the standards of personal independence and social responsibility expected of his age and cultural group" [Thain 1980]. Certain areas of functioning are commonly included in a definition of adaptive behavior. They are:

- Skills for meeting basic physical needs. These include eating, dressing, toileting, and personal hygiene.

- Skills for daily living, which include cooking, cleaning, laundry, shopping, home maintenance, travel, the ability to use money, and the ability to care for personal belongings.

- Social skills, including interpersonal relationship skills, the ability to cooperate, language and communication skills, the ability to initiate and carry out purposeful activities, understanding social roles, the ability to work, behaving appropriately in social situations, and the ability to assume responsibility.

When mental retardation was diagnosed solely on the basis of measured I.Q., many persons were inappropriately labeled, and received inappropriate treatment and educational programming. By including adaptive behavior measurements in the diagnosis of mental retardation, we help to insure that only those persons whose functioning is significantly delayed in all areas are diagnosed as mentally retarded. A good adaptive behavior assessment also delineates problem areas and areas of greater skill, which improves our ability to provide the proper interventions.

Comparable deficits in both intelligence and adaptive behavior are necessary for a diagnosis of mental retardation.

Levels of Mental Retardation

In general, mental retardation is determined statistically by measuring intelligence and adaptive behavior against the "normal" range for these traits. "Normal" is considered to be within two standard deviations on either side of the mean, or middle, of a normal distribution, and includes 95% of the population. The remaining 5% lie more than two standard deviations on either side of the mean. Approximately 2.5% of these are significantly delayed, or mentally retarded; the other 2.5% would be considered to possess exceptional intelligence and ability.

The general characteristics of persons in each category of mental retardation and the expected developmental and functioning abilities for each category are outlined below.

MILD MENTAL RETARDATION

In childhood, mild mental retardation is generally not clearly diagnosed until a child is of school age. During infancy and the preschool years, mildly mentally retarded children may progress in their motor, social, and emotional development close to the "slower" end of normal, but there are typically no serious developmental delays.

In general, higher order cognitive skills are most affected in persons with mild mental retardation. This includes abstract or hypothetical reasoning ability, the ability to perceive and accurately interpret subtle interpersonal or environmental cues, the ability to weigh and consider information in making judgments or solving complex problems, and in understanding the perspectives of others.

A person with mild mental retardation is likely to have considerable problems mastering academic skills. Generally, a person with mild mental retardation may learn basic reading, writing, and math skills to about the fourth grade level. Mild mental retardation has been referred to as "educable mentally retarded," which implies a capacity to learn some basic academic skills.

If there are no accompanying physical or emotional disorders, persons with mild mental retardation are often able to function independently in the community, provided the environmental demands are not too complex. They can work and support themselves, and can manage most daily activities, but may need direction and supervision from others during times of crisis or in matters which require more complex skills. They may also need help to avoid being exploited. Some persons with mild mental retardation can be adequate parents, if they are taught proper child care and parenting skills, and if they are given adequate support.

It must be remembered, however, that the mild range of mental retardation encompasses a continuum of 15 points in I.Q. and comparable adaptive behavior skills. Persons at the upper end of the range (I.Q. 70) will typically have more skills and potential for independent functioning than do persons who are closer to the lower end of the range (I.Q. 55). We must also remember that people with mild mental retardation are more like than unlike other people, and they are susceptible to all the emotional and psychological needs and problems we may see in persons falling into the "normal" or "above average" range of intelligence and adaptive behavior.

MODERATE MENTAL RETARDATION

Moderate mental retardation can generally be diagnosed during infancy and early childhood. Sensorimotor development is often significantly delayed. Moderately retarded children, for example, may sit up at 12 months, walk at two years, be toilet trained at four years, and learn to talk at six years.

Persons with moderate mental retardation have sometimes been referred to as "trainable." The implication is that while they do not possess academic potential, they are able to learn to perform many routine tasks. With appropriate training and supervision, persons with moderate retardation can learn to feed, toilet, bathe, and dress themselves; to assist in maintaining a living environment; and to perform functional work tasks, usually in a closely supervised or sheltered setting. Persons with moderate mental retardation can often live successfully in community–based group home settings, with proper help and supervision from family members and/or staff. Independent community living is generally not possible.

As with mild mental retardation, there are variations in the functioning of persons with moderate mental retardation, depending upon which end of the continuum they fall. Moderate mental retardation also spans a range of 15 points in I.Q., from 55 to 40. A person with an I.Q. of 55, and comparable adaptive behavior, will generally be more similar in functioning to a person at the lower end of the mildly retarded range than to someone at the lower end of the moderate range.

SEVERE AND PROFOUND MENTAL RETARDATION

Severe and profound mental retardation can generally be diagnosed early in infancy. The developmental delays are very significant in all developmental domains. Severely and profoundly retarded persons typically require full-time supportive care. Persons with severe and profound mental retardation do not develop and use language for communication. Some persons in the severely retarded range may use some words or combinations of words to communicate, but they do not develop basic language skills.

A small percentage may be taught some basic self-help skills such as self-feeding and toileting, but most individuals will need routine assistance in even basic self-help tasks. Many persons who are severely or profoundly retarded have physical disabilities as well. Because of the multiple physical factors which often accompany severe and profound mental retardation, including serious genetic abnormalities, many do not survive infancy or childhood.

Early Identification

The hallmark of mental retardation is delayed development that is comparable in all developmental domains–cognitive, physical, social, and emotional. If the child welfare worker knows the behaviors and abilities that represent the normal range for all developmental domains, recognizing delay is not difficult. The greater the discrepancy between development and chronological age, the more likely the child is mentally retarded. However, since many other factors can contribute to developmental delays, most psychologists do not diagnose children as mentally retarded until they are school age. Many children with early developmental delays have the capability to grow and develop, if given the proper intensive interventions. Therefore, any child with demonstrated delays in development should receive early intervention and developmental services, regardless of diagnosis.

Treatment and Intervention

Before any intervention program can be developed, a person with possible mental retardation should be thoroughly assessed and accurately diagnosed. This assessment should be performed by a competent psychologist who considers both I.Q. and adaptive behavior. Once an appropriate diagnosis has been made, an assessment of the person's areas of skill and strength, as well as service needs, should be completed. A comprehensive intervention program should then be provided to promote development, and improve adaptive behavior.

As is true with all developmental disabilities, the earlier the identification and intervention, the more we can maximize each person's functioning. Any intervention program should plan for developmental activities in all four developmental domains, and should include the following components.

EDUCATION AND/OR TRAINING

By definition, persons who are mentally retarded are slower in their development and in their rate of learning. However, they do learn. The degree to which they will progress in any area will be limited by the degree of retardation; however, the way learning experiences are structured and presented can significantly influence how far, and how quickly, they can progress.

Research has consistently demonstrated that early, intense educational intervention, including infant stimulation, structured preschool experiences, and specialized school programming, can significantly promote and improve a child's cognitive and adaptive development. Activities in the home which provide structured and consistent stimulation are also very helpful.

There are many technologies which have been developed to help children and adults with mental retardation acquire, generalize, and maintain skills in a wide variety of areas. Learning activities should be well planned and formalized using an Individual Education Plan (IEP) or Individual Habilitation Plan (IHP). Staff should be trained in specialized methods of teaching or training persons with mental retardation.

PHYSICAL AND HEALTH CARE

Many syndromes include both mental retardation and physical disabilities that can restrict a person's mobility, ability to manipulate objects, self-help activities, and the capacity to interact with others. These physical conditions must be treated and managed. Physical therapy, medical care, and the use of prosthetic devices can minimize the effects of many physical disabilities, and can enhance the individual's development of adaptive skills.

Each child with mental retardation should be routinely examined by a physician. Caregivers should know and recognize signs and symptoms of physical illness, since persons who lack verbal communication skills may have difficulty communicating illness or pain. Children with conditions that require medication and medical management should be treated by physicians who specialize in providing services to persons with developmental disabilities.

SOCIAL AND RECREATIONAL OPPORTUNITIES

It is often wrongly assumed that people with mental retardation don't have the same social and affiliative needs as other people, and they are often excluded and isolated from typical social and interpersonal experiences. Because their verbal communication skills may be limited, it is not unusual for other people to discount or ignore them. Isolation and exclusion have contributed to emotional problems, including depression, low self-esteem, and boredom in many people with mental retardation, particularly in the mild and high moderate ranges.

Structured recreational experiences, including games, activities, and outings into the community should be routinely provided. These opportunities can promote the development of relationships, and the learning of useful social skills, as well as create a pleasant, nurturing environment.

Persons of all ages with mental retardation have the same basic needs of nurturance, stability, affection, intimacy, and affiliation as do all people. Family members and caregivers should assure that these social needs are recognized and addressed.

NORMALIZATION AND INCLUSION

An important concept in serving persons with mental retardation is normalization, which refers to providing a pattern of life that is as similar as possible to the normal, or typical, life of the rest of the population. Inclusion refers to routinely involving persons with mental retardation in typical life events and social experiences.

In the recent past, persons with mental retardation were segregated into very atypical living and social environments in institutions and in segregated schools. This was often justified as being in the best interests of the person with retardation. We now know that a lifetime of segregation often promotes further developmental retardation, and makes integration into society impossible. Children with retardation who are raised in their own homes and communities not only progress further in all areas of development than children raised in institutional settings, but their adaptive behavior skills are better suited to functioning within the community environment. This is true for adults with mental retardation as well. In general, adults who are provided with a community–based living arrangement with proper services have a greater opportunity to develop appropriate skills, and to function within the community.

Any intervention program for a person with mental retardation should include as many activities as possible in normal social, recreational, educational, and vocational environments. Unnecessary isolation and segregation should be avoided.

⚘ Case Example: Gregory Gorman

Gregory, age three and a half, was referred to the child welfare agency by his Head Start teacher, who thought he was being neglected by his mother. Gregory was the youngest of five children cared for by a single mother. The Head Start teacher liked Gregory's mother, but thought her to be very limited in her abilities.

Gregory had started coming to Head Start about three months earlier. He had been enrolled by a welfare department caseworker, who was helping Gregory's mother explore job opportunities as part of her financial assistance grant.

The Head Start teacher reported that Gregory came to school hungry and dirty, and his clothes were not appropriate for the weather. He was not toilet trained, and he was often urine soaked, since his mother had him in training pants. The teacher also believed he was quite delayed in his development.

The caseworker met with the Head Start teacher in the classroom. Together they observed Gregory and did a gross developmental screening. Gregory's gait looked like that of a child who had just learned to walk. He stumbled often, and appeared to lack balance and coordination. He didn't seem to know what to do with the play equipment in the room, and he did not know how to climb. He generally used a full-hand palmar grasp, and only occasionally did he show good finger–thumb opposition. He tried to feed himself finger foods, but he would not hold a fork or spoon. He held a bottle, but would not drink from a cup. He chose simple toys, such as colored beads, and he amused himself by placing them into a bucket and dumping them. He often wandered around the room picking up objects and dropping them. He did not play with other children. He knew several simple words, but he did not speak phrases or sentences.

He was responsive to the Head Start teacher; he was affectionate, and liked to be cuddled.

The worker and teacher together decided, giving him the benefit of the doubt, that Gregory's development was generally more typical of a one to two year old than a three and a half year old. The caseworker made a referral to a psychologist who specialized in working with children with delays. The developmental assessment confirmed that Gregory was, on average, functioning between 12 and 18 months of age. The psychologist suggested that while Gregory was too young to make a final diagnosis, this represented a potentially moderate level of mental retardation, and that specialized services were essential immediately. Gregory was transferred to the intensive early intervention preschool associated with the county Mental Retardation and Developmental Disabilities program.

Gregory's mother was also assessed, and was determined to be functioning between low-normal and high-level mild mental retardation. She was linked with the proper services to provide her with in-home instruction on child care, and the essentials of home management. A volunteer was assigned to help her twice weekly. Her other children were also assessed, and found to be functioning at the low-normal/mildly retarded level of intelligence. The volunteer assisted Gregory's mother to improve her care of all her children.

The worker followed Gregory's development for six months. The Early Intervention Preschool indicated that he was progressing, albeit very slowly, and that the mother was actively involved with the program. The volunteer was still involved, and was committed to helping the family. Both the children and their mother referred to the volunteer as "Grandma." The preschool believed Gregory would always need some level of special education, and they assumed responsibility for his ongoing educational and developmental planning. The child welfare caseworker closed the case, since there was no further evidence of neglect, and the children were being monitored by other community professionals.

FRAGILE–X SYNDROME

Fragile–X syndrome is the most common known inherited cause of mental retardation. It is a sex-linked disorder with an estimated incidence of 1 in 1000 males. Females display the syndrome less frequently. Fragile–X syndrome was first identified in 1943 by Martin and Bell, who published a family pedigree that described a sex-linked form of mental retardation. The chromosome defect was first located and described in 1969, but the specific gene responsible for the syndrome was not identified until 1991.

Genetic transmission in fragile–X syndrome is similar to other X-linked chromosomal disorders, such as hemophilia and certain types of muscular dystrophy. All humans have 23 pairs of chromosomes. One of these pairs determines gender. Normal males have an XY chromosome pair, and normal females have an XX pair. In fragile–X syndrome, one of the X chromosomes is malformed. Males who inherit this defective X chromosome always exhibit the syndrome. The syndrome is less frequently expressed in females, because they have a second X chromosome in the gender-determined pair, which is usually normal, and appears to block or mediate expression of many of the symptoms. These women are called "carriers," since while they, themselves, exhibit no symptoms, the abnormal chromosome can be transmitted to their children.

The primary symptom of fragile–X syndrome is mental retardation. Most males with fragile–X syndrome exhibit moderate to severe mental retardation. Most females with fragile–X syndrome have normal I.Q.s, but they often have learning disabilities. However, 30% function in the borderline to mildly retarded range.

Autistic traits are also common in males with fragile–X. Common behaviors include avoidance of eye contact, hand flapping, self–injurious behavior such as hand biting, tactile defensiveness, unusual sensitivity to stimuli, and perseveration in speech and behavior. Hyperactivity, attention deficits, language delays with echolalic speech (repeating the speech of others), aggressive outbursts, and a pervasive lack of interpersonal responsiveness are also noted. Males with frag-ile–X also are more shy, socially withdrawn, emotional, and less energetic than males with mental retardation with other etiologies. Adaptive behavior appears to be similar to that of other persons with comparable mental retardation.

Physical features associated with fragile–X include a long, thin face with large, prominent ears, joint laxity, flat feet, cardiac abnormalities such as mitral valve prolapse, esophageal reflux, hypotonia (lack of muscle tone) and hyperextensi-bility of the joints, all suggesting an underlying connective tissue disorder. Infants with fragile–X have often been noted to have difficulty feeding, often resulting in failure to thrive.

Some children with fragile–X syndrome are misdiagnosed as autistic because of their autistic–like symptoms. However, most persons with autism do not have a fragile–X chromosome. Autism and fragile–X appear to remain distinct disor-ders, even though some of their symptoms are similar.

Children diagnosed with fragile–X should receive intensive early intervention to promote maximum development of both intelligence and adaptive behavior, although the prognosis for most is limited. Women can now receive genetic screening to determine whether they are carriers of the fragile–X chromosome. Genetic screening and counseling are recommended if a familial history of sex-linked mental retardation is noted.

DOWN'S SYNDROME (TRISOMY 21)

The first clinical description of Down's syndrome was published in 1866 by a British physician named John Langdon Down. Down had observed that several of his patients who were mentally retarded all had fairly similar physical fea-tures, including facial features he thought resembled those of Mongolian or Oriental peoples. At the time, the term "idiot" (from the Greek *idios*, meaning peculiar or unique) was a common diagnostic category of mental retardation. Down named his syndrome "Mongolism," and referred to persons with the syn-drome as "Mongoloid Idiots." As the English social structure of the time was strongly prejudiced against Oriental peoples, the term "Mongolism" quickly became derogatory. The syndrome is now widely referred to as Down's syn-drome, or Trisomy 21, which more accurately reflects the nature of the disorder.

Down's syndrome results from an abnormality in chromosome formation. The normal human chromosome configuration is 46 chromosomes organized into 23 pairs. A trisomy is an abnormal grouping of three chromosomes instead of a normal pair. Most people with Down's syndrome have a trisomy of the 21st chromosome pair, and a total of 47 chromosomes. This trisomy most often occurs through an error in cell division during the development of reproductive cells. The result is the development of a sperm or egg cell that carries an extra chromosome. If this reproductive cell is fertilized during conception, the resulting embryo carries the extra 21st chromosome in all its cells, producing the syndrome. Hence, the formal name for the syndrome is Trisomy 21.

Approximately 3 to 5% of Down's syndrome cases result from a chromosome translocation. In a translocation, a broken off portion of another chromosome attaches to a 21st chromosome, thereby changing its structure and its function. It is important to identify this group of individuals, since the translocated chromosome may have been transmitted by a parent who carries the chromosome abnormality, but who is developmentally normal. In such families the risk of recurrence of Down's syndrome in subsequent pregnancies is considerably higher (10–15%) than for the more typical trisomy (1%) [Bartoshesky 1980].

The incidence rate for Down's syndrome is approximately 1 per 700. Research shows that the risk of bearing children with Down syndrome increases with maternal age. Estimates are approximately 1 in 1,500 for mothers age 25; 1 in 1,000 for mothers age 30; 1 in 350 for mothers age 35; and 1 in 50 for mothers age 40 and over. The risk is also higher for young teenage mothers. Down's syndrome appears to occur equally in male and female children, and within all racial and ethnic groups.

Clinical Description

Children with Down's syndrome are most often identified at birth because of characteristic facial and physical features. However, positive identification of Down's syndrome should never be made without a chromosome analysis (karyotype) which confirms the presence of the chromosomal abnormality. In the past, some people who had similar facial features to persons with Down's syndrome were improperly diagnosed and placed in institutions, even though they were later determined to be of normal intelligence and ability.

Down's syndrome may be detected in the fetus through amniocentesis, wherein a sample of the amniotic fluid is extracted, and an assessment is made of individual cells to determine their chromosome configuration. This may be performed at the beginning of the second trimester of pregnancy.

The most common clinical features of Down's syndrome are as follows:

- *Short stature.* Almost all persons with Down's syndrome are shorter than average, and reach full height at about age 15. Typical height is around five feet.

- *Flat facial profile and flat nasal bridge.* Approximately 90% have flat faces and a very flat, almost absent nasal bridge.

- *Hypotonia and hyperextensibility of joints.* Evident in approximately 80% of people with Down's syndrome. Hypotonia, or lack of muscle tone, is noted at birth and tends to improve as the child develops. Hypotonia and joint hyperextensibility tend to contribute to delayed motor development.

- *Slanted eyes with inner canthal folds (epicanthal folds).* These are present in approximately 80% of people with Down's syndrome.

- *Short neck with excess skin on back of neck.* The head seems to sit close to the shoulders, which often appear rounded.

- *Microcephaly.* The head is often smaller than normal, and is typically flattened at the back.

- *Enlarged tongue and malformed, improperly placed teeth.* The malformations of the mouth and an enlarged tongue often result in protrusion of the tongue from the mouth.

- *Low-set and malformed ears.* The ears may be strangely shaped, and are very low on the sides of the head.

- *Transverse palmar crease.* Often referred to as a "Simian Crease." The "life lines" in the upper portion of the palm form a single linear crease across the palm.

- *Congenital heart disease and malformations.* Present in 40–60% of persons with Down's syndrome. Before the availability of open heart surgery, this constituted a major cause of death for infants with Down's syndrome. Corrective surgery has improved the prognosis for these children considerably.

- *Digestive malformations.* Persons with Down's syndrome may have problems with the stomach, esophagus, and digestive tract due to malformations in these organs.

- *High susceptibility to leukemia.* The incidence of leukemia in persons with Down's syndrome is estimated to be approximately 20 times greater than in the normal population.

- *Hearing deficits.* Hearing loss in some children with Down's syndrome contributes to delayed speech and language acquisition. Children should be screened to assure their hearing is not impaired.

- *Spinal cord malformation.* About 10% of individuals with Down syndrome have a malformation of the cervical vertebrae called Atlantoaxial Dislocation. Without early identification and corrective surgery, strenuous physical activity can lead to cervical and central nervous system damage. All persons with Down's syndrome should be screened by x–ray for this condition.

- *Adolescent/sexual development.* Females with Down's syndrome may menstruate, and some have been known to bear children. Males are generally infertile and have low serum testosterone levels. Adolescent sexual development is typically incomplete.

- *Cognitive development.* Almost all persons with Down syndrome are mentally retarded. The degree of retardation varies, ranging from mild to severe. The average level of cognitive development is in the moderately mentally retarded range. A few individuals with Down's syndrome have been identified within the low–normal range of intelligence.≠

- *Social development.* Many persons with Down's syndrome attain social and interpersonal skills which are more highly developed than would be expected for their general degree of mental retardation.

Prognosis and Treatment

At least 20% of infants with Down's syndrome are stillborn. While in the past, many children with Down's syndrome did not survive early childhood, advances in medical treatment, and management of the associated physical conditions have reduced the rate of infant deaths.

The developmental level of persons with Down's syndrome is affected by many congenital and environmental factors. Individual assessment of each person with Down's syndrome is essential to determine areas of strength and service need. Many persons with Down's syndrome are relatively competent socially, despite intellectual deficits, and they are able to function reasonably well in a family or group home setting. Because most persons with Down's syndrome are not seriously physically disabled, many have been able to learn vocational tasks, and can work in supervised or sheltered workshop settings. Most persons with Down's syndrome learn to talk, and use language to communicate with others.

Studies have consistently demonstrated that children with Down's syndrome who are raised at home in nurturing and stimulating environments typically outperform children raised in institutional settings in their cognitive, adaptive, and social functioning. Early intervention, including infant stimulation and preschool programs, also contribute positively to the child's development. This is of particular importance for child welfare professionals, who may have responsibility for permanency planning for these children. For children who cannot be maintained in their own home, adoption is the most appropriate placement.

The physical development of children with Down's syndrome is generally delayed. Speech and language acquisition are also delayed, and may be related to hearing deficits. Some persons with Down's syndrome also display behavior disorders, including hyperactivity, autism, and other affective disorders. These disorders should be considered additional disabling conditions, not a typical symptom of Down's syndrome.

Life expectancy is reduced for persons with Down's syndrome. They also tend to show physical signs of aging earlier. Decreases in infant deaths are lengthening the statistical life expectancy. Still, the life expectancy is about 50 years.

Services

Children with Down's syndrome in the child welfare system will likely need the full range of developmental and supportive services. Young children should be cared for in family settings with supportive educational, recreational, and respite services. This will generally require linking the family to dependable community resources and supports. Children in need of permanent placement should be adopted. Community–based settings that combine supervised group home living with vocational training are appropriate for older youth with Down's syndrome. Placement into nursing care or other institutional settings should be avoided, unless the individual is severely or profoundly retarded, and requires constant care.

♪ Case Example: Carrie

Carrie was three months old when she was brought to the child welfare agency by her 16-year-old mother, Lisa, who asked that Carrie be adopted. Carrie was Lisa's third baby in three years (she had given birth to twins a year earlier), and she felt Carrie would have a better life if adopted. Lisa's parents were currently caring for her twins, and they didn't feel they could handle another child. Carrie was placed in a foster home, and the mother and the worker began the necessary legal processes to give the agency permanent custody of the baby.

Carrie was small and low weight for age. She was severely hypotonic. She had no head control, she lay quietly wherever placed, and she rarely cried. She did not establish eye contact with the worker, and she did not turn toward her mother's voice. She appeared placid and vacant. She was also unusual in her appearance. She had a flat face, round head, short neck, she lacked a nasal bridge, and her tongue often protruded from her mouth. Her ears were set very low on her head, and she had epicanthal folds on her eyes.

Lisa had had no prenatal care. The baby had been born at home and was delivered by a local midwife. Lisa had difficulty feeding Carrie. Carrie was placid, didn't eat very well, and didn't seem to like the formula. Lisa said Carrie had never been seen by a physician.

The baby was placed in a foster home. The foster mother took Carrie to a pediatrician, who confirmed the baby was slow in her development and low weight for age. The doctor prescribed a regimen of high nutrient feedings, and asked to see Carrie again in two months, unless she didn't progress.

The caseworker saw Carrie in the foster home a month later. The baby had put on weight and was much more active, although she was still very delayed in her development. However, her strange facial features had become much more pronounced, and she clearly had the appearance of a child with Down syndrome. The worker began to make arrangements with the children's hospital in a large neighboring city for genetic testing.

The worker also decided to carefully document the baby's developmental milestones, and she did a brief developmental assessment. Carrie was still hypotonic and, while more active, had not achieved important developmental milestones. However, she did appear stronger, had developed head control, and was more responsive to her foster mother.

The worker returned a month later to do a full developmental screening. Carrie was now five months old. The worker found her sitting in the baby swing, reaching for and batting the colored disks on the rod in front of her. Her body strength was good. She was reaching with both hands for the toys. She grasped and shook a rattle. She attended to voices and smiled often at her foster mother. The worker stood Carrie in her lap; she bore weight on her legs, and bounced herself up and down while the worker held her. Carrie reached for and grabbed the worker's glasses and hair. The worker surmised that Carrie had apparently made up for her previous delays and appeared to be developing within normal limits. She still had an increasingly strong resemblance to children with Down syndrome. The lack of developmental delay was, however, confounding. The worker considered the possibility of a partial rather than full trisomy, which would limit the severity of the disability, or considered that there was perhaps some other genetic abnormality.

The worker pursued genetic testing. The genetic tests were normal, and the clinic said that while Carrie clearly had the facial features of a child with a genetic problem, her normal development would suggest that whatever the underlying condition, if indeed there was one, it was not interfering with her development.

Carrie was adopted at age seven months. She continued to develop normally, and eventually exhibited exceptional intelligence in many areas, even though she remained "different looking."

SPINA BIFIDA

Spina bifida is a congenital deformity of the spinal column. The defect occurs within the first six weeks of fetal development, when the cells that form the brain and central nervous system are in their early stages of development.

In spina bifida, the central nervous system cells forming the neural tube fail to fuse and close, usually at the lower end of the spine. The bony arches of the spinal column subsequently fail to develop properly, and they may also remain open. Portions of the central nervous system, including the spinal nerve cord fibers, the meninges (membranes which cover the nerves in the central nervous system), and parts of the autonomic nervous system, do not develop properly because of the defect. These neurological structures may also protrude through the open spinal column, and be exposed in the midline region of the lower back. In myelomeningocele, which is the most serious of several types of spina bifida, neural transmission through the spinal cord may be interrupted and impaired.

Etiology and Incidence

There are many factors that can lead to spina bifida. The highest incidence occurs in England, Ireland, and Wales, and in persons with this ancestry. Spina bifida is rare among people of African or Asian ancestry. The wide variation in incidence rates among different races would suggest some genetic etiological factors. Genetic factors are thought to sensitize the developing embryo to the effects of some environmental influence during the first month of intrauterine life, creating a complex interaction of genetic factors and an environmental "trigger." Incidence rates are between two and five per thousand births. It is more common in girls than in boys.

While spina bifida cannot be prevented, it can be detected prenatally through amniocentesis. Substances which are not normally in the amniotic fluid may leak from the open spine. The presence of these substances in the amniotic fluid sample generally indicates a cystic defect. Spina bifida may also be detected by an ultrasound examination.

Clinical Description of Spina Bifida

There are three main types of spina bifida: spina bifida occulta, meningocele, and myelomeningocele. Of these, usually only the myelomeningocele poses severe developmental problems for the child. However, as the first two types are also referred to as spina bifida, they should be mentioned.

SPINA BIFIDA OCCULTA

The neurological deformity is limited to a small, bony defect in the vertebrae of the spinal column, and can only be seen on x-ray examination. Most patients have no symptoms. There may be a dimple, a discoloration of the skin, or a growth of hair over the malformed vertebrae. Some persons may have mild motor weakness, or disorders of sphincter control, but these may not develop until later in life. Some studies suggest that as many as 25% of people have this benign form of spina bifida.

MENINGOCELE

The bony defect in a meningocele is confined to a few vertebrae, and is usually located in the sacral or lumbar (lower) regions of the spine. The defect, called a cyst or cele, consists of a sac of the meninges (the membranes covering the nerves in the spinal cord), which protrudes through the opening in the bony vertebra. This sac fills with cerebrospinal fluid. It is often covered by more or less intact skin, and the spinal cord and nerves are usually not involved. There is seldom weakness in the legs, lack of sphincter control, or any other neurological dysfunction. Surgical correction is necessary immediately after birth to prevent rupture of the sac and subsequent infection. The prognosis is good with surgical correction.

A secondary problem for persons with meningocele is hydrocephalus, which occurs in approximately 9% of affected persons. This is also surgically correctable, with a good prognosis.

MYELOMENINGOCELE

Myelomeningocele is the most severe form of the three types of spina bifida. It occurs four to five times more frequently than the simple meningocele. The defect consists of a wide opening in the spinal column, covering several vertebrae, usually in the lumbar or sacral region. A grapefruit–sized sac protrudes through the opening in the spine. The sac, formed by the meninges, contains spinal cord nerves and cerebrospinal fluid. The misplacement of spinal cord nerves typically impairs neural transmission, and may affect many motor, sensory, and autonomic functions.

The degree of disability resulting from the myelomeningocele depends upon several factors, including the location of the malformation, and the extent of involvement of neural tissues. While generally located in the lower areas of the spine, the defect may occasionally occur in the mid–back (thoracic), or even the neck (cervical) areas. The higher on the spine the defect occurs, the more likely there will be widespread and serious neurological dysfunction. The degree of disability from myelomeningocele may range from mild to severe, but a high percentage of people born with this type of spina bifida are seriously physically disabled.

Interruption of neurological transmission between the brain and the lower portions of the body may lead to paralysis, motor weakness, loss of motor control, impaired sensory functions, and autonomic nerve dysfunction in areas of the body which are typically innervated by nerves in the spinal cord below the level of the myelomeningocele.

Orthopedic problems such as hip dysplasia, "rocker–bottom" feet, and other deformities are caused by inconsistent innervation and stimulation to opposing muscle groups. This leads to unbalanced muscle tone and abnormal muscle tension on opposing muscles, creating disproportionate muscle development, and also bone and joint malformations. Some individuals are able to stand and walk with braces; others must use wheel chairs for mobility.

Persons with myelomeningocele often have difficulty controlling the bladder, which may lead to constant urinary dripping and failure of the bladder to empty completely. Retention of urine in the bladder for an extended period of time often leads to repeated urinary tract and bladder infections. When not treated, these may result in damage to the urinary tract or the kidneys. Historically, one of the largest causes of mortality for persons with spina bifida was kidney damage from untreated urinary infections. Poor innervation of the anal sphincter muscle and the bowel can lead to incontinence, or to the retention of fecal matter in the lower bowel.

Hydrocephalus is an abnormal accumulation of cerebrospinal fluid in the cavities inside and around the brain. Hydrocephalus occurs in approximately 65% of persons with myelomeningocele. It results from malformations in portions of the spinal cord which occur in the head and neck area. Hydrocephalus may develop prenatally or immediately after birth. If it is untreated, it typically leads to brain damage and mental retardation. This is a serious problem, because prenatal hydrocephalus is very difficult to treat. The infant with myelomeningocele may be born with serious brain damage due to prenatal hydrocephalus.

Some fetuses with myelomeningocele spontaneously abort prior to reaching full term. Difficult labor and delivery is common for children with myelomeningocele for several reasons. The child's head may be enlarged because of prenatal hydrocephalus. The child's lower limbs may be paralyzed and inappropriately positioned, and the birth position is often breech. The spinal deformity is very susceptible to birth injury, including injury to the nerves in the spinal cord. The open myelomeningocele is susceptible to infection, including spinal meningitis. This can lead to additional central nervous system damage or death. Most children with myelomeningocele are in poor condition at birth, and are more likely to be delivered with forceps, which can add risk to the child during the delivery. If it is known that the infant has myelomeningocele, a cesarean delivery may be used.

A percentage of children have pervasive neurological damage by the time they are born. Some do not survive. However, because of the wide variability of presentation of this condition, there are also many children born with normal cognitive abilities and manageable physical impairments, who can lead very normal lives, if they receive proper medical management.

Treatment and Management

Treatment for an infant with myelomeningocele begins immediately after birth. Medical intervention may be very complex because of the multiplicity of problems which may be present, but prompt medical attention decreases the probability of infection or subsequent injury.

Surgery is often performed immediately to repair the defect and cover the open spine to prevent infection or additional injury. Surgical insertion of a shunt may also be necessary to treat hydrocephalus and prevent subsequent brain damage. A shunt is a tube that is inserted into the head cavity and extends through the neck into the chest cavity. Excess cerebrospinal fluid drains through this tube, and is absorbed and disposed of by the normal body processes. Children with shunts must be evaluated periodically by their physicians to assure the shunt does not become blocked, causing subsequent accumulation of spinal fluid and neurological problems.

Orthopedic deformities may be surgically corrected to minimize their negative effects. Prosthetic devices such as wheelchairs, braces, and other orthopedic aids can increase mobility. Ongoing medical attention must be provided, particularly in growing children, to manage orthopedic problems and promote development.

Individuals must be checked often for the presence of urinary infection. In the past, surgery was often performed to detach the urethra and attach it to an opening in the abdomen to permit continuous drainage. This procedure, called urinary tract diversion, requires major surgery, and creates another medical condition which requires ongoing attention. More recently, the use of a nonsurgical procedure called intermittent catheterization has been adopted by many physicians for patients with myelomeningocele. A sterile catheter is used by the caregiver, or by the patient, to drain the bladder several times a day. This is currently the treatment of choice, as it is considerably easier than surgery, and it is more similar to normal bladder functioning.

An associated problem, however, is urinary tract infection that may result from unsterile catheters. The urinary infection may be quite advanced by the time it is diagnosed, since the person with myelomeningocele often lacks sensation in the lower body, and cannot feel and report urinary pain typical of bladder infections. Regular urinary screening for infection, and antibiotic therapy when needed, can eliminate this problem.

Mental retardation in persons with myelomeningocele is generally the result of hydrocephalus or central nervous system infection. If these underlying conditions are controlled or prevented, the degree of mental retardation is not progressive. However, children who have had any degree of hydrocephalus must be fully evaluated to insure that early developmental and educational planning include consideration of any special needs.

Persons with myelomeningocele who are also mentally retarded will have more difficulty being self-sufficient, particularly if mental retardation is severe. The effects of mental retardation in persons with myelomeningocele are the same as with other persons who have comparable degrees of intelligence and adaptive functioning. However, the need to manage the multiple physical conditions associated with the myelomeningocele may complicate the caregiving process.

PERVASIVE DEVELOPMENTAL DISORDERS

Pervasive developmental disorders include a group of conditions characterized by severe and pervasive impairment in several areas of development and adaptive behavior, primarily reciprocal social interaction, and verbal and non-verbal communication, or when stereotyped behavior, interests, and activities are present. These disorders are usually evident in the first few months to years of life. These disorders include autistic disorder, Rett's syndrome, childhood disintegrative disorder, Asperger's syndrome, and pervasive developmental disorder not otherwise specified (PDD) [American Psychiatric Association 1994]. Primary differentiating features are the age of onset of the symptoms, and the typical developmental course.

Autistic Disorder

Of all of the developmental disabilities, autistic disorder, often called autism, is one of the most difficult to understand and to diagnose. The symptoms of the condition may be quite variable, and a clear cause has not been determined.

Many behaviors displayed by autistic persons are also common in other conditions such as mental retardation, schizophrenia, fragile-X syndrome, other pervasive developmental disorders, and deafness-blindness. As a result, arriving at a diagnosis of autism is often difficult, and misdiagnosis is common. The common use of the description "autistic-like" for some conditions further illustrates the high degree of uncertainty in determining who should be diagnosed autistic.

Autism was first identified and described by Leo Kanner in 1943, and he continued to study and publish about the disorder for many years [Kanner 1973]. While a physician at Johns Hopkins University, Kanner recognized that a group of children who had been diagnosed "retarded," or "psychotic," had very consistent and similar behavior patterns. These included indifference to other people, abnormal speech patterns or absence of speech, and a peculiar and stereotypic preoccupation with objects. It was these children's emotional remoteness and social withdrawal that prompted Kanner to name the syndrome "Early Infantile Autism," from the Greek word *auto*, which means "self." Kanner hypothesized that autistic children were unable to form the normal emotional bonds with other people, and that the problem was probably present at birth.

Kanner also identified certain characteristics in the parents of autistic children, which he initially felt contributed to the onset of the disorder. He observed that many parents of autistic children appeared to be reserved and aloof, and lacked warmth in their relationships. He described these parents as "cold, humorless perfectionists of above–average intelligence, detached." Many of the parents were very committed and successful professionals.

While Kanner speculated about the relationship between these parental characteristics and the presence of autistic symptoms, he did not suggest that parental behavior alone caused autism in children. Kanner felt there were many factors to be considered as possible causes of autism. However, for many years following Kanner's initial publication, the preferred treatment for autism was family psychotherapy. This approach to treatment implied that the parents' own lack of emotional contact with their children contributed to the children's disabilities. As a result, parents of autistic children were often made to feel that they were responsible for their children's condition.

In retrospect, while Kanner's identification of autism as a distinct syndrome was diagnostically astute, his initial sample of children and their families was quite small, and his judgment regarding the role of parents in causing the disorder was premature. More extensive studies have illustrated that most parents of autistic children do not fit Kanner's early stereotype. Additionally, it is believed that the aloof behaviors seen in parents of autistic children may be related to the child's inability to interact emotionally with and rejection of the parent. Therefore, the conflictual and distant parent–child relationships are likely a result of the child's condition, rather than a cause of it.

ETIOLOGY AND INCIDENCE

Incidence figures for autism are very difficult to obtain, because there is still very little clinical reliability in diagnosis. Most researchers estimate the incidence of autism to be between five and 15 children per 10,000 births.

There appear to be no family, racial, or ethnic factors correlated with autism. Some research indicates that autism is four to five times more prevalent in boys than it is in girls, but girls with autism are more likely to be mentally retarded. There is some support for a genetic origin for the syndrome, and neurologic involvement is likely. Some youth with autism develop seizures, particularly during adolescence, and EEG abnormalities are common, even in the absence of seizures. However, a precise etiology for autism has not been determined.

CLINICAL DESCRIPTION

Autism is believed to be present at birth. There is typically no period of unequivocal normal development. However, some children's development may appear relatively normal for a year or two; the symptoms may not be obvious, or they may be so mild as to be overlooked or denied by parents. Some parents note that their infants were "strange" or "different," but they cannot always specify why.

Some autistic infants may cry less often, may appear content to be left alone for long periods of time, may become rigid or limp when held, may not mould to the parent when held, may not establish or maintain eye contact, and may not respond or interact socially. Autistic infants may be extremely irritable, may overreact to any type of stimulation, and may show early signs of feeding and sleep disturbances. The severity of unusual behaviors varies; in general, the more severe the behavior, the earlier the child will likely be diagnosed.

Most researchers and clinicians agree that symptoms are clearly evident by 24 to 30 months of age. For a diagnosis of autism, the disturbances must be evident by delays or abnormal functioning prior to age three. By this time, the child's apparent hearing deficits, language delays, and abnormal social interaction suggest developmental problems. This often prompts referral for speech and hearing assessment. Normal hearing, and the absence of physical speech deficits, suggest the possibility of other disorders, including autism. However, despite the prevalence of early symptoms, some autistic children remain undiagnosed until they are of school age.

Ornitz and Ritvo [1976] divide the common behavioral symptoms of autism into five major categories.

DISTURBANCES OF PERCEPTION

People with autism may be either hyperresponsive to sensory stimuli, or they may not respond at all. They may appear not to hear, see, or feel things. They may not respond to persons or objects in the environment. They may sustain bad falls, bumps, or bruises, and appear not to experience any discomfort. "Indifferent" and "remote" are adjectives often used to describe people with autism.

Conversely, they may be hypersensitive, and may overreact to visual, auditory, and tactile stimuli, becoming easily agitated and distressed. Bright lights, harsh or loud sounds such as sirens or vacuum cleaners, physical contact with rough fabrics or other uncomfortable objects, and physical contact with other people may cause significant distress for people with autism. They might close their eyes or put their hands over their ears to ward off sights and sounds, and they may actively avoid physical contact.

Some persons with autism may seek out visual, auditory, and tactile stimulation. They may create noises and listen to them intently, visually explore minute details of objects for long periods of time, or rub objects of varying textures. Whirling, rocking, hand flapping, and head rolling appear to be attempts to generate vestibular and proprioceptive stimulation (sensory feedback from movements of the body).

All of the above patterns of behavior are thought to be the result of an underlying neurological dysfunction. Persons with autism are believed to be unable to process sensory stimuli appropriately. They lack the ability to interpret or correctly use information from visual and auditory sensory input; the senses of smell, touch, and taste seem to be preferred by persons with autism. This is very different from the preferences of most children, who rely most on the senses of sight and hearing.

DISTURBANCES IN RATE OF DEVELOPMENT

The expected course of normal development is disrupted in children with autism, and these delays become more apparent as the child grows. The development of a child with autism is often characterized by spurts and plateaus, and the rates of development between the physical, cognitive, social, and emotional domains may be very inconsistent. Children with autism have been noted to sit without assistance at an early age, but then fail to pull themselves to standing. Others may unexpectedly stand and walk without preparatory motor experimentation and practice.

In many children with autism, motor development and coordination may be normal, while they remain significantly delayed in cognitive, social, and emotional development. Approximately 75% of children with autism show generalized cognitive retardation, usually at the moderate level. However, the profile of cognitive skills is usually uneven, regardless of the general level of intelligence, and some children display some peculiar or exceptional cognitive abilities.

DISTURBANCE IN SOCIAL DEVELOPMENT AND USE OF OBJECTS

Persons with autism show characteristic disturbances in both their relationships with other people and in the way they use objects. Relationships with people are often characterized by failure to make eye contact; absence of social smiling; an aversion to physical contact with others; a tendency to relate to only parts of a person (i.e., a hand or an arm) rather than to the whole person; disinterest in social interaction, games, and activities with others; and delayed, absent, or over-reactive anxiety in response to strangers.

It is common for persons with autism to play with toys and use other objects in a bizarre and very inappropriate manner. This is different from the imaginative play typical of young children, who may ride a broom handle as if it were a horse, or create a tent under the dining room table. For example, a child with autism may turn a bicycle upside down and spin the wheels for very long periods, yet never attempt to sit on or ride the bike. Or, the child may place a toy on the floor and repeatedly run around it in circles. Adults with autism may flick, twirl, spin, bang, or otherwise use objects in unusual ways. At other times, a person with autism may pay no attention to objects at all.

These inappropriate relationships with people and objects are thought to be symptoms of the more basic disturbance in perception. A person cannot relate appropriately to his environment, if he is not able to make sense of or integrate his perceptions into a consistent picture of reality. If a person does not understand what is happening around him, he cannot relate to his surroundings in normal ways. It is especially hard to be involved in social relationships, where the recognition and understanding of subtle social cues are necessary.

DISTURBANCES OF SPEECH AND LANGUAGE

Many persons with autism do not talk at all, while others develop some verbal communication ability. However, those who do learn language often display characteristic abnormalities in their language and speech patterns. Persons with autism often speak in a flat, toneless, mechanized manner. Voice inflections and verbal expressions of feeling are noticeably absent. Speech patterns often include echolalia (the imitation and verbatim repetition of the speech of others), and continuous repetition of selected words or phrases, as if the goal of speech were the production of rhythmic sounds, not interpersonal communication.

Persons with autism often interpret and associate speech concretely. For example, an eight–year–old boy with autism was given a candy bar. He replied, "Look at that bear." The phrase was meaningless when spoken in the middle of his living room in response to receiving a candy bar. However, his brother recalled that the last time the boy had been given a candy bar was at the zoo, near the bear cage. The child with autism had evidently associated the phrase "Look at that bear," to the receipt of a candy bar, rather than to the bear at the zoo.

Pronoun reversal is also common. Autistic children may refer to themselves as "you" and to other people as "I." This use of pronouns replicates the speech patterns used by other people; it is a concrete repetition of what is heard, rather than the utilization of pronouns in proper context.

DISTURBANCES IN MOTILITY

Persons with autism are often described as having bizarre behaviors, and peculiar, stereotyped actions. These may include atypical gross and fine motor activities, such as rocking, swaying, lunging, darting, lurching, toe-walking, hand flapping, posturing, and twirling. Researchers concur that these behaviors are also related to an underlying central nervous system dysfunction. Some persons with autism also exhibit self-injurious behaviors.

TREATMENT AND PROGNOSIS

The prognosis for persons with autism is variable, although most persons with autism may be considered severely to profoundly developmentally disabled.

A small minority of children with autism have relatively normal motor development, and use language in appropriate ways to communicate by the age of five. These children appear to be less severely affected. They may often attend school and learn in a classroom setting, and they may be able to acquire some vocational skills. They typically remain shy, introverted, and passively social as adolescents and adults.

Approximately 2/3 of persons with autism are classified as mentally retarded or mentally ill (psychotic) as adults. These persons need care and supervision throughout their life. They display severe limitations in cognitive, social, and emotional functioning.

Autism cannot be cured, and there are few treatment interventions that can successfully minimize the effects of the disorder. While biological processes are believed to contribute to the disorder, these are not well understood, and there are no medical or drug treatments that can significantly modify the child's condition. Behavior modification strategies may be used to encourage the development of language, or to help persons learn basic adaptive skills, but these have varying degrees of success.

Because persons with autism may be emotionally withdrawn, remote, and very difficult to manage behaviorally, their families often need a great deal of support. Special programs for caregivers of autistic persons provide families with the skills and resources needed to manage chronic stress. Caregivers can often benefit from periods of respite, where someone else assumes primary care of the person with autism. Placement in a group home or other community–based living arrangement, where staff can share caregiving responsibility and support one another, may also be an appropriate alternative to family care for persons with autism.

Other Pervasive Developmental Disorders

The other conditions in the classification of pervasive developmental disorders can be differentiated from autistic disorder primarily in their age of onset and by some specific differences in their characteristics [American Psychiatric Association 1994]. These disorders appear to be much less common than autistic disorder.

Rett's syndrome has been diagnosed only in females, and its multiple deficits follow a period of normal development after birth. The pattern of developmental regression is highly distinctive, and the loss of skills is generally persistent and progressive. Children with Rett's syndrome have apparently normal psychomotor development for the first five months of life, and their head circumference at birth is within normal limits. Between the ages of five and 48 months, head growth decelerates, and there is a loss of previously acquired purposeful hand skills. The child often develops characteristic stereotyped hand movements that resemble hand–wringing or hand washing. Interest in the social environment diminishes in the first few years after the onset of the disorder. Children with Rett's syndrome also have severe impairments in expressive and receptive language. Severe or profound mental retardation is typical, and various nonspecific neurological symptoms or signs may be noted, including increased frequency of EEG abnormalities and seizures.

In childhood disintegrative disorders there is marked regression in multiple areas of functioning, but only after a period of at least two years of apparently normal development that includes age–appropriate verbal and nonverbal communication, social relationships, play, and adaptive behavior. At some time after two years, but before age 10, there is a clinically significant loss of previously acquired skills in several areas. These children eventually exhibit the social and communication deficits and behaviors typical of children with autism. Eventually, these children become severely mentally retarded, and nonspecific neurological symptoms may be noted, including an increase in EEG abnormalities, and seizure disorders.

In Asperger's syndrome, children exhibit severe and sustained impairments in social interaction, as well as repetitive and restrictive patterns of behavior and activities, similar to that of children with autism. For example, children with Asperger's syndrome lack social or emotional reciprocity, and they show a marked impairment in the use of nonverbal behaviors, such as eye contact, facial expressions, or gestures, to regulate social interaction. They may inflexibly adhere to specific, nonfunctional routines or rituals. They may also exhibit a persistent preoccupation with parts of objects, or with stereotyped and restricted patterns of interest that are abnormal either in focus or in intensity. However, Asperger's syndrome differs from autism in that the children usually exhibit no significant delays in language, in cognitive development, in the development of age–appropriate self–help skills, or in adaptive behavior (other than social interaction). Children with Asperger's syndrome also display normal curiosity about the environment. There may be some delay in motor development, and motor clumsiness may be evident.

The general category of "pervasive developmental disorder not otherwise specified" is used when the presentation of the child's disorder does not meet the specific criteria for the other pervasive developmental disorders. This category includes "atypical autism" because of late age at onset, unusual symptoms, mild symptoms, or all of the above [American Psychiatric Association 1994].

ATTENTION–DEFICIT/HYPERACTIVITY DISORDER

Attention–deficit/hyperactivity disorder (ADHD) is a relatively common condition in children. It is estimated that 3–5% of school-age children have the disorder. It is more prevalent in males than females, with ratios of males to females ranging from 4:1 to 9:1. ADHD is believed to be the result of an underlying neurologic disorder; however, the cause and exact nature of the condition have not been determined. It is more prevalent in certain families, suggesting possible genetic determinants.

ADHD is characterized primarily by the child's difficulty with maintaining attention and concentration. This inability to maintain sustained mental effort leads to considerable difficulty adjusting in academic, occupational, and social situations.

While most individuals with ADHD have symptoms of both inattention and hyperactivity–impulsivity, there are some persons in whom one pattern is more predominant than the other. The signs and symptoms of the disorder also vary with the child's age and developmental level.

The primary symptoms of ADHD, inattention, hyperactivity, and impulsivity, are described below [American Psychiatric Association 1994].

The signs of innattention may include the following:

- Individual has difficulty with tasks that require sustained mental effort or close attention; is unable to persist with tasks until completion; and frequently shifts from one uncompleted activity to another.

- Tasks that require sustained mental effort are experienced as unpleasant and markedly aversive; individuals typically avoid or have a strong dislike for such activities.

- Work is messy and is performed carelessly, without considered thought; careless mistakes are often made in school work and other tasks.

- Individual often fails to follow through on requests or instructions.

- Individual has difficulty organizing tasks and activities; work habits are often disorganized, and materials needed for the task are scattered, lost, or carelessly handled and damaged.

- Individual is easily distracted by irrelevant stimuli, and frequently interrupts ongoing tasks to attend to trivial noises or events that are easily ignored by others.

- Individual is "forgetful," in daily activities, misses appointments, forgets to bring things.

- In social situations, individual may appear not to listen to others, may not stay focused on the interaction, fails to follow details or rules of a situation, and exhibits frequent shifts in conversation.

The signs of hyperactivity in children often include the following:

- Fidget continuously, squirm, bounce or rock; they do not remain seated when expected to do so;

- Run, jump, or climb excessively in situations where it is inappropriate;

- Have difficulty sitting still to play quietly or engage in sedentary leisure activities;

- Appear to be always "on the go" or "driven by a motor";

- Fidget with objects, tap hands, shake feet or legs excessively; and

- Talk excessively, make excessive noise during quiet activities.

Impulsivity in behavior is another common symptom of ADHD. Indicators include the following:

- Children may exhibit considerable impatience, have difficulty in delaying responses, blurt out answers before questions have been completed, make comments out of turn, initiate conversations at inappropriate times, and have difficulty waiting for their turn.

- Children often interrupt or intrude on others, grab objects from others, touch things they are not supposed to touch, and clown around. Impulsivity may lead to accidents and engaging in potentially dangerous activities without considering the possible consequences.

In adolescents and adults, the behavioral symptoms of hyperactivity may subside, and are often replaced by feelings of restlessness, fidgetiness, or an inner feeling of jitteriness and discomfort in situations that require sedentary activity or sustained attention. Difficulty in sustained attention may persist into adulthood.

ADHD may often present as soon as a child learns to walk or move around independently. However, it is important that toddlers and preschoolers not be prematurely diagnosed with ADHD, since overactivity is a hallmark of this developmental stage, and many excessively active toddlers and preschoolers do not exhibit either inattention or hyperactivity during the school years. In general, ADHD is first diagnosed during elementary school years, when school adjustment is compromised.

It is also important not to automatically diagnose ADHD whenever a child exhibits excessive activity or inattention. This is particularly true in populations of maltreated children, or children who have experienced traumatic separations. Inattention and overactivity, particularly in a school setting, are common symptoms of anxiety in children, and may reflect a pressing preoccupation with other worries and concerns. Inattention is also common when children are inappropriately placed in academic settings, either from boredom because they are not sufficiently challenged, or in response to feeling overwhelmed because the classroom demands exceed their intellectual ability. Children from chaotic and disorganized home environments may also exhibit disorganized and chaotic behavior, and may not be able to sustain goal-directed behavior. Finally, some individuals may resist work or school tasks that require self-application because they are unwilling to conform to others' demands. Most children with ADHD fail to conform to expectations because they cannot...not because they don't want to. However, after years of negative responses to their disruptive behaviors, many children and youths with ADHD develop negative and oppositional attitudes about school, work, and conforming to social expectations.

Early identification, proper diagnosis, and appropriate intervention are critical in helping children with ADHD. For many children, and for many adults who have had ADHD since childhood, medication can significantly reduce hyperactivity, counteract feelings of restlessness, and make it easier to focus and sustain attention. Ritalin, or methylphenidate hydrochloride, is a mild central nervous system stimulant that appears to have a paradoxical, calming effect in many persons with ADHD. Ritalin is the most frequently used drug to treat ADHD. However, in some cases it may exacerbate rather than reduce symptoms. (Many parents have also found their children to be unusually sensitive to many common chemicals in foods, and restricting their children's intake of preservatives, excessive sugar, and other chemicals also helps to lessen their hyperactive behavior.)

Treatment must include an appropriate educational placement, and, when appropriate, supportive counseling to help families understand the disorder and to learn appropriate responses. Parents or caregivers must first understand that their child's behavior is not under the child's control, and that punishment for hyperactive behaviors and inattention will often exacerbate the child's emotional distress. Parents must help the child set realistic and achievable expectations (for example, helping the child focus and concentrate for five minutes at a stretch rather than 25) and reward the child for small, but successful efforts at self-control and attentiveness.

There are a number of behavioral strategies that parents and caregivers can implement to help children with ADHD to better learn and adapt to their environments. Parents can reduce environmental distractions, including lights, objects, and noise when the child is trying to attend to tasks. Parents can direct children to take frequent, but controlled breaks, while working at a task. They can help the child to expend excessive energy in nonharmful ways, such as running outside rather than in the house, or throwing a sponge ball rather than a softball. Parents should intervene early in misbehavior, redirect the child whenever possible, and ignore less problematic hyperactive or impulsive behaviors. Positive rewards for small achievements is necessary to promote the development of self-esteem and self-confidence.

FETAL ALCOHOL SYNDROME (FAS) AND FETAL ALCOHOL EFFECTS (FAE)

In 1973, Jones and Smith described a distinct pattern of physical abnormalities and central nervous system dysfunction in 11 children whose mothers were chronic alcoholics [Jones & Smith 1973]. Fetal alcohol syndrome (FAS) is now recognized as one of the most frequent syndromes associated with impaired cognitive functioning. A less severe pattern of malformation that primarily affects behavior has been called fetal alcohol effects (FAE) [Caruso & ten Bensel 1993; Coles 1993]. The widespread use of alcohol makes it the most common major teratogen (environmental insult) to which a fetus can be exposed.

Incidence of FAS is estimated at one to three per 1,000 live births. Studies estimate that 10 to 20% of mild mental retardation and low–normal cognitive functioning are the result of prenatal exposure to excessive alcohol [Smith 1982]. Among alcoholic women who drink during pregnancy, approximately 35 to 40% of their infants will have fetal alcohol syndrome, and up to three times as many will have fetal alcohol effects.

The primary symptoms of fetal alcohol syndrome are:

- Prenatal and postnatal growth deficiency (failure to grow.) FAS children tend to be lower in birth weight and demonstrate generalized growth retardation. Average is below the fifth percentile for age.

- Typical facial features include flattened mid face, epicanthal folds on the eyes, short, up–turned nose, thin upper lip.

- An average I.Q. of about 68 to 70, which falls within the mild range of mental retardation.

- Irritability in infancy, hyperactivity and other emotional and behavior disorders throughout childhood, including attention deficit disorder (ADD), with hyperactivity (ADHD), and poor social judgment.

- Mild to moderate degrees of microcephaly. (Microcephaly is small head circumference. It is usually associated with varying degrees of mental retardation and abnormal brain development.)

- Dysfunction in fine motor control, such as weak grasp, poor eye–hand coordination, and tremulousness.

Fetal alcohol effects (FAE) is generally the diagnosis when there are few physical deformities and the child does not meet the criteria for FAS. However, these children do manifest many of the behavioral and central nervous system disturbances, such as attention deficit disorder (ADD), with hyperactivity (ADHD), poor social judgment, and delayed learning. These children also have a subnormal I.Q., which helps to differentiate them from children with ADD or ADHD from other causes [Caruso & ten Bensel 1993].

Research suggests that the extent of disability is highly correlated with the amount of prenatal exposure to alcohol. Low infant birth weight has been associated with maternal ingestion of as few as two drinks per day. With four to six drinks per day, additional clinical symptoms become more evident. Heavy maternal alcohol consumption is generally defined as five or more drinks per day. The most severe effects of FAS were seen in children born to alcoholic women whose average intake was eight to 10 drinks per day or more.

It is sometimes difficult to isolate the effects of alcohol on development from the effects of other factors. Mothers of FAS children frequently have no prenatal care, and take other drugs, such as cocaine and/or marijuana. Many studies report that FAS/FAE children seldom remain with their birth mothers; a high percentage are placed in foster care, relatives' homes, or are adopted [Caruso & ten Bensel 1993]. In one study, many FAS infants were reportedly taken from their alcoholic mothers because of constant neglect or the risk of severe deprivation; some were institutionalized because of acute life-threatening circumstances [Spohr et al. 1993]. These factors would be likely to exacerbate the developmental problems resulting from prenatal alcohol exposure.

Longitudinal and follow-up studies of children with fetal alcohol syndrome suggest that as these children grow, the characteristic physical features and minor physical abnormalities diminish or disappear, and there is improvement in internal organ functions, growth patterns, and skeletal abnormalities. However, the prognosis for cognitive and emotional development is not as good. Most children remained mentally retarded. In addition, several psychological disorders were common, including conduct disorders, hyperkinetic and attention deficit disorders, emotional disorders, speech disorders, and problems in social relationships. In general, the greater the prenatal exposure to alcohol, the greater the severity and duration of intellectual and emotional impairment [Steinhausen et al. 1973; Spohr et al. 1973].

Recommended interventions include:

- Preventive education and counseling to pregnant women regarding the risks to their babies from ingesting alcohol during pregnancy. It is important to note that the most susceptible period in embryonic development to alcohol abuse is from day nine to day 41–often before the mother is even aware she is pregnant [Caruso & ten Bensel 1993]. This does not suggest, however, that drinking later in pregnancy is safe.

- Referral of pregnant women who abuse alcohol to medical services and alcoholism programs to help them reduce or eliminate alcohol consumption during pregnancy.

- Developmental assessment of children thought to have been exposed prenatally to alcohol.

- Referral of affected children to infant stimulation, early intervention, and special education programs. Children with FAS must be assessed to determine the degree of developmental delay or mental retardation. Educational programs should be planned accordingly.

- Training parents or caregivers to plan and implement activities that will address developmental delays and emotional problems.

- Appropriate educational programming. Vocational programs have been found to be more successful than traditional school programs in teaching youth with FAS useful living and working skills [Caruso & ten Bensel 1993]. However, case planning for each child should follow from individual assessment.

PRENATAL EXPOSURE TO DRUGS

The research is consistent in its reporting of the effects of fetal exposure to drugs, including crack cocaine, on prenatal and postnatal child development. Studies have repeatedly confirmed that prenatal drug exposure has significant negative effects on early infant growth and development.

In a review of several research studies published from 1988 to 1994, there were several outcomes consistently associated with prenatal fetal exposure to crack and cocaine, either alone or in combination with other drugs, such as heroin or methadone [Anday 1989; Azuma 1993; Chasnoff 1989a,b,c; Cherukuri 1988; Ross Laboratories 1989; Dobercza, 1988; Fulroth 1989; Griffith 1994; Hadeed 1989; Howard 1989; Kaye 1989; Little 1989; MacGregor 1987; Scherling 1994; Zuckerman 1989].

Cocaine–exposed infants typically had lower birth weight and growth retardation. The weight, length, and head circumference growth curves for these infants were typically below the 25th percentile. Birth weight of cocaine exposed infants averaged 423 grams less than controls. Infants exposed to cocaine also had an increased risk of preterm delivery, with gestation averaging 37 weeks rather than the typical 39 to 40 weeks.

Infants exposed to cocaine had a smaller head circumference. Seventeen percent of infants in one study and 21.4% in another study were microcephalic. A third study indicated that these infants were 2.8 times as likely to have a head circumference that was below the 10th percentile. Small head size appeared to persist at least through age two.

Infants exposed to cocaine had a higher rate of perinatal complications (immediately before, during, or immediately after birth.) Complications included mild abnormal neurobehavioral symptoms, increased meconium (the presence of bowel excretions in the amniotic fluid, which increases the risk of infection); tachycardia and other heart abnormalities, and impairment of orientation and motor activity. A high percentage of cocaine–exposed children had central nervous system irritability and abnormal EEGs during the first week. The brain wave patterns did appear to revert to normal after several months.

Crack was noted to be worse than cocaine with respect to adverse neurological signs and low birth weights. Also, mothers who used more than one drug placed their infants at considerably higher risk than did single drug users. For instance, simultaneous use of crack cocaine and heroin, or crack cocaine and methadone appeared to greatly increase the risks of negative developmental consequences. These infants were also more likely to need treatment for symptoms of withdrawal at birth.

Initial studies conclude that the effects of cocaine exposure persist into the toddler and early preschool years, with resulting problems in attention, cognitive organization, affect and emotion, socialization, and play.

Research suggests that children exposed to crack are often difficult to care for from birth. They are likely to be born prematurely, with all the risks normally associated with premature birth. They may be irritable, or extremely lethargic. They often have poor sucking ability that hinders feeding, and alternative feeding methods or schedules may be required. Their sleep patterns may also be irregular. These infants also often demonstrate poor or insecure attachment.

Chasnoff et al. [1989a,c] studied two and three year olds who had been prenatally exposed to crack. Their intelligence on standardized I.Q. tests was found to be generally comparable to the intelligence of children from similar environments, but who had not been exposed to drugs. However, the ability of the cocaine–exposed children to concentrate was impaired. They were distractible and easily frustrated, they had difficulty organizing and responding in planful ways to their environments, and they had considerable difficulty playing in unstructured settings. They appeared to be unable to organize their own play activities.

Howard, Beckwith, and Rodning [1989] compared 18 toddlers who had been exposed to cocaine prenatally with a control group of 18 premature children, who had not been exposed to drugs. All children were from similar socioeconomic environments. In the study, although the children exposed to cocaine performed within the normal range on developmental assessments, their developmental scores were significantly lower overall than those of children not exposed to drugs. The cocaine–exposed children also performed better in the highly structured environment of the developmental assessment than they did in free play situations; they appeared to have difficulty in structuring and organizing their own activities. The toddlers exposed to cocaine did not play appropriately with toys; they scattered and batted at them and manipulated them without apparent goal or purpose. They also engaged in significantly less representational play, fantasy play, or curious exploration. They demonstrated little initiative; many would play only if an adult initiated the activity. They had trouble playing with and talking with other children.

The drug–exposed children also showed little emotion, and were described as "joyless" and "dispassionate." They did not show strong feelings of pleasure, anger, or distress in appropriate situations; they appeared to be withdrawn, apathetic, and had flat affect. They demonstrated insecure attachment characterized by disorganization, rather than avoidance or ambivalence. They showed minimal anxiety and separation distress when left by their caretakers. Their attention span was significantly less than that of nonexposed children. Because of the demonstrated link between representational play and the development of language, the investigators anticipated problems in the children's later language development.

Many studies have also suggested that the quality of the children's home environments was often adversely affected by ongoing parental drug abuse. Children in substance abusing families typically experience neglect, physical abuse, disorganization, and inconsistent care. Chronic drug use distorts a parent's thoughts and perceptions, and affects memory and attention. Some physicians suspect that some children may also be further injured by breathing the crack–filled smoke in their homes.

In some respects, drug–exposed children reared by caregivers addicted to crack cocaine may be at significantly higher risk of long–term developmental harm than are drug–exposed children who are reared in drug-free environments. This is related to the often serious neglect and abuse experienced by children of addicted parents. The drug addiction is often so strong that it overwhelms all other considerations of either maternal health or child well-being. Children of addicted parents are often neither fed nor nurtured. They are often abandoned, or are left in the care of unreliable caregivers. They may be exposed to crime, drug dealing, and childhood prostitution. Family financial resources are often directed toward maintaining the addiction, rather than providing healthful care for the child [MacGregor, et al. 1987; Scherling 1994; Howard 1994;

Zuckerman 1994]. (Refer to Section IV-C, "Conducting the Family Assessment," for further information on the effects of parental drug use on child development and well-being.)

Intensive interventions are necessary if children exposed to drugs are to be successfully maintained with their parents without risk of serious developmental problems. The following strategies are recommended:

- Prevention is the best intervention. Pregnant women should always be counseled regarding the risks to their offspring of any drug use. Referral of mothers early in their pregnancies to medical services and substance abuse programs is essential.

- Thorough medical, developmental, and psychological assessments should be performed when children are believed to have been prenatally exposed to drugs to identify any health or developmental problems.

- Many children will benefit from infant stimulation, early intervention, and special education programs. They may require highly structured and consistent school environments. Low pupil-teacher ratios in preschool settings can provide the one-to-one attention that is often necessary to help the children acquire social and play skills.

- Parents and other caregivers should be trained to provide activities that promote healthy development, and can mitigate the negative effects of drug exposure. The home environment should be highly structured and consistent. Parents will probably need training in methods to manage the children's behavior and to structure daily activities.

The continuing abuse of drugs by parents creates a high risk of abuse and neglect for their children [Besharov 1994]. Parents should routinely be referred to drug treatment programs. They often need intensive education in parenting skills as well, specifically in providing nurturance and structure for their children. Several studies reviewed by Chavkin [1993] suggest that maternal drug users consistently experienced feelings of shame, guilt, and failure for providing inadequately for their children or for exposing them to drug-dominated environments. Some mothers are, therefore, receptive to therapy designed to help them build relationships with, and care for their children. Chavkin also reports that concern for their children's well-being has motivated many addicted mothers to enter drug treatment. Treatment must, however, be broad-based, and address the complex social, environmental, and emotional contributors to drug use.

However, we do not yet have longitudinal studies of sufficient scope to determine the long-term developmental implications for children exposed to intrauterine cocaine. Many researchers stress the difficulty in distinguishing the direct effects of prenatal drug exposure on child development from the effects of other maternal and environmental factors, including abuse and neglect resulting from parental polydrug use and addiction. Early data suggest that while a structured and stimulating home environment can foster secure attachment, and mitigate the impact of drug exposure on development, it does not entirely eliminate the long-term negative effects. Further study is necessary to determine the long-range effects of prenatal exposure to crack and cocaine on children's development.

LEARNING DISABILITIES

The term "learning disabilities" is commonly used to describe a variety of conditions characterized primarily by an inability to take in, process, express, and/or retain sensory information. Learning disabilities can include impairment in one or more aspects of a broad range of cognitive functioning, including attention, memory, visual perception, receptive language, expressive language, motor output, and higher order conceptualization.

The most common type of learning disability is known as dyslexia, which derives from the combination of *dys* meaning "hard or difficult," and *lexia*, from the Greek *lexikos*, meaning "pertaining to words." Difficulties with words and letters is called dyslexia, which can manifest itself in speaking, reading, or writing.

Many children with learning disabilities also exhibit behavior disorders, including disruptive behavior, hyperactivity, and difficulties in social and emotional interaction. Thain et al. [1980] believe that the combination of learning and behavior disorders represents a syndrome that includes these primary symptoms. Other theorists suggest that the associated emotional and behavioral disorders are secondary, and may be a consequence of the primary problem of difficulty in learning.

It is generally agreed that learning disabilities have their roots in brain dysfunction; however, theorists vary widely in their explanations of how this occurs. Some clearly object to the use of such terms as brain damage or minimal brain dysfunction, as these connote brain pathology. Alternative explanations for learning disorders can be made in terms of the existence of maturational or developmental lags, perhaps caused by failure to establish unilateral brain superiority with a definite pattern of hemispheric dominance, and of other constitutional origins, probably genetically determined, and unlikely to be the product of damage to the brain at birth [Levine 1980].

Considering the foregoing, it is not surprising that much confusion exists in diagnosis and intervention for the many conditions included under the rubric of learning disorders.

Learning disorders occur in boys approximately five to nine times as often as in girls. Estimates of the numbers of school children affected are as high as 10%. Learning disabilities should be differentiated from mental retardation. Children with learning disabilities are generally impaired in only a few specific cognitive or perceptual skill areas, while mentally retarded children typically show comparable degrees of delay across all developmental areas. Special education programs that provide alternative means of learning can help children with learning disabilities develop to their full capacity, while minimizing the effects of the learning disability. Early identification and intervention are critical to prevent subsequent social and emotional problems.

CONGENITAL MALFORMATIONS

"Congenital" means present at birth. Malformation refers to a structural abnormality of any part of the body, including all internal and external organ systems. Cleft palate; harelip; club foot, or other orthopedic deformities; extra digits, or missing limbs; and structural defects in internal organs, such as the heart or intestinal tract, are congenital malformations. Many are surgically correctable, and often do not significantly affect the child's development. Other conditions may be more problematic. There will be increased interference with the developmental process when malformations are not correctable, are severe, or exist in combination with other developmental disabilities.

VISUAL AND AUDITORY DISORDERS

These disabilities include varying degrees of dysfunction in the visual and auditory sensory systems, resulting in impaired vision or blindness, or impaired hearing or deafness.

Strabismus is a condition often seen in infants and young children, in which one or both eyes are abnormally aligned. Strabismus usually results from weaknesses or abnormal tension in the muscles of the eyes. As a result, the eyes may twist upward, downward, or appear to be crossed. Some degree of misalignment is not uncommon in infants and small children, as the muscles of the eyes are still developing. This condition often corrects itself as the child matures. However, if the condition persists after the age of two, surgical intervention may be needed to align the eyes properly. Without such intervention, the child's vision may be permanently affected. Any child who displays strabismus should be evaluated by a pediatrician or ophthalmologist to diagnose the problem, and determine the need for intervention.

Visual and hearing losses can also be associated with other developmental conditions. Both blindness and deafness can result from prenatal exposure to rubella. Meningitis and other infections that affect the central nervous system can result in hearing or visual loss. Severe blows to the head can cause brain damage and injury to either sensory system, resulting in visual or auditory impairment. Perinatal exposure to gonorrhea in the birth canal, if not treated, can cause blindness. In the past, the overadministration of oxygen to infants in incubators caused blindness from a condition called retrolental fibroplasia. The apparent inability to hear is also a symptom of absence seizures and of autism; however, in these two conditions, the problem is not in the auditory organ system, but in an underlying brain dysfunction.

Milder forms of visual and auditory impairment are generally modifiable or correctable, and therefore may pose no significant developmental problem for a child. The more severe disorders can seriously delay development when not recognized, or when left untreated. As with all such conditions, early diagnosis and intervention can greatly minimize the long-term negative effects of the condition on the child's development.

D. Services for Children with Developmental Disabilities and their Families

1. Conceptual Framework

2. Application

3. Case Example

Conceptual Framework

In the early 1970s, strong political and legislative advocacy resulted in a redefinition of appropriate services for persons with developmental disabilities. Historically, many people with mental retardation and other disabilities were cared for in institutions. Some were placed at birth, and others in later childhood or early adulthood, when their care became too challenging for their families. Parents who preferred to rear their children at home often could not. Many parents lacked the skills and resources to meet their children's special needs, and community–based supportive services were rare or nonexistent. For many years, the prevailing view among both professionals and lay persons was that institutionalization was in the best interests of persons with disabilities, as well as their families. In fact, one of the original functions of institutions was "to relieve the family of the perceived burden of caring for a child who had mental retardation" [Wikler 1986].

The broader civil rights movement of the 1960s and 1970s prompted a re-examination of society's treatment of persons with disabilities. Advocates were successful in gaining passage of federal legislation that assured people with disabilities the right to grow, be educated, live, and work in typical family and community environments. This legislation also required "reasonable accommodation," to enable persons with disabilities to have access to and function more independently in those environments. A proliferation of structural changes resulted, including the installation of wheelchair ramps at curbs and in buildings; installation of motorized lifts on buses; increased public transportation options; installation of electronic door openers; mounting telephones and drinking fountains within easy reach; posting signs and instruction panels in braille; and widespread availability of accessible bathrooms, hotel rooms, and apartments. The legislation also generated federal funding to support special education, as well as health–related, employment, and family support services, and created fiscal sanctions for noncompliance.

One of the most important outcomes of the advocacy movement was deinstitutionalization. Large congregate care institutions, once the placement of choice for persons with disabilities, were found, at best, to be overly restrictive, unnecessarily segregating, and incapable of supporting healthy development. At worst, these institutions were destructive and dehumanizing environments, that frequently failed to meet even the most basic of human needs. Many persons with disabilities were subsequently discharged from institutions into community-based living environments, and many of the institutions were permanently closed. Unfortunately, many communities lack the array of supportive services needed by many persons with developmental disabilities.

These changes have had a profound impact on the nature of services to children with developmental disabilities and their families. The goal for all children with disabilities is to provide a healthy, developmentally stimulating environment, in a family setting whenever possible, with community-based supportive services to meet the child's special needs. This goal is entirely consistent with the goals and premises of a family-centered approach to services for abused and neglected children. To achieve this goal, we must understand the family's service needs, and we must develop and provide a wide array of developmental, therapeutic, and supportive services. Since children with disabilities have the same fundamental needs as all children, we can serve them effectively within the framework of other family-centered services, with linkage to special services as needed. We must also understand the unique stresses and needs experienced by families parenting children with developmental disabilities, and we must address these special needs as well.

CRISIS INTERVENTION THEORY

Crisis intervention theory is particularly useful in understanding a family's response to a child with a disability, and in assessing their strengths and service needs [Parad & Caplan 1965; Wikler 1986; Dyson 1991; Beckman 1983].

Crisis intervention theory is based upon the interaction of three dynamics that together cause crisis: 1) the nature and severity of the stress experienced by a family; 2) the family's coping strategies, including the supports and resources available to them; and 3) the family members' perceptions of their situation.

Stress

McCubbin and Patterson [1983] describe a stressor as a "life event or transition impacting upon the family unit which produces, or has the potential of producing, change in the family social system." Stress is a state that arises when there is an imbalance between a demand for change and a person's inherent resources to cope with that change. The presence of a child with a developmental disability should be considered a potential stress factor for nearly all families. At times, the stresses associated with caregiving may become severe enough to precipitate a family crisis. Such crises may place a child at higher risk of abuse or neglect [Petr & Barney 1993].

Several factors have been shown to correlate with increased stress in families of children with developmental disabilities. It must be remembered that a stressful event does not, by itself, determine the degree of psychological distress experienced by family members. The relative weight of any stressor must be determined within a context that also considers: 1) whether the family has sufficient resources and supports to cope with the stressor; and 2) the family's perception of the meaning of the stressful event, including their perception of its effects on family life. The responses of different families to comparable events will vary considerably. Thus, while the factors listed below may generally increase the likelihood of family distress, each family's response must be evaluated individually.

- *The degree and severity of the child's disability.* A chronic (long-term) or severe condition tends to result in more stress, than a condition that is correctable or of less severity. In general, the more the child's disability limits the child's functioning and interferes with normal growth and development, the greater the potential for family distress.

- *The child's life expectancy.* Family stress can be considerably greater when a condition, such as cystic fibrosis or internal organ deformities, is life-threatening, or is likely to reduce a child's life expectancy. The stress is especially acute if the quality of the parents' care can influence the child's survival.

- *The degree of specialized care required.* Some disabling conditions require considerable special care, often creating excessive demands on the caregiver. Feeding, bathing, toileting, and transporting a child may be time-consuming and difficult tasks for family members, and may disrupt normal family routines and activities. Children with disabilities may be more dependent upon other people for a long period of time, and some persons with disabilities require nursing care for life. This can place additional stress on the family.

- *Visibility.* A condition that is highly visible, or results in an unusual physical appearance often evokes unpleasant reactions from other people. Parents of children with disabilities are regularly confronted with negative stereotypic attitudes about their children, and inappropriate behavior from strangers. Wikler [1986] suggests that the stigma associated with mental retardation in our society is a constant stress factor for families throughout the child's life, particularly when friends and extended family members display negative attitudes toward and about the child.

- *The child's temperament and responsiveness.* Research has suggested that family stress may be related to the child's temperament, and particularly to the child's ability to give and receive affection. As would be expected, children who were more socially responsive, affectionate, and less demanding were rated less stressful by their caregivers than children who were difficult to satisfy, and who were socially nonresponsive and unable to reciprocate affection [Beckman 1983; Wikler 1986].

- *The presence of stressors unrelated to the child's condition.* The total amount of life stress experienced by a family, including stresses not directly related to the child's disability, can contribute to the development of crisis. A family with limited income, or multiple other problems, may experience the effects of a child's developmental disability with more intensity than a family that has few other sources of stress.

Coping

Families have varying capacities to cope with stress. Families that have a variety of coping skills and strategies can generally mitigate stress, maintain stability, and prevent crisis. Families with limited coping capacity are much more likely to experience a stressful event as a psychological crisis.

Several factors can affect a family's ability to cope with stress. First, families with considerable skill in constructive planning and problem solving are generally less vulnerable to stress, and more likely to manage their situation effectively. A family with a history of successful management of stress or illness may be more likely to respond with more confidence, as they can draw upon a repertoire of effective coping skills. Conversely, families whose coping abilities are limited, or who are already overtaxed from other problems, are more vulnerable to the effects of even minor stresses. The unusual needs of a child with a disability can promote crisis in these families.

The availability of emotional support, and access to community resources are significant assets in managing stress. Conversely, the absence of such resources and supports can greatly exacerbate stress. Wikler [1986] reports several coping strategies that are correlated with decreased stress in families that have children with disabilities. These include: the ability to organize formal support networks, such as parent associations; regular contact with a supportive kinship network; frequent church contact and a strong personal belief system; and a satisfying marital relationship prior to the birth of the child. Unfortunately, social isolation is a frequent occurrence in families of children with mental retardation and other disabilities. These families have been found to have a diminished circle of acquaintances; they belong to fewer organizations; they share fewer leisure time activities; and they lack vacation and respite time [Wikler 1986].

Perception of the Situation

The family's perception of their situation also influences the degree of distress experienced by the family. Rapoport [1965] contends that stresses are generally perceived in one of three characteristic ways, and that this perception affects the emotional response to the stressor. Stress can be perceived as a threat, with resulting fear and anxiety; it can be perceived as a loss, with resulting grief and depression; or it can be perceived as a challenge, with increased productive coping responses.

A child with a disability may be perceived as a threat to the family in many ways. Normal family routines may be permanently disrupted. Parents may have to quit jobs to care for their child, resulting in lowered family income. Relationships between spouses, siblings, and with extended family members may become strained and conflictual. Siblings may feel threatened by the increased time and attention paid to the child with the disability. Parents may experience a threat to their own self-esteem and parenting competence, particularly if their parenting activities appear to have little positive effect on the child's health or development.

Most families also feel some degree of loss when they have a child with a disability. Losses may be concrete, such as the loss of time for a spouse, other children, or themselves; loss of financial stability; or loss of personal freedom and mobility for the parents. Losses may also be entirely psychological, such as parents grieving the loss of the child they might have had. Such feelings are normal in the early stages of adapting to a child with a disability, and an initial period of mourning is to be expected. Mourning beyond the initial period, however, is commonly referred to as chronic sorrow. In families where this occurs, chronic depression may interfere with the family's ability to cope.

If stressors are perceived primarily as a challenge, families are more likely to be mobilized to respond with positive, goal-directed, problem-solving activity. This goal-oriented mobilization is often directed toward providing experiences that help the child develop to his or her potential; to provide experiences in which family members can interact with and enjoy one another; and to assure that the developmental and emotional needs of other family members are met. This is effective both in its positive effects for the child with a disability, and in reducing the family's susceptibility to crisis.

Wikler [1986] reports congruence in the literature on the effects of several common parental perceptions on parental stress. First, mothers appear to perceive their mentally retarded child as more of a hardship in direct proportion to their child's level of incapacitation and helplessness. Similarly, mothers' ability and enthusiasm for caregiving are adversely affected when the mothers perceive their children as unaffectionate and undemonstrative. Lower I.Q. levels of the child are related to increased stress and more frequent placement. Parents' social values, social standing, and socioeconomic class also can affect the ways in which they perceive mental retardation. In general, parents with higher levels of education tend to perceive mental retardation as more of a "tragedy." Wikler suggests that the "impact of the child's retardation may be triggered less by the child's capacity as measured on an absolute scale than by the discrepancy between the *actual* performance and the *expected* performance." Fathers reportedly have increased difficulty coping with mental retardation when the child is male; their perception seems to be related to concerns about the eventual performance of their sons in roles outside of the home. Wikler also reports that while parents generally appear to have accurate perceptions of their child's capabilities, there are "some dramatic exceptions."

A parent's perception of the impact a child with a disability has on the family may also be distorted. For example, a mother who must expend considerable effort caring for a child with special needs may feel that doing so is damaging to her other children. She may feel both anxious and depressed. However, reality may be quite different from her perception of it. Her children may gain emotional gratification by helping her care for their sibling; they may receive considerable attention and affection from grandparents and extended family members; and they may not equate their mother's lack of time with a lack of love for them. When helped to examine the situation from a more accurate perspective, the mother may realize that, while her concern remains valid, the real effect is considerably less than imagined.

Many parents' unrealistic fears and concerns are exacerbated by widely held negative attitudes, stereotypes, and misconceptions about persons with developmental disabilities. Attitudes such as, "This is permanent; it will never be better;" "This is a terrible tragedy;" "Persons with disabilities can never live normal lives... function independently...live in the community...get around on their own..." and others, create hopelessness and despair. The truth is often far different than the stereotypes would suggest. With developmental services and supportive resources, and with the benefits of technology, many persons with disabilities can, and do, live in independent or semi–independent situations. They learn and grow. They develop self–help skills. They may work, either in the community or sheltered job settings. And they enjoy and benefit from typical family and community activities. Only a very small percentage of persons with developmental disabilities require extensive, long–term nursing care.

Helping families achieve a realistic perception of their situation includes recognizing how their perceived fears and losses may increase their stress; recognizing and learning to trust their own strengths and internal resources; developing positively realistic expectations for their children's growth; and learning to view their situation as an achievable challenge, with potentially positive outcomes for themselves and their children.

SERVICE NEEDS OF FAMILIES OF CHILDREN WITH DISABILITIES

Services for families of children with disabilities must address all three factors of the crisis equation: the reduction of situational and psychological stress; strengthening a family's ability to cope and to access supportive services and resources; and, helping the family achieve a realistic perception of their situation.

The service needs of families with children who have developmental disabilities typically fall into several major categories.

When the child's condition has a medical or physiological component, ongoing medical care, monitoring and supervision, and/or rehabilitation services are necessary. The nature of the child's medical condition must be accurately assessed and continually reevaluated. Therapeutic interventions must be closely monitored. Families may need special medical equipment and medications. In some situations, the most appropriate specialized medical resources may only be available in a large hospital or other specialized clinic located far from the family's home.

The special needs of many children with disabilities can create serious financial stresses for their families. Even with health insurance, the costs of care and management can become immense. The family may have to incur child care costs, or one parent may have to quit work to care for the child. Additional money may be needed for rehabilitative and therapeutic equipment, such as wheelchairs, braces, hearing aids, feeding utensils, and hospital beds. Homes may need to be renovated for wheelchair access. Total costs often exceed a family's financial resources. Although financial assistance programs are available, many families will need help in locating and applying for financial help. Again, because these special services are not available in many communities, travel costs may increase.

When a child's disability precludes the child's involvement in typical childhood activities, special educational and recreational resources may be needed to promote healthy development. Such activities will change as the child grows. In infants, developmental activities will be needed to master sensory and motor skills, and to stimulate cognitive development. As the child reaches preschool and school age, opportunities to develop positive peer relationships, and to acquire social and self-help skills become important. If the adolescent with a disability is to be emancipated to semi-supervised or semi-independent living, self-care and home management skills must be learned. Throughout the child's life, the child should be involved in activities that are pleasurable, and that enhance self-esteem and accomplishment. Special service programs may include infant stimulation, structured preschool, individual skill development, recreational programs, group socialization programs, special educational experiences, and work-study programs. These should be carefully planned to meet the needs of each child, combining these with participation in as many typical family community activities as possible.

Even when services are readily available, managing them is often a complicated process. Many families need a variety of services offered through multiple agencies, and locating and accessing the most appropriate services is typically time consuming and stressful. Most families are unfamiliar with service systems and rules of eligibility, and they may become overwhelmed with the discouraging routine of seemingly endless referrals. Once service needs are identified, careful planning and coordination are essential to prevent the frustration associated with service gaps and overlaps, agency-hopping, and dead ends. Having a relationship with a primary caseworker who provides case management, advocacy, and interagency coordination can significantly reduce the family's stress.

Respite care is an essential service for many families. Respite care refers to child care provided by someone other than the parents or primary caregiver, allowing the family a period of relief from the stresses associated with the care of the child. The child may be placed temporarily in a substitute-care family, or a formal child care facility. In-home child care services can also be provided. The respite period may be a few hours to several days in length. Extended respite allows family members to take vacations, to give parents time to themselves, or to enable parents to give special attention to their other children. Respite care helps to avert crisis by intermittently relieving tension, reducing stress, and allowing families to rebuild their strengths.

Most parents will need specialized training to learn how to meet their child's special needs. This may include using special equipment to manage medical conditions, techniques to feed their child, or strategies to enhance their child's mobility. Formal therapeutic programming often must be maintained by parents at home through physical exercises or other types of programmed stimulation. Parents must also recognize warning signs of medical problems, and they must learn to manage unusual behaviors.

Finally, family responses to the presence of a child with a disability vary. In some families, members develop increased strength and cohesion. In others, there is a painful disruption of family relationships, high levels of grief and anxiety, and an inability to function effectively. Some families will require considerable supportive and therapeutic counseling to help them deal with their feelings, and to understand and resolve the resulting problems. Other families manage well from day to day, but may need supportive intervention when confronted with new problems and challenges as the child grows. The help of a knowledgeable counselor, the opportunity to resolve issues that interfere with family interaction, and the opportunity to participate in support groups with other parents can reduce stress and strengthen family integrity.

Application

Child welfare agencies regularly serve a large number of children with developmental disabilities. Most of these children enter the child welfare system as a result of abuse or neglect, or because they need temporary or permanent care. Because developmental disabilities have typically been perceived as secondary to the primary presenting problems of abuse and neglect, services for children with disabilities have not always been formally integrated into child welfare programs. When available, these services may be poorly planned or inconsistently applied, and delivery often depends upon the ingenuity and determination of the individual worker or agency. If we are to maintain children with disabilities in family and community settings, we must advocate for and deliver supportive, developmental, and therapeutic services to these children and their biological, foster, and adoptive families.

SERVICES

Many regular child welfare services are appropriate for children with disabilities and their families, and some could routinely be made available with little or no program modification. Others could be expanded with few additional resources, and could be offered as a regular component of child welfare interventions. In addition, establishing formal linkages and service agreements with other community agencies and service providers can greatly expand the type and scope of services child welfare agencies can offer to the families and children they serve.

Early Screening and Identification

The preventable nature of many developmental disabilities, and the importance of early intervention have been previously discussed (See Section VII-A, "Understanding Developmental Disabilities.") Successful early intervention depends upon the existence of systems for regular screening of high-risk children, and the prompt identification of disabling conditions.

Many children with disabilities are first diagnosed in the medical system because of obvious physical problems. However, other disabilities have no immediately apparent symptoms, and a child's condition may remain undiagnosed for months to years. Most families will not recognize developmental delays, or understand their potential significance unless the delays are pronounced. Of course, failure to properly identify developmental disabilities makes it impossible to provide the early intervention services that promote healthy development and mitigate long-term negative effects.

Disabilities that are often not properly recognized or diagnosed include:

1) *Absence seizures.* These may be infrequent enough that they do not appear during medical examination. When they are witnessed by parents, teach-

ers, or other caregivers, they are often mistaken for daydreaming or inattention.

2) *Cerebral palsy.* Mild involvement may not be evident at birth. The symptoms are manifested as delayed or abnormal motor development as the child grows. Some of these children may not receive routine medical check-ups, and their parents may not recognize the early signs of the condition. Many children with mild or moderate cerebral palsy are not properly diagnosed until they are in school.

3) *Mild mental retardation.* While there is usually some evidence of early developmental delay, most children with mild mental retardation are not diagnosed until they begin school and demonstrate difficulty learning in an academic setting. Their delays become more pronounced as they get older.

4) *Autism.* Many early cases are misdiagnosed as hearing problems, or simply identified as emotional and behavioral dysfunctions of unknown origin.

5) *Learning disabilities.* Learning disabilities are generally first diagnosed in school. The child may be thought to be mentally retarded and/or may exhibit behavior problems.

6) *Psychomotor epilepsy.* The symptoms of psychomotor epilepsy include severe behavioral and verbal outbursts, which are often misdiagnosed as emotional disturbance or conduct disorders. Many children are punished for their behavior, not treated.

7) *Attention deficit hyperactive disorder.* These children may be thought to be willfully overactive and oppositional, and are often diagnosed with behavior and emotional problems. Identification of the disorder often occurs after the child begins school and has difficulty attending to academic tasks. However, some mild to moderate cases remain undiagnosed.

Child welfare workers have regular and frequent contact with a population of children at high risk of developmental disabilities. Many of these children do not receive regular or adequate medical care and assessment. Until they reach the age of mandatory public school attendance, the child welfare caseworker may be the only social service professional to have contact with them. Yet, many child welfare workers have no training in developmental disabilities, do not know how to recognize disabilities in children, and remain unaware of the importance of early identification and intervention. A minimum of training and education can adequately prepare most child welfare staff to recognize many disabilities and provide effective interventions.

To increase agency effectiveness in the identification of developmental disabilities, a formal comprehensive screening and assessment process can be developed. Staff can regularly conduct general screening for developmental delays in children on their caseloads, either by comparing children's development against age-expected milestones, or by using a formal screening instrument. A resource network of more specialized medical, psychological, and educational diagnosticians can be used for follow–up and more complete assessment. Children who show signs of developmental delay or abnormal patterns of development should be immediately referred for a more comprehensive evaluation.

Case Management, Resource Linkage, and Interagency Coordination

The purpose of case management is to direct families to those community agencies, programs, and resources that most appropriately meet their identified needs. Many families will need concurrent assistance from several service systems and professional disciplines. These might include: medicine, education, supplemental income, developmental programs, mental health and social services. However, these services are generally offered through an array of programs, which are not usually organized into a cooperative network. Most families find "service shopping" a tedious and often fruitless process.

In addition, some families may feel uncomfortable working with formal social service agencies. The identification and development of community–based and culturally appropriate services is helpful in assuring that families will utilize needed resources, and will continue to be involved with them after the child welfare agency case is closed.

Case management and case planning form the foundation of social service delivery in any setting. Complex family needs make case assessment and planning the essential first step in any service intervention for a child with a disability. Case management should be carried out by professionals who can oversee assessment of the child's and family's needs, set goals with the family, and manage the development of a clearly defined intervention plan. Workers must also follow up to determine the effectiveness of services. Case management professionals must be thoroughly familiar with community resources, if they are to guide families to appropriate services in a timely and consistent manner.

In addition to the usual range of family support resources, child welfare agencies must be linked to special programs and services for children with developmental disabilities, and should develop formal interagency agreements with these service providers. This will facilitate referral, case coordination, and collaborative case planning. Coordination by service agencies, with the family as a central member of this planning team, can greatly increase the effectiveness and efficiency of all services.

Respite Care

In a recent survey of biological, foster, and adoptive parents of children with developmental disabilities, respite care was one of the most frequently cited service needs [Petr & Barney 1993]. Respite care should be viewed primarily as a form of support. Locating competent persons to care for a child with exceptional needs is a major problem for many parents. Simple activities, such as grocery shopping or going to a movie, may not be possible for a family when appropriate child care is not available. Parental employment outside the home is often impossible.

Typical child welfare services such as homemaker, day care, parent aide, protective day care, emergency shelter care, and regular foster home care could be utilized to offer short-term respite services. Homemakers with special training could provide in-home child care while parents run errands or attend to other family responsibilities. Placement of the child in a day care or day foster home might enable a parent to work outside the home. These resources can also provide short-term child care. In situations of potential child abuse, protective day care can be incorporated into the case plan. Regular foster homes may also be used to care for children on a 24-hour basis for short periods.

Child welfare agencies currently operate substitute care systems that can be modified or expanded to care for children with disabilities who need placement. Families who have had experience in caring for children with disabilities could be recruited, licensed, and trained as day care or foster care providers. Many families in the community might be willing to provide substitute care for brief periods, rather than accepting placement responsibility for a child for weeks or months. Financing such homes can be supplemented by the usual babysitting fees paid by the family. The equipment needed for care of a child with special needs can often be provided by the child's family for the duration of the respite period.

Trained foster families can also be used as mentors to educate, train, and support parents in providing proper care for their children. Parents can learn skills to provide care to their child in the foster home, under the direction and supervision of specially trained foster caregivers. The direct involvement in caregiving can help to maintain the parent-child relationship, while assuring that the child's special needs are met. Foster families can also provide intermittent respite care for the family after the child returns home.

Respite services are not available in some communities, and are very limited in others. A comprehensive community network of respite services would be a valuable service addition in most communities, particularly if such a network could be funded, organized, and managed collaboratively by the child welfare agency, the local mental retardation/developmental disabilities service system, and the local children's mental health system.

Specialized Foster or Kinship Care Placement

Some children with developmental disabilities need longer-term placement in substitute care. Assessing the child's need for substitute care and planning for permanence does not differ from such planning for any child. Issues relating to separation trauma, visiting, and adjustment reactions to placement are universal. Foster caregivers for children with developmental disabilities must also have the skills and resources to meet the child's special needs. They may have to be specially recruited and trained. The home study for these families should be similar to that carried out for older-child adoption, with particular attention given to the family's prior experiences with disabilities, and the availability of external support systems. Families may have to be trained in medical management, special aspects of daily care, behavior management, and location of community services and resources. Foster or kinship care families will also need the continuing support of the agency and other foster caregivers to manage and plan for the child.

Adoption

Child welfare's emphasis on permanence for children with special needs has increased the numbers of children with disabilities available for adoption. Yet, systemic barriers to the successful adoption of these children remain. Misconceptions held by many child welfare workers and managers have been identified as one of these significant barriers. Coyne and Brown [1985] noted that:

> Developmentally disabled children are usually perceived as especially hard to place for adoption. This perception appears to be based on informal discussions among workers and on the assumption that seriously handicapped children are extremely hard to parent and thus less desirable to potential adoptive parents. Also, their adoptive placements are thought to be more likely to disrupt than those of other children

Wimmer and Richardson [1990] identify similar barriers. They state:

> Children [with disabilities] who were legally free for adoption were often not brought to the attention of potential adoptive families. Many children were not listed on exchanges or in photolisting books because child welfare workers, supervisors, and agency directors considered the children unadoptable. Social workers often feel that they would not wish to parent a particular child and question the motives of interested adoptive families. Eighteen percent of...foster children [with disabilities] had as their goal "permanent foster care" and 17% had "continued foster care" rather than goals that provided permanence.

Coyne and Brown [1985] collected data that contradict these assumptions. In a survey of 799 agencies in 49 states, eight provinces and the District of Columbia, during a 12-month period, 1,588 children with developmental disabilities had been placed for adoption. Of those, 44.5% were of school age, and 9.5% were age 13 or over when they were adopted. Only 26% were adopted by foster parents; at least 70% were adopted by other families. The majority of the children placed were mentally retarded or had cerebral palsy. Placement workers had identified 31% of the children as having mild impairments; 38% with moderate impairments; 18% with severe impairments; and 5% with profound impairments. Boys and girls were adopted about equally. Of these children, 66% were white, 14% black, 5% Hispanic, 4% Asian, and 2% Native American. Over half (53%) of the adoptions were supported by an adoption subsidy. The authors also reported an overall placement disruption rate of 8.7%. Disruption was only 3.3% when the children were seven years of age and younger when adopted; the disruption rate for children eight and over was 17.7%. The general disruption rate for foster parent adoptions was 4.4%, and for adoptions by a new family, 10.4%. The authors concluded that a large number of children of all ages and disabilities had been successfully placed for adoption, with a low rate of disruption.

Many child welfare agencies have modified existing adoption programs or have developed special adoption programs for children with disabilities. There are several factors in adoption programming that increase the likelihood of successful placement of children with disabilities:

1) *Recruitment and education.* Potential adoptive families have to be recruited and trained regarding the special needs of children with disabilities, and the special responsibilities of the families who adopt them. Targeted recruitment can help identify parents who have already reared children with disabilities. In addition, relatives and foster caregivers should routinely be considered as prospective adoptive families for the children in their care who cannot be returned home.

2) *Adoption subsidy.* The availability of subsidy money may determine whether a family can adopt a child with a disability. The adoption can be supported by providing the family with the necessary financial resources to fund medical and other special services.

3) *Home study.*The home study process will not differ significantly from any well-formulated home study for older children or other children with special needs. It should prepare a family for adoption, as well as assess their interests, capabilities, and limitations. Discussion regarding the special aspects of an individual child's care should be regularly included in the study.

4) *Postplacement supportive services.* Most families will need considerable postplacement follow-up. Support groups which include other adoptive, foster, and biological parents of children with disabilities can offer families a helpful support system and resource network. The groups also can be educational or therapeutic in nature. Adoptive families should also be linked to the proper community services.

5) *Developmental services.* Developmental services include activities that promote development, and provide compensatory strategies to help assure optimum growth. Developmental services should include a program of parent education in the skills and attitudes necessary for the care and management of children with disabilities. Topics of frequent interest include: behavior management strategies; leisure time activities; time and home management; how to access and use supportive community resources; issues of sexuality for persons with disabilities; providing for the needs of other children in the family; estate planning, wills, and trusts; coping with negative community attitudes and prejudices; and activities to enhance a child's growth. Parent education groups often provide a support network for the participants as well.

Programs that offer recreational and social opportunities appropriate for children with disabilities should be accessed. Many agencies operate children's therapy or activity groups. Inclusion of children with disabilities, where possible, into these peer groups can promote healthy social interaction and a beneficial growth experience for all participants.

Infant stimulation programs can train parents to provide developmental interventions. Regular participation can enhance normal development and minimize developmental delay. Preschool programs can address the developmental needs of many children with disabilities within the integrated preschool environment. Supplemental educational and recreational activities for children can also be provided.

Special Education

In 1975, Congress passed Public Law 94–142, The Education for Handicapped Children Act. Prior to this time, public schools were not required to provide educational programming for all children with disabilities. P.L. 94–142 required that school districts provide a "free, appropriate, public education" for all children with disabilities in the least restrictive environment. Individual Education Plans (IEPs) were also required, based on a complete assessment of the child's educational and developmental needs.

Since 1975, there has been considerable evidence of the benefits of early identification of children with disabilities, and of early intervention. In 1986, P.L.99–457 was passed, amending P.L. 94–142 to include children between the ages of three and five. The law set forth provisions to identify and provide intervention for infants and toddlers as well. These amendments are now known as the Individuals with Disabilities Education Act (IDEA) of 1991.

These laws set forth different service requirements for children at different ages. The infants and toddlers age group includes children who have diagnosed disabilities, as well as children who are at established risk because of a diagnosed medical, physical, or mental condition that has a high probability of resulting in developmental delay. Individual Family Service Plans (IFSPs) are developed to provide early intervention services to eligible children and their families. These plans are written with parental involvement and consent, and generally involve a variety of community agencies in providing these services. Every local jurisdiction has an interagency collaborative group that coordinates early intervention services.

Children age three to five who have an identified disability are eligible for preschool services. Parents and educators jointly develop an IEP (Individualized Education Plan) for these children, based on an assessment of the child's developmental needs. Public schools are responsible for providing preschool programming for these children in the least restrictive environment.

School-age children with disabilities also have an IEP developed annually. This plan guides individualized and group instruction, in the least restrictive environment, to meet the educational and developmental goals for the children.

The IFSP and IEP processes are based upon several underlying premises. Families are considered essential contributors in planning services for their children, and have the right and ability to make decisions about their children. These include, but are not restricted to, choices of services, location of services, and the providers of the services. Parents also retain the right to review and receive copies of their children's records, the right to participate in meetings about their children, and the right to request testing for the child by an interdisciplinary team. Parents can also request that someone else represent them at a meeting with school personnel. If parents cannot attend, a guardian for the child, or educational surrogate, can attend in place of the parent. If a parent disagrees with findings in an evaluation, or a decision made about the child's education, a due process hearing can be requested, at which time the parent's concerns will be heard and considered.

Parents have specific responsibilities related to educational and service planning for their children. They should be prepared to participate in the IFSP or IEP process, should participate with school personnel and other professionals in a collaborative manner, and should contribute information to assist in developing the most appropriate plan for the child.

The IFSP is, in many ways, similar to a child welfare case plan. Both address developmental goals for the child; both provide in-home and supportive services to families; and both utilize a variety of community service providers. The child welfare case plan includes an additional component, when necessary, to assure safety and protection for the child. When child welfare agencies serve children from birth to three, with or at risk of disabilities, the family assessment and case planning process should be conducted collaboratively with personnel responsible for the IFSP. Otherwise, there is a strong possibility of duplication of effort and confusion for the family.

Many parents will need assistance in negotiating the school environment, and in advocating for their child's developmental and educational needs. Petr and Barney [1993] contend that interventions to provide special education are a vital, but underemphasized component of efforts to maintain children with disabilities in their families; and, Barth [1988] found that special education problems were a critical variable in adoption disruptions. Advocating for children in the educational environment is an essential child welfare intervention.

Counseling and Emotional Support

Most families of children with disabilities will, at some time, need significant emotional support. The birth of a child with a disability can promote crisis in some families. Depression and anxiety are common. Considerable stress may be placed on the marital relationship, and siblings may develop behavior or emotional problems. In addition, children and youth with disabilities may also exhibit depression or anxiety, which contributes to behavior disorders. This may often remain unidentified by caregivers, and by some mental health practitioners.

Families of children with disabilities report several sources of emotional support. These include extended family, intimate friends, church contacts, neighbors, community groups, clubs, work place acquaintances, and human services professionals [Wikler 1986]. However, Petr and Barney's [1993] study sample indicated that parents could not always depend upon these resources for the consistent, reliable, and empathic support they needed. Rather:

> The most reliable and inspirational source of support was other parents of children with similar disabilities. These parents share a common bond that allows for understanding and support at the deepest levels. These relationships can enrich the total experience by helping parents see the positive aspects of raising a child with special needs, and by helping them appreciate their own personal growth... [Petr & Barney 1993].

This has significant implications for child welfare practice, particularly considering the previously mentioned finding that families of mentally retarded children are very often socially isolated [Wikler 1986]. Agencies should make extensive use of parent groups that include biological, foster, and adoptive parents of children with disabilities. Such groups can serve multiple functions, including education and training, recreation and leisure, counseling, and peer support. It is important that group affiliations be continued even after the child welfare agency is no longer involved. For this reason, groups should be sponsored and supported by agencies that serve children with disabilities, local community agencies, advocacy groups, and the parents themselves.

The caseworker should also be alert to the need for formal mental health counseling, and should help the family access the most appropriate service provider. The worker should be able to recognize families near, or in crisis, the presence of acute or chronic depression or anxiety, marital and family conflict, and other signs that the family is experiencing severe stress. Counseling resources can include professional counselors, members of the clergy, local mental health agencies, counselors through mental retardation and developmental disability agencies, and culturally specific community providers.

Advocacy

Advocacy is action on behalf of, or in the interest of others. There are probably as many different types of advocacy as there are arenas wherein people need help. Advocacy can assist in accessing services, in assuring maintenance of individual rights, or in negotiating complicated systems. The need for advocacy can reflect a person's inability to independently negotiate a system, as is true for persons with developmental disabilities; or, it may reflect the general complexity of the system, which may overtax the capability of most in the general population.

Some systems of advocacy are an institutionalized part of our society, such as the child welfare systems, the courts, and policing agencies. Others are of grass roots or citizen origin. Both may become legislated entities.

There are several types of advocacy. These include:

1) *Legal advocacy*, which is generally performed by attorneys, is an effort to ensure that the legal rights and entitlements of an individual or group of individuals are not denied.

2) *Systems advocacy*, which promotes the common rights of a particular population, by negotiating and altering a designated system. Examples are advocating for better conditions in a residential institution, or for the installation of ramp–style curbs on city streets.

3) *Citizen or volunteer advocacy*, which is carried out by individual community members who assist a person in day–to–day activities, and in negotiating service systems. Activities might include assisting a person with budgeting, obtaining adequate housing, filling out an application form, or locating a lost assistance check.

4) *Case management advocacy*, which is generally performed by professionals with case management responsibility for a family. These professionals ensure that the family's needs are fully assessed, they draw up and

implement a comprehensive case plan, and they locate and access the most appropriate service providers. Case management advocacy may require monitoring the services provided by other agencies, and intervening to assure that such agencies deliver what they have agreed to deliver.

Advocacy activities specifically for children with disabilities and their families should address the following objectives:

- Protecting an individual or group of individuals from abuse, neglect, or exploitation. This may include identifying when decisions to withhold or terminate care for infants with life-threatening medical conditions constitutes abuse or neglect.

- Promoting equal access to services and resources, such as education, employment, housing, social services, and health care resources; and assuring that resource providers make "reasonable accommodations" to enable participation of persons with disabilities.

- Promoting awareness of the rights and entitlements of a person or group, and ensuring such rights. This includes educating people about their rights, and assuring that service providers fully understand and implement their responsibilities under the law to provide specialized services.

- Ensuring physical accessibility to community buildings or services. This includes construction of ramps and wheelchair-accessible doorways, and making restrooms accessible.

- Ensuring that certain persons or groups are afforded a representative voice in decision making and legislation, particularly as it affects them.

The child welfare worker has many advocacy responsibilities. Protective service is an institutionalized form of advocacy designed to protect children from abuse, neglect, or exploitation. Part of a social worker's responsibility includes aggressively assisting the client in gaining access to and negotiating social service systems. Activities performed by child welfare workers when advocating for children with disabilities might include:

- Attendance at educational planning conferences with school personnel and parents to make sure that an Individualized Education Plan (IEP) or Individual Family Service Plan (IFSP) is developed for the child and family; and to assure that the child is not placed in a more restrictive, segregated educational environment than is necessary to meet the child's needs. This may also mean helping parents pursue due process when they are dissatisfied with a school's plan for their child.

- Supporting parents in their efforts to obtain appropriate services, including: evaluating and identifying the best provider or resource; initiating referrals; expediting the application process; attending planning sessions; and helping parents overcome obstacles caused by negative stereotypic attitudes and restrictive policies.

- Using professional influence to deal with systems to assure that the rights of children and their families are not violated; linking with formal advocacy agencies; and obtaining legal representation, when necessary.

5) Assuring that the child's best interests are reflected in the agency's case plan for that child.

6) Advocating for expedient and effective interagency coordination on behalf of the family. The child welfare caseworker, as a case management advocate, will often intervene to provide direction to other service providers to assure service coordination. Parent aides, volunteers, and foster caregivers can also be trained to serve in a case management and coordination role, once the case plan has been developed.

PARENT–PROFESSIONAL RELATIONSHIPS

Families in Petr and Barney's [1993] study had strong opinions about the qualities of professionals they found to be helpful–and not helpful. Most often, criticism of professionals was related to the perception that many professionals believed the children would be "better off in placement," despite parents' wishes to keep their children at home. While parents understood this to be based on well–intentioned concern for meeting the child's therapeutic or educational needs, it was perceived as intrusive and unwarranted. Parents communicated their desire that their children be integrated as much as possible into the "mainstream" of community life, so their children's lives could be as normal as possible. They wanted professionals to help them do so. This required avoiding labels and preconceived ideas about the child's disability, in other words, "see the child and not the disability."

Families also listed the qualities and behaviors they found helpful in their caseworkers. They appreciated when workers:

- Spent more time to get to know the child and family, to understand their issues, and to become a part of their support network before offering solutions or advice; and related to parents as peers and collaborators rather than as "distant experts";

- Demonstrated an ability to listen and show respect for the parents' opinions and feelings, and allowed the parents to disagree and have a different view without jeopardizing the relationship;

- Were not inappropriately pessimistic about the child's potential; expressed realistic optimism about the child's successes and gains;

- Avoided negative stereotypes and misconceptions, and helped families promote normalization and community integration for their children;

- Provided families with essential information to help them access special services or programs;

- Avoided unwarranted criticism or blame about what was wrong in the family or what the parents had done wrong; and

- Helped the family access services that could prevent the exacerbation of stress and crisis that could lead to placement.

Case Example

⚐ Elena

Elena was injured by her 19-year-old uncle, Tony, when she was seven months old. Tony was babysitting while Elena's mother, Diane, went grocery shopping. After Elena had cried nonstop for several hours, Tony picked Elena up and shook her. When Diane came home, she could not wake Elena. She became frightened and took the baby to the emergency room. Elena had suffered a severe subdural hematoma, or blood clot in the brain, as a result of having been shaken. The hospital called the child welfare agency, and referred Elena for suspected abuse. The case was opened and transferred to a family services caseworker.

The worker learned that Diane and Tony were relatively new to the city, having moved there from a small town to find work after their mother had died. They had no other family and few friends in the area. Their only relatives were distant cousins in another state. The whereabouts of Elena's father were not known.

Elena remained in the hospital. Diane visited her daily. As the days passed, the seriousness of Elena's injuries became evident. She developed seizures. She was initially severely hypotonic, with a serious lack of muscle tone, but then developed increasing spasticity. She was eventually diagnosed with epilepsy and cerebral palsy, both believed to be the result of a serious head injury from shaking. It was too early to determine whether she would be mentally retarded.

Diane was devastated. She reacted by angrily attacking the doctors, and demanding additional opinions. She threatened a lawsuit against the hospital. She then went into clinical crisis. She was alternately angry and profoundly depressed. She threatened to kill her brother, and then swore she would kill herself. The child welfare worker immediately called the crisis center at the mental health agency, and transported Diane to the first appointment. The crisis counselor saw Diane every day for a week, and three times weekly, afterward. The child welfare worker continued to contact Diane regularly, and confer with the crisis counselor. The crisis counselor helped Diane begin to deal with her situation. Diane said she was strongly considering placing Elena for adoption, since she did not believe herself capable of caring for a child with a serious disability.

The crisis worker and the child welfare worker met jointly with Diane to map out a plan that would help her eventually make a realistic decision about her ability to care for Elena. Activities included attending a support group of parents whose children had disabilities, run by the early intervention center in the local mental retardation/developmental disabilities agency. Diane then visited a classroom where early intervention and infant stimulation activities were being conducted. She talked with parents whose children were severely disabled, and with parents whose children were making significant developmental strides in spite of their disabilities. Throughout this period, the crisis worker helped Diane begin to come to terms with the injury to her child. The crisis worker reported Diane to be very angry, and deeply depressed.

The child welfare worker, concerned about Tony, asked Diane's permission to contact him. The worker explained that most people did not understand that shaking a child was dangerous, and wondered whether Diane thought her brother had intentionally harmed Elena. Diane didn't think so, but thought him immature, and seriously lacking in judgment. She was still too furious at him to even talk to him, and didn't know whether she ever could.

The child welfare worker called and set an appointment to talk with Tony. He agreed to meet with her only after considerable prodding, and the reassurance that his involvement would ultimately be important to Elena and Diane. The worker also communicated she was greatly concerned about him. When they finally met, Tony was extremely upset. He told the worker he felt totally responsible for the "accident." He cried throughout the interview. He reported being unable to go to work. He looked like he hadn't slept for weeks. With encouragement, Tony allowed the worker to schedule an appointment with the crisis counselor that afternoon. The worker transported him. The crisis counselor continued to see Tony for several weeks, and was eventually able to do joint counseling with Diane and Tony.

After several weeks, Elena was discharged to the rehabilitation unit of Children's Hospital, where she was to stay while she received physical therapy and ongoing medical intervention. The worker suggested that Diane stay with Elena during the week and participate in the rehabilitation activities. Diane refused. She felt if she were going to place Elena for adoption, she should do so, and not prolong the inevitable. However, she said she wasn't ready to sign any papers just yet, and asked to be left alone.

The child welfare worker arranged a joint meeting with Diane and the crisis worker to discuss Diane's concerns. During this session, Diane was helped to understand that her desire to place Elena resulted from terror that she would hurt Elena, and her despair that, if she retained custody of Elena, she would never have a life for herself. Yet, she could not bring herself to give up her child. The crisis worker assured Diane that her ambivalence was very normal, and that it was probably premature to make a final decision. The child welfare worker suggested a three-month trial period, wherein Diane could be taught to care for Elena, and the worker would help her plan her own life as well. At the end of three months, they would again evaluate Diane's feelings. The worker made it clear that whichever course Diane chose, adoption or keeping Elena, the worker would help her develop the best permanent plan possible for Elena.

The child welfare worker contacted hospital social services, and arranged for Diane to stay in a boarding home near the hospital. The agency paid the nominal cost for room and board. Tony offered to transport her each week so she could stay with Elena, and to transport her home on the weekend. Diane grudgingly agreed.

The hospital social worker involved Diane in the activities of the rehabilitation center. The physical therapist taught her how to exercise and stimulate Elena without hurting her. The psychologist talked to Diane about the importance of stimulation and affection, and helped her be less afraid of handling Elena. Under the guidance of the psychologist, Diane began taking over more responsibility for parenting Elena at the hospital. At first, Diane was very upset because Elena didn't seem to recognize or respond to her. With ongoing support from the psychologist, she continued to cuddle, hold, and talk to Elena, and eventually, Elena began to respond to her by smiling and cooing. This was very reinforcing for Diane.

When Elena was ready for discharge a month later, Diane was still too afraid to have sole responsibility for her. She wanted the baby to remain in the rehabilitation unit, and when told this was not possible, she resumed talk about placing Elena for adoption. The child welfare worker provided Diane with a third alternative. She located a woman, Eloise Watkins, through the mental retardation/developmental disabilities early intervention center, who had raised her own child with cerebral palsy, and who now did volunteer work at the center. Ms. Watkins agreed to care for Elena on a temporary basis, and to work with Diane. The child welfare worker arranged for Diane and herself to visit the Watkins home. After meeting Eloise, seeing her home, and meeting her 21-year-old daughter with cerebral palsy, Diane agreed to the placement.

The worker arranged for Diane to visit Elena in the foster home each day. Under the guidance of the foster mother, Diane took on more and more responsibility for Elena's direct care. At Eloise's prodding, she sometimes brought Tony with her. He had returned to work, but consistently expressed a desire to learn how to care for Elena so he could help Diane. Diane was initially reluctant, said emphatically she would never leave Elena home alone with him again, but eventually agreed to have him along.

Diane also accompanied Elena and Eloise to the early intervention center, where she participated in infant stimulation. Eventually Diane picked up Elena at the foster home, and took her to the center independently. As Diane gained confidence in caring for Elena, she agreed to a trial period with Elena at home. The foster mother and child welfare worker helped Diane acquire the necessary equipment she would need at home. Elena began going home for weekends. Finally, at age 14 months, Elena went home under Diane's care.

Diane received ongoing services and support from the early intervention center, and from the child welfare agency. She often became overwhelmed, but her brother insisted she become involved, and stay involved, in the parent support group. He also attended these groups, and he utilized the group support to deal with his own guilt and emotional pain. Diane kept contact with the crisis worker, and on occasion, went in for counseling sessions. The child welfare worker provided continued case management and advocacy to assure that Diane was linked to all the necessary medical and support services. She also helped Diane apply for financial subsidies.

Elena was enrolled in the county infant stimulation program under IDEA, where she could receive ongoing services. At the end of the three-month trial period, Diane agreed to parent Elena permanently, but expressed considerable fear about being left without support. The child welfare worker made certain that Diane remained linked to community support services before she closed the case. She called Diane periodically to see how she was doing.

Epilogue

Elena's seizures were eventually controlled by anticonvulsant medication. As Elena continued to develop her motor skills, she eventually learned to sit and stand with assistance. Her diagnosis was changed to cerebral palsy of moderate involvement, and it was thought that with continued physical therapy, Elena might be able to walk with braces. Early indications were that Elena would likely be within the normal range of intelligence. She was alert, interested in her surroundings, and appeared to understand words at about 18 months. Tony visited often, played with Elena, helped with her physical therapy, and brought her toys and books. Diane often called him to watch Elena to enable her to work around the house, read a book, or relax; however, she refused to let him stay alone with Elena, and continued to take Elena to the Watkins home for respite and babysitting. Diane continued to be involved with parent support groups, and other community services. She eventually began to talk about returning to school to train for a career.

E. CHILD WELFARE SERVICES FOR THE CATASTROPHICALLY ILL NEONATE

A Confusion of Responsiblity*

On October 17, 1991, a Superior Court Judge in Fulton County, GA, ruled that a hospital could not discontinue life support for a comatose child without her parents' permission. The judge ruled that the rights of the parents, not the child's best interests, were paramount in the case. The girl's mother testified that she could not decide what to do, but could not bear the thought of being held responsible for her daughter's death. Physicians had testified that the only sensation the young girl felt was pain, and that keeping her alive constituted child abuse [Columbus Dispatch 1991a].

What stance should a child protective services agency with jurisdiction in this case take? In passing the Child Abuse Amendments of 1985, Congress gave public child welfare agencies the responsibility to police bioethical decision making for catastrophically ill neonates. The public child welfare system was thus made responsible for assuring that bioethical decisions regarding medical treatment are in a newborn's best interests, and do not constitute abuse or neglect. Despite the 1985 amendments, however, public child welfare agencies have provided little or no protective services to developmentally disabled neonates with life-threatening medical complications [Barnett 1990; U.S. Commission on Civil Rights 1989]. This is not because clear and consistent decisions are routinely made for such children. In fact, hospital personnel, medical societies, and health professionals appear factious, and their decisions are not guided by a consistent, universally applied bioethical paradigm. Literature and research suggest that the majority of health care and child welfare professionals believe that the Child Abuse Amendments do not provide an adequate bioethical decision-making criterion. Most professionals either feel the Child Abuse Amendments are unclear, or they disagree with the Amendments' ethical premises [Chalnick 1989; Barnett 1990]. The fact that the child welfare profession does not have its own clear criteria for determining when "treat/no treat" decisions are "in the child's best interests," has likely contributed to the lack of protective service activity in these situations.

Since 1970, approximately 100 "wrongful life" lawsuits have been filed in the United States on behalf of children [Columbus Dispatch 1991b]. Typically, in wrongful life lawsuits, those bringing suit argue that for "a severely disabled child to have no life would have been preferable to one filled with pain and suffering" [Liu 1987]. Most lawsuits regarding treatment decisions for catastrophically ill children are, however, brought to continue treatment rather than discontinue it. These suits often contend that to discontinue treatment constitutes child abuse. Herein

* © 1993. Child Welfare League of America. Originally published as "Child Welfare Services for the Catastrophically Ill Newborn: Part I: A Confusion of Responsibility," and "Part II: A Guiding Ethical Paradigm. " *Child Welfare, Vol. LXXII*, 4 & 5, July–August and September–October.

lies the dilemma for child welfare professionals. How do child protective service workers decide what constitutes child abuse, in the milieu of treatment decision making for developmentally disabled neonates, with life-threatening medical complications? Do the "child's best interests" constitute the final criteria? If so, how can it be determined if it is in a child's best interests to continue, or discontinue, medical treatment? How is it that the child welfare system in this country finds itself with the responsibility to assure that decisions in the medical setting do not result in neonatal abuse or neglect, yet does not have consistent criteria to determine when treatment decisions are in a child's best interests? To answer these questions the bioethical issues involved must be examined.

Thousands of developmentally disabled children are born each year with life-threatening medical complications [Lyon 1985; Driscoll 1982; Todres 1977]. For each of these children, a decision must be made to provide or withhold vigorous medical treatment. For the vast majority of children, decisions are quickly and routinely reached to provide medical treatment [Shaw 1973; Duff & Campbell 1973; Lorber 1971]. But some of these children have such serious neurological problems, so limited a prognosis for social, emotional, and cognitive development, and so certain a prognosis for a short and painful existence, that a formal decision-making process to determine whether to treat or withhold treatment appears to be an ethical necessity. For some children, decisions are made to terminate, or not to begin, rigorous medical treatment. Reasons given for withholding or terminating treatment include: (1) treatment would only prolong the dying process and thus would be inhuman [Kuhse & Singer 1987; Mahon 1988]; (2) the potential good achievable from treatment would not justify the certain and horrific consequences of treatment [Fleischman 1986; Brennan 1986; Mahon 1988]; (3) the prognosis for the infant's posttreatment quality of life in the best possible scenario suggests that the beneficent option is not to prolong the life [Keyserlingk 1987; Fleischman 1986; Kuhse & Singer 1987]; (4) the limited potential benefit to the child from treatment would not outweigh the potential harm to the integrity of the family brought about by the child's condition [Berkowitz 1986; Mason & Meyers 1986; Simms 1986; Battle 1987]; and, (5) social justice or social utility would be better served if society's limited resources were used otherwise to more efficiently and effectively save and maintain life [Lister 1986; Taft 1987; Subramanian 1986].

These decisions can be complicated by a number of situational variables, including: (1) the neonates are often in life-threatening distress and require immediate medical decisions [Battle 1987; Lyon 1985]; (2) treatment prognoses are often inherently equivocal [Lyon 1985; Shelp 1986]; and (3) parents may be extremely emotionally distraught at a time in which rational decisions are vitally needed [Simms 1986; Davis 1986; Mahon 1988].

But these decisions are difficult for other more fundamental reasons as well. Although the Child Abuse Amendments clearly assign responsibility to the child welfare system, there is no consensus within the social work profession, or in our society, regarding who should make these decisions, or what the criteria for decision making should be [Lang 1985]. Before we look at the variously championed loci of decision-making authority in our pluralistic society, or the problems associated with our society's lack of a consensus-guiding ethical paradigm for decision making, let us consider the history of treatment for catastrophically ill newborns.

AN HISTORICAL PERSPECTIVE

Until recently, decisions to provide or withhold treatment for developmentally disabled children with life–threatening medical problems were made by the newborn's parents, within the guidelines and sanctions of their respective cultures and their own conscience. Literature provides us with details of such bioethical decision making through time and in diverse cultures. Most cultures appear to have adopted a utilitarian ethic. Decisions were often made after assessing a newborn's estimated future social utility–that is, after calculating the infant's net potential assets and deficits for the family unit or to society. Irrespective of the validity of the guiding ethical paradigm, these calculations were often characterized by ignorance and prejudice. Many children who were thought to be a net potential burden to their family or to society were allowed to die or were killed [Fraser 1976]. Plato, in the *Republic*, advocated the killing of children born with deformities in order to improve the state [Cornford 1945]. Toward this same goal, the laws of some Greek city–states called for infanticide of newborns with obvious physical deformities [Fraser 1976]. Several hundred years later, the Roman Seneca also argued for the routine killing of physically disabled newborns, a common practice in the Roman Empire [Lyon 1985]. Although Christianity generated some of the first sanctions against infanticide, malformed children were often exempted from protection. For example, while the Christian Emperor Justinian supported the church's sanction against infanticide in general, he declared that the fathers of malformed children could destroy them [Lyon 1985].

Although Christian theology in western cultures clearly evolved an ethic stressing the inviolability of life, secular realities of poverty, disease, lack of birth control, and limited resources combined to support decisions based upon utility. Infanticide for developmentally disabled newborns was a common phenomenon in western Europe during the Middle Ages, and continued up through the eighteenth and nineteenth centuries in England and France [Rosen 1976].

Selective infanticide of newborns was also a common and accepted practice in many non–Western and non–Christian societies. North American Eskimos, the Aborigines of Australia, the Maori of Polynesia, the Yanomamo Indians of Venezuela, and the Zhun–twasi Bushmen of Africa have all culturally sanctioned selective infanticide, especially of physically deformed infants [Lyon 1985]. It has also been a part of the cultural history of the Chinese and Japanese, and of the city–states of India [Rice 1990].

Although selective infanticide and the calculated withholding of support for developmentally disabled newborns have historically been condoned, only recently has the decision–making process informing these decisions become a public issue. This can be attributed to changes in the newborn's milieu, and to advances in the technologies of treatment. At the turn of the century in the United States, childbirth took place at home. Prevailing medical philosophy stressed nonintervention; the infant was protected from infection and otherwise provided with support, with as little additional interference and handling as possible. Most developmentally disabled children with life–threatening medical complications died under this philosophy of benign neglect. After World War II, significant technological developments combined to move childbirth from the home to the hospital, and to change the treatment approach dramatically. Nonintervention was supplanted by increasingly sophisticated interventions, including indwelling feeding tubes, and specialized neonatal surgical techniques. The 1960s saw the advent of electronic monitoring, respirators, sophisticated blood analysis, and the specialization of neonatology. Large numbers of catastrophically ill newborns who formerly would have died were sustained, although with varied prognoses. Whereas decisions to treat or withhold treatment had formerly been privately made at home by parents, they were now being made in public care facilities with a confusing convergence of shared authority and responsibility.

The mid-twentieth century also saw an explosion of sociomoral issues brought about by scientific and technological advances in the social, biological, and medical sciences. Bioethical dilemmas with respect to treatment decisions for catastrophically ill neonates became a public social issue as a result of these technological advances and the ensuing dilemmas of social justice. Bioethical review committees began to appear as a means of deciding moral issues. Sterilization review committees were established in the 1950s to protect the rights of persons with developmental disabilities. In the 1960s, dialysis committees were established to select the few among many who would benefit from scarce medical resources [Fox & Swazey 1978]. Federally mandated review boards were also established to standardize research involving human subjects, and to protect human subjects from the potential abuses of dangerous and/or intrusive science. The 1970s saw a considerable social and legal impetus for the formation of formal ethics committees to review decisions regarding the withholding or termination of medical treatment. The Karen Ann Quinlan case in 1976 was an important impetus in its recommendations that ethics committees be established to verify the validity of prognoses [In Re Quinlan 1976]. This trend continued through the 1980s. In 1983 the President's Commission for the Study of Ethical Problems recommended ethics committees as a means of resolving medical ethics dilemmas [The President's Commission for the Study of Ethical Problems 1983]. The Child Abuse Amendments of 1985 strongly encouraged the establishment of Infant Ethics Committees for all hospitals caring for newborns [U.S. Department of Health and Human Services 1985], and by 1985 the American Hospital Association reported that 60% of the respondents in a survey it conducted had institutional ethics committees [Hosford 1986].

The Baby Doe Case

It was within this social environment of increasing moral awareness that the case of "Baby Doe" focused this country's attention on the bioethical issues associated with treatment decisions for developmentally disabled children with life-threatening medical complications. On the evening of April 9, 1982, a child was born in a Bloomington, Indiana, hospital, severely hypertonic, blue from lack of oxygen, not breathing, with an erratic heartbeat. It was immediately evident that the child had Down's syndrome. Further examination revealed that the child had a constricted aorta, esophageal atresia, and a tracheo–esophageal fistula, a combination of disorders that would be lethal if left untreated. After consultation with the attending physicians, the parents decided it was in the child's best interest not to provide treatment, a decision that meant death within days for the newborn. Baby Doe died six days later.

Many similar scenarios have ended shortly thereafter with the death of a child in relative anonymity. The legal, theological, political, and medical machinations that followed Baby Doe's death, however, so focused attention on the medical and ethical dilemmas associated with treatment decisions for mortally ill, developmentally disabled infants, that henceforth, the Baby Doe case would acquire historical significance and notoriety. From the very beginning, those involved with the case were divided with respect to who should make the case decisions, and what constituted the proper treatment for the infant [Lyon 1985]. Three attending physicians consulted with the parents to facilitate their decision making. Two of the physicians recommended immediate and extraordinary medical intervention. The other physician, after considering the child's and the parents' best interests, recommended no treatment of the infant as the best possible case outcome. Two physicians believed the local protective service agency and the local courts should make the treatment decision. The third physician believed the decision should remain entirely with the parents. The Baby Doe case represented in microcosm a society's confusion and disagreement about who should make such life and death decisions, and what the decision-making criteria should be.

The Child Abuse Amendments of 1985

After the media attention given to the Baby Doe case, national politics began to play an increasingly important role in this bioethical issue. Both the executive and legislative branches of government became involved. Using civil rights legislation for its authority, and with regulatory initiative through the Department of Health and Human Services, the Reagan Administration strongly endeavored to effect policy that approached medical treatment of infants from a strictly deontological, or sanctity of life, philosophical perspective [Victoroff 1986]. The courts repeatedly found these efforts unlawful and set them aside [Barnett 1990].

The Reagan Administration then tried to promulgate nearly identical policies in the form of child abuse legislation. From early 1982 through early 1984, Congress grappled with various versions of compromise legislation to regulate treatment decisions for catastrophically ill newborns with developmental disabilities. Senators from across the ideological spectrum encouraged representatives of the various interest groups involved in this issue to negotiate a compromise amendment, which was passed by Congress, and was signed by the president into law on October 9, 1984. The Child Abuse Amendments (P.L. 98–457) and their implementing regulations became effective one year later [U.S. Department of Health and Human Services 1985].

This compromise was not wholly successful, due to the impracticality of trying to make two inherently dissonant ethical paradigms compatible, and due to the difficulty of enforcing regulations ideologically incompatible with the beliefs of the majority of the health care workers affected by them [Chalnick 1989]. The final law was one with which most of its ideologically divergent authors could agree, as long as they could disagree about the definition of key words and phrases within the amendment, such as "virtually futile," "imminent," "near future," and "merely prolonging dying." A final attempt by the Reagan Administration to insert clarifying definitions that were concordant with a deontological/sanctity of life ethical paradigm into the amendments ended as a compromise–the definitions were attached to the amendment as nonbinding, interpretive guidelines.

Although the law's wording and instruction represent a degree of compromise and, in some instances, are open to interpretation [Murray 1985; Barnett 1990], its content represents a significant success by those committee members who wanted to produce legislation whose content removed both "quality of life" and "social utility" considerations from the treatment decision making for catastrophically ill newborns. In practice, however, the results have been equivocal [Barnett 1990]. A majority of physicians, nurses, and other professionals working with catastrophically ill neonates with developmental disabilities disagree with the deontological/sanctity of life ideology that informs the final language of the Child Abuse Amendments. And, whether from differing interpretation, calculated noncompliance, or lack of enforcement, the law has not resulted in consistent treatment decision making [Barnett 1990]. In a report issued by the United States Commission on Civil Rights in 1989, Commissioner Robert Destro suggested that most states still were "not certain which children are covered by the law and which aren't," and that inappropriate decisions to withhold treatment for these children continued with tacit approval of federal, state, and local government agencies, and had resulted in potentially hundreds of "Infant Doe" cases since the passage of the Child Abuse Amendments in 1984 [U.S. Commission on Civil Rights 1989].

In contrast to the continuing uproar regarding applicability and enforcement of the Child Abuse Amendments, the fiscal consequences of noncompliance are relatively insignificant. States that do not comply with the amendments can lose funds under the Child Abuse Prevention and Treatment Act. These funds are relatively meager and, as a result, the financial incentive for compliance is not great.

Although the amendments do not provide clear and effective guidance, they do clearly enjoin states to assign regulatory authority to their respective child protective services systems. Thus, state and local departments of child welfare and individual workers find themselves with legal authority and responsibility, but without clear and effective guidelines, or the operational decision-making criteria they need to do their jobs.

THE LOCUS OF DECISION–MAKING AUTHORITY: WHO SHOULD DECIDE?

Although the amendments assign final authority to the child welfare system to police neonatal bioethics, society remains divided regarding the proper locus of decision–making authority. Many loci of decision-making authority have been suggested as appropriate–the parents of the child, attending physicians and other medical staff, infant bioethics committees, structures of the state, such as child welfare agencies and the courts, and theological institutions.

The Parents

Parents are considered by many to be the proper locus of final decision-making authority. Broad parental rights are a fundamental and established legal and cultural tradition within our society. Parents have considerable latitude in making decisions for their children in such areas as education, religion, and discipline. The legal and cultural traditions of parental rights, prerogatives, and responsibilities are based upon the presumed emotional bond and commitment of parents to their children [Battle 1987; Kuhse & Singer 1987; Cranford & Doudera 1984; Taft 1987]. It is often believed that this intrinsic bond and commitment will ensure that parents, more than others, will advocate for the neonate's best interests.

Although few would argue against the basic right of parents to direct medical treatment of their children, many do argue that parents should not have unconditional decision-making authority. Many believe that because of potential conflicts of interest, parental decisions cannot be assumed or assured to always be in the seriously ill infant's best interests. The parents' own interests, and the interests of other family members can impinge upon their decisions. In a universe of limited resources, some parents may conclude that the time, money, and emotional energy needed to meet the often considerable needs of a seriously ill newborn may be at the expense of other family members. Some would argue that in spite of these potential conflicts of interest, parents should still retain final decision-making authority, even though the self-interests of the parents or the family unit may potentially conflict with the neonate's interests. Proponents contend that parents have special rights and responsibilities that supersede societal goals when family goals are threatened, and therefore, parents may have the right and responsibility to subordinate a developmentally disabled neonate's interests to the countervailing interests of the family [Schoeman 1985]. The assignment of final decision-making authority to parents is often questioned and challenged by various factions of the medical establishment, by theologians and theological institutions, a plethora of political arenas, and in the courts, which clearly assert their responsibility to intervene in situations of abuse or neglect.

The Medical Community

The medical community is often considered to be the proper locus of authority for treat/no treat decisions for critically ill neonates. Physicians have historically assumed responsibility for many such decisions, both because they believed they had the responsibility, and because others had abdicated responsibility. There is considerable support in recent literature for a medically based locus of decision-making authority. Siegler [1986] writes that bioethical deliberation and decision making for newborns should be the responsibility of physicians and nurses in the neonatal environment, because this is where the "anguish of the moral dilemma" is played out. He believes experiencing this anguish is an essential element of the moral deliberation; therefore attending physicians and nurses are the proper locus of decision-making authority. Many physicians contend that the bioethical principle of "do no harm," derived from the physicians' Hippocratic Oath, requires that physicians make these treatment decisions, and advocate for the patient's best interests when conflicts arise between those interests, and the interests of other involved parties, such as the parents [Gustaitis 1988; Young & Stevenson 1990]. Brennan [1986] agrees, stating that neither parents, nor ethicists, nor jurists are familiar with the medical and emotional nuances associated with the care of acutely ill and dying patients, and therefore, the treatment decisions should be left to physicians.

Mahon [1988] contends that nurses have no choice but to assume a shared responsibility for making treatment decisions. Although physicians often write the treat/no treat orders, the nurses usually carry them out. These circumstances conspire to assign nurses moral culpability. Mahon contends that nurses should ultimately act in the child's best interests, even if such actions are in conflict with a physician's or parent's dictum.

By contrast, there are those who feel that final moral decision–making authority should not rest with physicians and nurses. The medical director of a large pediatric hospital reported that some children are "salvaged" because of the "professional challenge" such activities afford the physicians, rather than to meet the best interests of children [Battle 1987]. Some physicians believe that while it was an assumed responsibility in the past, physicians should no longer be the arbitrators of life–and–death decisions concerning developmentally disabled infants [Weil 1986]. Some feel that physicians, because of their positions of authority, have undue influence over parents in the decision–making process, and should not be making the decisions [Lister 1986]. Cranford and Roberts [1986] state that a physician's training affords little skill outside of medicine, and therefore, a physician should not be construed as possessing special abilities in moral decision making. Asch et al. [1987] cite the lack of consensus among physicians regarding treatment policies, and the possibility of conflict of interest, as justifications for not assigning exclusive authority to medical professionals in bioethical decision making for seriously ill newborns.

The Ethics Committee

Many authors have recently suggested that some form of an ethics committee on infants would be the best locus of decision–making authority [Asch et al. 1987; Cranford & Doudera 1984; Weil 1986; Lyon 1985; Ross et al. 1986; Hosford 1986; Cranford & Roberts 1986; Doudera 1986; Bioethics Committee of the Canadian Paediatric Society 1986; Victoroff 1986; Fleishman 1986; Taft 1987]. Although the suggested makeup of infant care review committees varies somewhat from author to author, and the makeup of existing committees also varies somewhat, most hospitals use similar guidelines for establishing committee membership. The aim is to include members representing the service providers (physicians, nurses, hospital social workers, and psychologists); representatives of the community being served (local community lay members); professional moralists (clergy, ethicist–philosophers); representatives of the state (child protective service workers); and legal experts. The rationale for using bioethics committees is that discourse among representatives of the various interests in a milieu of guided ethical decision making can best bring about consistent and just ethical decisions. This common–sense rationale would appear to have some intrinsic validity. In practice, however, the consistency and logical validity of various committees' recommendations is being questioned. The literature has little supporting documentation, and no supporting research for the conclusion that by assembling such a group, consistent and logical bioethical decisions are more likely to be achieved than with other, more homogeneous groups, or by individuals.

Lyon [1985] states that infant care review boards were founded to standardize treatment decision making, but in fact, have not done so. Many reasons are suggested for the contended lack of standardization and potential inconsistency, including the lack of philosophical sophistication of members of infant ethics committees [Wolf 1986; Siegler 1986]; the lack of medical sophistication of members of infant ethics committees [Brennan 1986]; and the utilization of different philosophical paradigms by different committees as guiding principles for decision making [Wolf 1986; Hughes 1989]. Wolf [1986] suggests that ethics committee members generally have no formal training in ethics, and are not experts in moral reasoning. She believes their decisions are suspect as a result. In research concerning the dynamics of decision making by an ethics committee on infants, Hughes [1989] concluded that inter-committee reliability can be significantly compromised because ethics committees lack a standardized guiding ethical paradigm. Thus, the neonate could receive differing treat/no treat decisions depending upon which hospital, which ethics committee, and which guiding ethical paradigm was used to make the decision. Siegler [1986] states that the usual ethics committee is an unmanageable collection of uninvolved professionals, who have no special expertise in moral reasoning; he believes that the role of interdisciplinary ethics committees should be education only, and the resolution of bioethical dilemmas should be left to committees of specialized nurses and physicians. Brennan [1986] argues for physicians retaining responsibility since "ethicists...are not familiar with the medical and emotional nuances associated with the care of acutely ill and dying patients." Despite suggested problems of subduction of physician authority and responsibility, and suggested problems associated with uninformed lay committee members, others warn against physician–dominated bioethical decision-making committees, and testify to the utility of more diverse committee membership. Victoroff [1986] warns that, in his experience, bioethics committees dominated by physicians are usually much less effective than those whose membership consists of a majority of other professionals.

The Theological Community

The theological community is an often championed locus of bioethical decision-making authority. Given the nation's secular government, a theological locus may never be a legally compelling authority; however, theological institutions may have ascribed authority, and are often freely sought and chosen for ethical guidance by individuals within our society. Parents who find themselves thrust by circumstance into situations where they must make profound and conflicting moral decisions often look to theological authority for guidance. Submitting to the traditional and absolute authority of theological imperatives in situations replete with ethical and emotional dilemmas can often be psychologically compelling and comforting. In addition, various voices within the theological community, representing various religious traditions, often do not accept a secular moral decision–making authority. Many theological traditions consider the ethical imperatives regarding matters of life and death to be transcendent, and therefore, feel that all involved parties have a moral responsibility to follow the tradition's guidelines for conduct and behavior [Ashley & O'Rourke 1978;

Francoeur 1983]. These guidelines are often believed to be absolute and categorical, communicated by God or other transcendent sources [Rosner 1983; Beauchamp & Childress 1983]. Problems arise, however, as a result of the inconsistencies that can result from attempts to interpret and utilize absolute moral principles as practical guidelines in situations replete with relativistic contingency. For example, while all Judeo–Christian traditions place a high value on life, practical differences exist among denominations in their normative rules of conduct. The sanctity of life is a common fundamental presupposition for many denominations of the Judeo–Christian tradition [Rosner 1983]. For many, adherence to this principle requires that an attempt to sustain life must be made, regardless of how heroic and extraordinary the effort, and without consideration of expenditure of resources, or the quality of the life that is perpetuated [Veatch 1981; Lyon 1985]. Yet, the *Declaration of Euthanasia* of the Catholic Church uses the premise of sanctity of life as a justification for sometimes withholding treatment. The rationale is that one must protect life's sacredness from the potential dangers of the humanistic excesses of medical technology [McCormick 1978], and when there is neither hope nor benefit for the patient, treatment may be withheld or withdrawn. Thus, nearly dichotomous interpretations can be derived from the same absolute principle.

With our societal tradition of strict separation of church and state, it is extremely improbable that any theological locus of decision–making authority could be legally assigned. The moral authority of theological institutions notwithstanding, any legal authority for a theological locus of decision–making authority will be derived from parental rights arguments pertaining to religious freedom prerogatives.

The State

Structures of the state, including juvenile courts and child protective service agencies, are viewed by many as the appropriate final authority for treatment decision making. Arguments for or against these structures of the state as loci of decision–making authority usually take the form of arguments for competing rights, compelling responsibility, or prescribed authority. Those who champion parents as the appropriate locus of decision–making authority argue the relevance of individual privacy rights pertaining to medical treatment, the confidentiality of the physician–patient relationship, and the supereminence of parental rights [Crossley 1987]. Physicians may claim moral responsibility and legal authority derived from historical professional guidelines such as the Hippocratic Oath, requirements and responsibilities related to the fiduciary relationship between physician and patient, and medical legislation. Religious institutions may claim a "higher authority," or authority derived from individual rights of religious freedom.

The state conditionally recognizes and sanctions these legal rights and jurisdictional claims through its various legislative and legal canons. Individuals may choose what they believe is medically in their own best interests when those interests are the only compelling interests affected by such choice, even if the choice is obviously a lethal one. Legislation and common law also generally support and protect parental rights and the integrity of the family unit [Garibaldi 1987]. There is also strong legal precedent supporting the rights of privacy and confidentiality in the physician–patient relationship [Gustaitis 1988]. Federal and state legislation prescribing professional medical authority, responsibility, and privilege is a significant part of our legal and social culture. Laws protecting religious freedom and supporting religious institutions encourage religious fellowship.

Yet, in addition to all of the above, our government has clearly retained authority to intervene to protect children from harm. There is a long-standing legal tradition of formal state interest in protecting children from harm expressed in the doctrine of parens patriae–the parental role of the state. Countervailing interests of the state begin at the point of viability of the fetus and newborn [Victoroff 1986; Crossley 1987]. The infant is generally protected by child welfare law from being put in situations at risk of harm by intentional acts of the parent or caregiver, by inaction, or by the parent's or caregiver's inability to protect the child. The courts have consistently ruled that privacy rights or parental rights cannot supersede the state's compelling interest to protect a child from serious harm [Sassaman 1983; Avery et al. 1978; Curran 1978; Damme 1978]. Historically, the public child welfare system, as the delegated agent of the state, has been given protective service responsibility.

The Child Welfare System

In a very real sense, the Child Abuse Amendments reaffirmed and precisely delineated what was almost certainly an already–existing, but neglected area of child welfare responsibility. The child welfare system's mission is to protect children from abuse and neglect, and in doing so, to always be guided by the child's best interests. This responsibility is not contingent upon the setting in which the harm occurs. Even though the milieu of potential abuse may be the strange land of a hospital neonatal nursery, and even though an assessment of risk may involve unfamiliar medically related variables, the responsibility for determining whether abuse or neglect exists remains a categorical responsibility of the child welfare system. In addition, local child welfare agencies are more and more finding themselves with primary legal responsibility for medical treatment decision making for catastrophically ill and developmentally disabled neonates and young children. In the last several years, the number of children born with catastrophic illness as the result of HIV infection has increased dramatically. Many of these children are abandoned at birth, or otherwise become the legal responsibility of local child welfare agencies. The agencies then have guardian responsibility for life–and–death treatment decisions. There will continue to be discussion and disagreement regarding the proper locus of decision-making authority. The Child Abuse Amendments of 1985, however, invest the public child welfare system with the responsibility and authority to police bioethical decision making for catastrophically ill newborns. This may be a well–placed responsibility, but it would require the child welfare field, at a minimum, to be able to employ a consensus-guiding ethical paradigm for decision making.

THE LACK OF CONSENSUS ON AN ETHICAL PARADIGM FOR DECISION MAKING

Assigning responsibility for decision making must be accompanied by an adequate, workable, and acceptable criterion to guide these decisions. The Child Abuse Amendments do not provide such a criterion, in spite of attempts to do so. The "best interests of the child" criterion, which is used as the decision-making criterion in other child protective service interventions, has not been operationalized for catastrophically ill neonates. There is no consensus regarding what would be in the best interests of children in these situations. This lack of consensus is not unique to the child welfare system. Our society has still not made the difficult, but necessary choice, of a consistent ethical paradigm to guide bioethical decision making for all developmentally disabled neonates with life-threatening medical complications, and catastrophically ill children are subjected to inconsistent treatment decisions that vary, depending upon where they are born, who their parents are, and who attends their birth. Until consensus-guiding principles are adopted, neither the child welfare system, nor infant ethics committees, nor any other potential locus of decision-making authority will be able to consistently and justly discharge this responsibility. The absence of a consistent decision-making criterion for the child welfare profession also makes it extremely difficult to challenge a hospital's treat/no treat decision for a severely ill newborn. Since the inception of the Child Abuse Amendments, few child welfare agencies have done so [U.S. Commission on Civil Rights 1989].

Treatment decisions for catastrophically ill newborns are critical decisions. They often require choices between life or death–choices that can involve pain and suffering. If one is involved, one cannot abdicate responsibilities. Doing nothing can be anything but benign, leading to the most dire consequences. Inaction *is* an ethical choice with moral consequences. If we conclude that child protective service workers have a moral and legal responsibility to act, we must have a guiding ethical paradigm to inform our decisions if we are to meet our responsibilities validly and consistently. A standardized ethical paradigm to guide our profession's activities is more than just a practical necessity. It is an ethical necessity. It is imperative that we develop a consensus bioethical paradigm to guide child protective service activities for catastrophically ill newborns.

Summary

The majority of these difficult bioethical decisions should properly be made by parents, with input from physician and health care workers utilizing the resources and guidance of infant ethics committees within the involved hospitals. The child protective service system should have the final authority, however, to assure that the decisions of the "caregivers" do not constitute abuse or neglect. This will require that the child welfare system sometimes walk the razor's edge between protecting the child's best interests and preserving, facilitating, and empowering families in these difficult circumstances. But this is an ethical dilemma the child welfare system negotiates daily, and is perhaps the reason used to justify assigning the child welfare system with this responsibility. It will also require that the child welfare field have a consensus bioethical paradigm for treatment decision making for children born with catastrophic illness. Consistent treatment decisions in the best interests of our most vulnerable children cannot be assured, or even expected, without such standardized guidelines.

A Guiding Ethical Paradigm

Each year, thousands of children are born suffering from a catastrophic illness and with a severe developmental disability [Lyon 1985; Driscoll 1982; Todres 1977]. For the majority of these children, formal decisions are made to provide treatment; for some, decisions are made to withhold treatment [Shaw 1973; Duff & Campbell 1973; Lorber 1971]. Yet, there is no consensus in our society about the proper locus of decision-making authority for these bioethical decisions, and there is no consensus regarding the proper ethical paradigm to guide this decision-making process—whether a child receives treatment may depend upon the place of birth, the parents, who attends the birth, or the local agency with responsibility to police these decisions. Without a consistent criterion with which to guide these bioethical treatment decisions, there are no assurances that these children will receive medical treatment in their best interests, or that they will not be unintentionally neglected or abused.

In passing the Child Abuse Amendments of 1985, Congress gave public child welfare agencies the responsibility to police bioethical decision making for catastrophically ill neonates. These amendments, however, in spite of their intent, did not establish a consensus regarding what bioethical principles should guide the decision making. As a result, child welfare agencies find themselves responsible for policing these decisions, but with no clear criteria to guide their actions.

JUSTICE AND CONSISTENCY

Since at least the time of Aristotle, the concept of justice has been an essential consideration in deciding the ethicality of an action. Justice, according to Aristotle, consisted of treating equals equally, and unequals unequally, proportionate to their differences. The just application of standards and rules implies their consistent application—"the right...to be treated alike." Questions of justice, according to Hume, Mill, and other philosophers, presuppose conflicts of interest [Benn 1972]. A claim of medical benefit or a claim of treatment rights is a claim most often based upon rights justified by some standard or rule of justice. Most ethicists agree that justice necessitates consistency in bioethical decision making, and in the delivery of medical services, and that an important aspect of the concept of justice is the right to equal treatment.

The right to equal treatment appears to imply that individuals in similar circumstances require the same moral consideration. Consistency in bioethical decision making, therefore, should be expected and demanded [Crossley 1987; Greenstein 1987]. For justice to be served, similar cases should receive similar consideration, and similar medical treatment. Fost [1981] advocates the use of a standardized criterion in ethical decision making for one essential reason—to facilitate consistency. Basson [1983] contends that traditional ethics insist on logical consistency in moral thinking, or else how could we decide between conflicting opinions or intuitions? Basson also questions how we can deal with a system that has no obligatory doctrine requiring that similar cases be treated similarly. He suggests that if this doctrine of justice is abandoned, the decision may as well be left to chance. Beauchamp and Childress [1983] suggest that an ethics system cannot be considered as such if it fosters inconsistent decisions, since it would not yield similar results when used by different persons, or even the same persons at different times. Brody [1981] suggests that inconsistency be the criterion for eliminating inadequate moral systems. He states that no one can claim ethical validity for a decision unless a rigorous and rational analysis proves that decision to be logically consistent.

Professional social workers with the responsibility to protect children should insist on the just and consistent application of bioethical decision-making guidelines in treatment decisions for developmentally disabled neonates with life-threatening medical complications. To do so, the profession must adopt a guiding ethical paradigm as the standard. Until it does, consistency and justice will be beyond the scope of its activity, and "best interests of the child" may mean many different things to the many child welfare workers who must operationalize this concept. How does one know, then, that what is being done is in the best interests of the catastrophically ill neonate?

GUIDING PARADIGMS

If consistency and justice in bioethical decision making are a necessity, then a guiding set of principles must be established and used to inform the decision-making processes. The philosophical discipline of ethics provides such a set of principles [Popkin & Stroll 1956]. Ethics as a discipline can be simply defined as the study of deliberate actions in an attempt to determine which actions are "right or wrong" and/or "good or bad." Child welfare agencies are, therefore, charged with the responsibility of making sure that treatment decisions for newborns are "right" and "good." The literature on bioethical decision making suggests that two conflicting philosophical paradigms are most often used to guide ethical behavior in society–the utilitarian (a consequentialist ethic), and the deontological (a duty-based ethic).

The Utilitarian Paradigm

Utilitarianism is a teleological ethic that eschews us to consider the consequences or ends of actions to determine the morality of conduct. States of being that are free of pain and infused with pleasure are considered intrinsically good. States of pain and distress are considered to be intrinsically negative. The rightness of an action is derived from its consequences; "right" conduct produces net benefit over harm. Utilitarianism injects a strong social variable into the formula for ethical conduct. The morality of conduct depends not upon the consequences of action for any individual, but rather, the net effect for all. In moral decision making, one must calculate the consequences of all discernible actions and inactions, and choose the one that will produce the maximum net social benefit over harm [Mill 1987].

The Deontological Paradigm

Deontological means literally "the study of duty." The deontological tradition in normative ethics defines "right" conduct as conduct consistent with duty–morally obligatory, regardless of whether its consequences produce human weal or woe [Kant 1959]. The motto, "Let justice be done though the heavens fall," conveys the spirit. Moral rules are believed by most deontologists to be universally valid and admitting of no exceptions [Olson 1967]. Some deontologists may go so far as to suggest that one moral rule may conflict with another in the world of human affairs. With respect to these moral dilemmas, however, an assessment of an action's consequences is not a valid moral means of disengaging oneself from the dilemma's impaling horns. The rules that deontologists hold in absolute regard may be derived from many sources: one's own personal communion with God, conscience, intuition, revelation, theological canon such as the Ten Commandments, and rational necessity, such as Kant's categorical imperatives [Kant 1959), or the discernible necessities of natural law.

Few deontologists refer to their guiding ethical paradigm as deontological. Instead their references are to "duty," "moral obligation," "normative rules," and "individual responsibility," all of which are often based upon obligatory rules of conduct and are, therefore, elements of a deontological ethic.

Although the sources of moral guidance may vary, the defining characteristic of a deontological approach is the reliance upon immutable rules for guidance in the decision making process. Rosner [1983] provides a good example of deontological ethics in his statement of reliance on the Torah for "eternally valid answers to even newly formulated queries." Rosner indicates that since "every moment of human life is also of infinite value," any life that can be prolonged should be prolonged.

A COMPARISON OF PARADIGMS

Each of the two paradigms has its advocates. Battle [1987] argues strongly that physicians should take a utilitarian approach when deciding whether to treat seriously ill neonates. She contends that many physicians are driven to save some children by the "professional challenge and their own egoist pleasure of success which reaffirms (their) own omnipotence." As chief executive officer and medical director of the Hospital for Sick Children in Washington, D.C., Battle walks each day among the consequences of technology and professional egoism that have "allowed us to create a new agony, an existence somewhere between life and death," with devastating repercussions for the families involved. She suggests that the child's potential quality of life, and the impact of the child's survival on the child's family and upon society's limited resources, should be considered in each decision to treat or to withhold treatment.

Taft [1987] examines this issue from the perspective of a hospital manager. She believes that the reality of limited resources may force a rationing system that should include utilitarian decision making as the selection process. She states that some infants have medical bills totaling one million dollars, and contends that if better cost control is not achieved, limitations in resources may require explicit ranking of cases based upon cost–benefit assessments.

Recent research on family dynamics related to the birth of severely disabled children concludes that a utilitarian approach to treatment decision making should be utilized because of the potential destructive effects such births can have on families [Simms 1986; Pahl & Quine 1984]. Kuhse and Singer [1987] state that the "principle of equal consideration of the interests of all those affected by a decision" is such a fundamental principle in ethics that it cannot be disregarded. They identify many factors that should be considered when deciding whether to provide treatment, including the interests of the parents and other children in the family. They claim that "the survival of a handicapped child is also the creation of a handicapped family." Lister [1986], in a straightforward argument for a utilitarian approach to decision making, states that physicians must always consider the social costs involved in maintaining an infant's life. Although he would prohibit the interests of the child's family from overriding the infant's interests, he states that an infant "should only be treated if the costs are within established societal limits."

A strict utilitarian approach to treatment decision making could require a decision not to begin treatment if: (1) the net pain and suffering of the child's life would not be offset by the potential for positive human experience; (2) the net pain and suffering of others (parents and other family members) exceeded the benefits of treatment for the newborn; (3) more lives could be saved by using limited medical resources in a different and more efficient manner—for example, a utilitarian argument could be made to justify using the million dollars for saving the life of one catastrophically ill newborn, to instead, fund preventive medical strategies in prenatal care to save many lives; and (4) decisions to terminate treatment could be made, as well as decisions not to begin treatment.

Many critics of utilitarian-based treatment decision making, or any other selection process that could result in selective nontreatment of infants, argue that we must adhere to a deontological principle of sanctity of life. Although many would argue that sanctity of life standards are vague, and therefore of little use in guiding decision making [Annas 1989], general principles are discernible. Sanctity of life advocates embrace a deontological, or duty based ethic. Sanctity of life means literally that human life has intrinsic absolute value [Lyon 1985], and therefore must be viewed as its own end with transcending value. We have a duty, therefore, to value all human life equally, regardless of our opinions of the relative worth or utility of a particular life. For sanctity of life advocates, all human life, regardless of its objective or subjective quality, must be considered as having transcendental value, requiring sustaining effort from all involved. The most obligatory, or deontologically pure, form of the sanctity of life position is often referred to as "vitalism." Paris [1982] illustrates this position when he states that "life is the ultimate value...to be preserved regardless of prognosis, regardless of cost, and regardless of social considerations."

AN ALTERNATIVE ETHICAL PARADIGM BASED ON BEST INTERESTS

In our pluralistic society, with colliding and evolving cultural perspectives, and with the intellectual rencontre that is the hallmark and strength of a free society, the debate continues regarding the appropriate guiding ethical principles of treatment decision making for catastrophically ill newborns with developmental disabilities. There is no consensus regarding appropriate guiding principles, and in any case, a consensus would not prove validity.

Recent literature does suggest, however, that there are two principles that although not always clearly developed or delineated, do serve as guiding prin-

VII. E. Child Welfare Services for the Catastrophically Ill Neonate

ciples for many professionals with treatment and case management responsibilities for seriously ill newborns. [Fleischman 1988; Kuhse & Singer 1989; Walters 1988; Singer & Kuhse 1988; Kinlaw 1990]. These principles are "quality of life," and "social transcendence." The quality of life principle can be described as the need to assess and consider the future quality of a person's life as an important variable in deciding whether to intervene to prolong life [Caplan & Cohen 1987; Brennan 1986]. A quality of life perspective assumes that some life situations can be worse than death, and in such situations, it may be unethical to support or prolong life [Caplan & Cohen 1987]. The principle of social transcendence can be defined as the requirement that decisions not be based upon the potential relative social utility of a person's life. It requires that treatment not be withheld on the basis of assessments of a child's future potential to contribute to society or upon the priorities of social utility. Individual treatment decisions should transcend considerations of social utility. Quality of life and social transcendence are concordant with the intent of the historical child welfare principle of best interests of the child.

In recent years, many health care, social service, and bioethical organizations have begun to identify and delineate these principles as appropriate decision-making criteria. The Bioethics Committee of the Canadian Paediatric Society [1986] states that both quality of life (referred to as the best interests of the child), and social transcendence principles should be used in treatment decision making. The society states that careful consideration must be given to all potential outcomes of both treatment and nontreatment, and defines best interests of the child as the sum of the potential benefit minus the harm that can be derived from potential treatment. Adherence to social transcendence is apparent in their statement that no outside interest of parents, family, or other care providers can override the interests of the child, or be considered a reason to withhold treatment. For example, they suggest analgesics be used to control severe pain in severely ill infants, even if they hasten death, and even when contrary to the parents' requests.

For the Infant Bioethical Review Committee of the Albert Einstein College of Medicine, the overriding principle is that care should be provided that is "reasonably thought to be in the infant's best interests" [Fleischman 1986]. The principles indicate that parents have the right and responsibility to make the decision in most cases, but they cannot be allowed to choose an action contrary to the infant's best interests. These guidelines indicate that a determination of the child's best interests should be the sum of the benefit minus the harm of any treatment considered. The guidelines also indicate that treatment should be withheld, or withdrawn, if it imposes a burden without compensating benefits for the infant.

A report of the President's Commission for the Study of Ethical Problems in Medicine and Biomedical and Behavioral Research, "Deciding to Forego Life-Sustaining Treatment," presented specific recommendations and conclusions regarding how decisions should be made, and who should make them [President's Commission 1983]. The commission established the infant's best interests as the criterion for treatment decision making. Although the words "quality of life" do not appear in the recommendations, the commission's position on treatment is clearly concordant with a general quality of life criterion

[Ross et al. 1986]. The commission report appears equivocal on social utility as a medical decision-making criterion. While it strongly affirms the developmentally disabled infant's best interests as the appropriate standard for treatment decisions, other sections of this same report suggest that social decisions regarding limited availability of treatment may supersede patients' autonomous choice for vigorous treatment [Ross et al. 1986].

In December 1987 the Hastings Center undertook a comprehensive effort to articulate a decision-making criterion based upon principles of quality of life and social transcendence. The center sought to determine whether a broader consensus regarding the ethics of neonatal care existed than was apparent from public debate. After assembling a group of "knowledgeable participants," to "grapple with the controversy of existing ethical paradigms," they concluded that "a child-centered best interest standard" was most appropriate, and that quality of life judgments were ethically proper and in a practical sense, inevitable. The report asserted that quality of life should not refer to the social worth of a person's existence as determined by a utilitarian criterion–"measured by balancing the burdens and benefits to others, especially to family members." Rather, quality of life referred to, "the present and future characteristics of the infant, judged by standards of the infant's own well-being and not in terms of social utility." Further, the center indicated that a consensus existed to equate quality of life with the best interests standard, and concluded that this standard should be used to determine if continued life would be in the infant's best interests; that certain states of life, marked by severe and intractable pain and suffering, can be viewed as worse than death; and that an infant's best interest could possibly lie in withholding or withdrawing medical treatments, resulting in death [Caplan & Cohen 1987].

This author suggests that although there continues to be considerable contention regarding the appropriate guiding principles for decision making, and considerable opposition among various groups to one or both of the principles of quality of life and social transcendence, these basic principles should be considered in the formulation of a guiding ethical paradigm for child protective service workers and agencies with the responsibility to police treatment decision making for catastrophically ill newborns.

Vicarious Egoism

If the child welfare profession adopts standards for case investigation of catastrophically ill newborns based upon the combined principles of social transcendence and quality of life, neither a utilitarian nor a deontological paradigm would be appropriate. Utilitarianism is based upon social utility, a concept that social transcendence repudiates. And a deontological paradigm would not consider the concept of quality of life an appropriate value base. Instead of either of these paradigms, a philosophical paradigm based upon the principle of ethical egoism would appear more appropriate.

Ethical egoism is one of the oldest ethical traditions. Its roots lie in Greek philosophy's earliest attempts to describe human motivation and behavior. Its fundamental proposition is that all human motivation and behavior are derivations of calculated efforts to achieve satisfaction and contentment, and to avoid pain. This elegantly simple moral philosophy is often assailed for its fundamental reliance upon self-interest as the basis for human conduct. Many biologists, sociologists, and anthropologists, however, tell us that the most complicated altruistic behavior, and the most exalted moral motivation, can be traced to the collective attempts of individuals within a social milieu to achieve their individual and shared self-interests. In any case, regardless of the validity of ethical egoism as a moral paradigm for general humanity, it is an imminently attractive alternative for the catastrophically ill neonate. These infants are born into a world of competing interests, with no power, little means of communication, and compelling needs; their existential situation demands that we develop a consistent and just criteria to champion their best interests.

To apply an egoistic ethical paradigm to a situation in which a person is incompetent, such as in the case of a catastrophically ill newborn, the guiding ethical paradigm would have to be applied by either a competent person, a group of persons, or an advocacy agency charged with the responsibility of acting in the child's best interests. A paradigm of ethical egoism, when applied with vicarious consideration of a catastrophically ill neonate's present condition and future possibilities, would provide a basis for determining whether treat or no-treat decisions were in a child's best interests, and would require that treatment decisions be made utilizing the guiding principles of quality of life and social transcendence.

Case examples can help us to compare and contrast the potential outcomes of treat/no-treat decisions using utilitarian, deontological, and vicarious egoism paradigms to guide decision making. The following are actual cases of neonates referred to infant care ethics committees for guidance in treatment decision making.

Case # 1: Bobby

Bobby is nine months old. Born to a drug-addicted mother, Bobby was two months' premature, of low birth weight, and showed evidence of drug toxicity. He remained in the hospital's intensive neonatal care unit for several weeks; ventilation was required to assist his breathing. As a result, Bobby's lungs were badly scarred, and he developed a condition called bronchopulmonary displasia. He now needs the ventilator for an indefinite amount of time, perhaps permanently, at a cost of $3,000 per day.

Bobby's mother abandoned him in the hospital shortly after he was born. His father is unknown. Bobby was placed in a specialized foster home when he was released from the hospital.

Bobby is restricted to his crib. His physical development is delayed, as he is essentially bedridden because of his dependence upon the ventilator. He appears to be socially and emotionally responsive, smiling and responding to conversation and social contact. He has not learned to vocalize, as the throat tube of the ventilator has prevented development of verbal expression.

Without treatment, Bobby would die within hours. With treatment, Bobby's life can be prolonged indefinitely, although lung disease could be reasonably expected to cause death in the first two decades. Although Bobby is not in pain, he will probably remain bedridden and on the respirator throughout his life, and he will need continuous nursing care. Although his social and cognitive development are delayed due to environmental deprivation, a normal potential probably exists. There is no locatable family.

If the treat/no-treat decision were made based upon the deontological ethic of sanctity of life, the decision would certainly be to continue treatment. A decision based on a utilitarian ethic would be questionable. Considering the net benefit to everyone concerned, a utilitarian ethic could advocate the discontinuance of treatment based on the cost alone. The cost of ventilator treatment at $3,000 a day totals over one million dollars a year. If Bobby lives an expected 20 years, the total cost to society would be in excess of $20 million. Utilitarian ethics would consider that this money could, in a limited resource economy, potentially be used instead to save the lives of many other children for whom there is a better prognosis for a happy and successful life. Since Bobby has no family, family foster care or residential care would be an additional cost to the state.

Vicarious egoists would almost certainly advocate that continued treatment would be in Bobby's best interests. He is in no pain, he is alert, socially involved, and expected to be cognitively normal. He has the capacity to experience pleasure, to be cognitively productive, and to derive enjoyment and meaning from life.

Case # 2: Baby Bill

Baby Bill, a newborn, was born four weeks postmature. He has been diagnosed as anencephalic, a condition in which significant portions of the brain, including the cerebral cortex, have not developed. Baby Bill responds to stimulation in a gross manner. His medical condition is stable. He has many reflexes, including a partial sucking reflex. No other organ deficiencies were noted. His level of comfort or pain is difficult to determine, but he appears to be in considerable distress. He is an otherwise healthy baby.

Without treatment, Baby Bill will die within a week, due to inability to eat. With extensive intervention, including continuous life support and hyperalimentation, Baby Bill's life could be maintained for several years. He would remain profoundly mentally retarded and physically disabled, and would be expected to have no social interaction and a life of considerable discomfort.

Baby Bill was born to an indigent 32-year-old mentally ill woman. She is unable to make an informed decision.

Most deontologists would probably choose to treat: sanctity of life is often operationalized as "life is sacred, no matter what, even for a moment, and all things should be done at all times to preserve it." An alternative sanctity of life interpretation, however, is that the sacredness of life means life should be beyond the humanistic meddlings of overintrusive science. Preventing the natural course of life and death through the artificial interference of excessive and extraordinary medical treatment could be interpreted as inappropriate within a deontological ethic. In this case, this could mean withholding heroic treatment and allowing the child to die a natural death.

Utilitarians, by contrast, might advocate treatment to maintain the child's life for the purposes of research. This could enable scientists to better understand the principles of brain development, and to determine the causes of anencephaly, which in the long run might lead to prevention of the same condition in other infants. The infant could also be kept alive to harvest his other vital organs for transplant, which could, in effect, save the lives of infants whose lives are at risk because of organ failure. These benefits would have to be balanced against the costs of maintaining the child's life. There are no countervailing family interests.

Vicarious egoists would advocate not to treat. It would not be in this child's best interests to prolong life when the infant has no possibility of any positive cognitive or emotional experience of life, when pain is his only awareness, and when the extraordinary medical interventions necessary to maintain life or research activities would potentially be experienced as additionally painful.

Case # 3: Katie

Katie has just turned three years old. She has been hospitalized for six weeks. She has AIDS, and is in the terminal stages of the illness. She weighs 18 pounds, and is extremely ill with a host of infections, including pneumonia. She shows increasing signs of cerebral neuropathy, and is in extreme and continuous discomfort. Katie has no chance of recovery. If antibiotic therapy is not increased, Katie will die within hours. With more heroic intervention, including drugs increased to the level of effective relief of pain, Katie could live for several weeks, but with increasing discomfort.

Katie is in the custody of a child welfare agency and in family foster care. Her mother died of AIDS last year. Her father, a recovering alcoholic, has recently expressed the desire to reestablish custody of Katie. Based upon his religious beliefs, he is advocating continued heroic treatment, and threatens a lawsuit if treatment is not forthcoming. Katie's father says his religious beliefs require that every effort be made to maintain Katie's life, regardless of the consequences for her, him, or anyone else, because "it's the right thing to do."

Katie's father's guiding ethical perspective appears to be deontological. He is advocating heroic treatment irrespective of the consequences.

A utilitarian approach would weigh everyone's interests. If Katie's physical pain and suffering could be relieved with pharmacological intervention, then a decision to treat could be made in the interests of Katie's father's religious beliefs and emotional well-being. If Katie's suffering could not be alleviated, or if the high cost of continued treatment could not be justified given scarce resources and the almost certain lack of efficacy of such treatment, then treatment would be discontinued.

Vicarious egoism would consider only Katie's best interests. If there were no hope of recovery, and no good means of alleviating Katie's suffering, treatment would be discontinued. If Katie's suffering and pain could be controlled, and if there were some slight chance of arresting the disease, treatment would be continued.

CONCLUSION

The above case examples illustrate the complex issues in treatment decision making for catastrophically ill newborns and young children. They are meant to illustrate the differences associated with using various ethical paradigms to guide decision making. Others may arrive at different case decisions even within the same ethical paradigm. It is this author's contention, however, that more consistent and just bioethical treatment decisions will be forthcoming if the child welfare profession adopts vicarious egoism as a guide.

Treat/no-treat decisions for catastrophically ill neonates are being made inconsistently throughout this country, depending upon whether a utilitarian, deontological, or some other poorly defined or personal criteria is used. Decision makers frequently do not consciously select an agreed-upon and consistent paradigm to guide their decisions. Many decision makers are not trained in, or lack knowledge of, principles of ethical decision making.

The criteria they use are often subjective. Many of those making decisions consider principles of quality of life and social transcendence only tangentially, if at all. As a result, treatment decisions for children with similar conditions and in comparable circumstances vary widely.

The Child Abuse Amendments of 1985 require states to assign their state child welfare systems the responsibility to assure that treatment decisions for catastrophically ill newborns do not result in abuse or neglect. As with any other case of potential child abuse or neglect, it is the responsibility of the child welfare system to investigate reports or allegations of abuse and neglect. Few investigations have taken place. The reasons for this lack of activity are many and complex: (1) child welfare responsibilities are perceived to overlap with the responsibilities of others; (2) the treatment decisions are medically difficult; and (3) there are no clear decision-making criteria.

In this shadowy arena of converging responsibilities and feelings, of questionable prognoses and questionable treatment efficacies, and of uncertain personal and professional ethical guidelines, social workers cannot help but be hesitant and unsure if called upon to provide protective services for catastrophically ill newborns. Although the government has assigned them the responsibility to police life and death bioethical decisions, it has not provided a consensus bioethical paradigm to guide their actions. If we are to achieve consistency and justice in moral decision making for catastrophically ill newborns, the child welfare system must be given a consensus-guiding ethical paradigm. The two most often championed ethical systems, the utilitarian and the deontological ethical paradigms, are potentially incompatible with the guiding principles of best interests of the child. The author would recommend the integrated principles of social transcendence and quality of life. If such standards are used, an egoist ethical paradigm, applied with a vicarious consideration of the neonate's present condition and future possibilities, can produce case management decisions in the child's best interests.